Contents

Doing Pragmatics

PETER GRUNDY

Department of Linguistics and English Language
University of Durham

Department of English
Hong Kong Polytechnic

Edward Arnold
A member of the Hodder Headline Group
LONDON   NEW YORK   SYDNEY   AUCKLAND

First published in Great Britain 1995 by
Edward Arnold, a division of Hodder Headline PLC,
338 Euston Road, London NW1 3BH

Distributed exclusively in the USA by
St. Martin's Press, Inc.
175 Fifth Avenue, New York, NY 10010

British Library Cataloguing in Publication Data
A catalogue record for this book is available from the British Library

ISBN 0 340 58965 5 (Pb) ✓
ISBN 0 340 62514 7 (Hb)

 2 3 4 5   96 97 98 99

Typeset in 10/11 pt Times by Scribe Design, Gillingham, Kent.
Printed and bound in Great Britain by Mackays of Chatham plc, Chatham, Kent.

Preface

Some students find that learning pragmatics and learning syntax are mirror images of one another. Because pragmatic data consist of everyday utterances, the first impression of pragmatics tends to be that it is really quite easy: the examples and the ways they are described seem to accord closely with our intuitions about everyday talk. In contrast, when we study syntax for the first time, the formal representation of the examples often seems very challenging. But as time goes on, we realize that the underlying ideas in pragmatics are really very difficult indeed, whereas the underlying ideas in syntax have a simplicity and elegance that makes syntax seem easier the more we study it. My main motive in writing this book has been to try and extend the sense felt in the early stages of pragmatics—that it is really a very accessible area of linguistics—to the second stage, when we have to grapple with the more challenging underlying ideas.

There are already a number of very good pragmatics textbooks available, and new ones seem to be appearing all the time: for this reason I have recommended chapters from several of them in the suggestions for further reading which appear at the end of each chapter. If this book is different, I hope it is because you will feel that it is a genuine 'entry-level' book and that it justifies its title, *Doing Pragmatics*, which is meant to reflect its strong pedagogic orientation. Wherever possible I have also tried to use real examples of talk that I've collected over the years rather than rely on invented examples. A book about the use of language ought to work with 'live' examples.

The materials in this book have been extensively tested over several generations of students at Durham. I have been fortunate to have had the opportunity to teach pragmatics at undergraduate and postgraduate levels for many years, and to have benefited from large and extremely lively lecture groups where I have frequently been caught out and corrected by students at every level. And I have to admit that reading pragmatics essays and projects is often a learning experience too—students very frequently have insights and react to data in ways that I have found enlightening and shaming. As well as all the faults that are owed to me, in this book you will also find many insights that are owed to generations of students. In particular I have acknowledged some by name in the text of the book: Andrew Caink, Roger Maylor, Csilla Szabo, and especially Kelly Glover, who has contributed ideas and read and commented insightfully on parts of the manuscript of this book, thereby saving me from a number of mistakes. But because this is pragmatics, I'm sure that as you read this book you will see things that I have missed and even got wrong—please write and let me know when this happens.

Although I have never had a colleague at Durham who was first and foremost a pragmaticist, I have been fortunate to work alongside stimulating colleagues in a department that takes its linguistics seriously, and in which all our different interests and approaches have always been understood to be interdependent and to have the same ultimate goal. As with deixis, the point of origin has been important to this book.

I also owe a debt to my two editors at Edward Arnold: Lesley Riddle, who threw caution to the wind in allowing me to write this book in the first place, and Naomi Meredith, who bore with me when it took longer than it should have done. Naomi also suggested the title, which is much better than the three previous ones I had toyed with. I am also grateful to Sophie Oliver, who managed the production schedule much more efficiently than I had managed the writing schedule.

How to get the best out of this book

If you look at the contents page, you will see that each of Chapters 2–6 has two sections. The first section in each chapter sets out a basic position and the second section then wrestles with more difficult ideas. One way to work with this book might be to read and work on the first sections of each of these chapters in class and leave the second sections for optional private reading, or until your second-year pragmatics course.

I have also grouped what needs to be said about pragmatics under three major headings which appear on the contents page: indexicality, relevance, and intentionality. You will see that each of these themes is addressed in Chapters 2–6 and again in Chapters 7–9. Chapters 7–9 have a strong practical orientation, and demonstrate the extent to which the pragmatic descriptions suggested in Chapters 2–6 can be applied. I could imagine a thematic pragmatics course which followed the indexicality or the relevance or the intentionality route through this book. Thus you might read the general Chapter 1 first and then choose between three pragmatics courses:

- the indexicality course: the first half of Chapter 2, followed by Chapter 7 and then the second half of Chapter 2;
- the relevance course: the first half of Chapters 3 and 4, followed by Chapter 8 and then the second halves of Chapters 3 and 4;
- the intentionality course: the first halves of Chapters 5 and 6, followed by Chapter 9 and then the second halves of Chapters 5 and 6.

Another motive in writing this book has been the hope that it may help you to do your own pragmatics. There are three ways in which this book overtly addresses this motive.

Checking understanding sections: throughout this book you will be challenged by sections that are designed to check that you have understood the theory being described and can apply it yourself to data. A key with solutions and suggested answers is provided at the end of the book (but it is important that you should try the checking understanding sections before looking at the key). In the case of the most difficult chapter in this book (Chapter 3) there are 19 checking understanding sections to guide you. In fact, you could spend a whole year's pragmatics course just working through Chapter 3 if you did all the checking understanding sections really carefully.

Raising pragmatic awareness sections: at the end of each chapter there are a number of activities which you can try for yourself, or with friends, or in a tutorial group. These are sensitizing activities, which involve you in tasks like eavesdropping on conversations and reporting your findings to your colleagues, or writing entries for a dictionary of pragmatics. Each of these activities is meant to be do-able either as a task set by the teacher or on a self-study basis.

Project work: Chapter 10 contains several suggestions about possible types of project, and in particular gives advice on data collection and transcription techniques. I have read many excellent student projects in pragmatics, but have frequently felt that they would have been even better for the kind of advice that I have tried to give in this chapter. I hope this chapter will help you in planning and carrying out your project work.

P.G.
University of Durham
March 1994

Part I

Pragmatic meaning

1

Using and understanding language

'We all know what light is; but it is not
easy to tell what it is' (Samuel Johnson in
James Boswell's *Life of Johnson*, 11 Apr.
1776)

Keywords: utterance, appropriacy, use, indirectness, inference, context,
relevance, deixis, implicature, speech act.

I am not going to try and define pragmatics in this first chapter, although by
the end of it you should have a much better idea of what we mean by
pragmatics than you probably have now. Instead, I am going to write about
some of the aspects of language use that are of particular interest to
pragmaticists such as you and me. Let's begin by eavesdropping on a
fragment of conversation I overheard in the corridor between two freshers
queueing up to register at the beginning of the academic year:

1 P: What's your name by the way
   S: Stephen
   P: You haven't asked my name back
   S: What's your name
   P: It's Pat

I don't know if they are still together, but they each frighten me in their own
different ways. Look at some of the pragmatic effects of their utterances.

P: What's your name by the way
Pat's 'by the way' serves as a warning to Stephen that what she is saying now
is not quite as relevant to what went before as his knowledge of the rules for
talk would normally lead him to expect. 'By the way' is not part of the way
we ask someone their name, more a comment on the status of 'What's your
name' at this stage in their conversation. Perhaps it suggests that corridor talk
has gone far enough and a little intimacy may now be risked. Pat's 'What's
your name' is a conventional but indirect way of saying *tell me your name*—
indirect because, although it takes the form of a question, it is intended as a
request. It is also more polite than *tell me your name*, which we would not
expect to occur in conversations between people of more or less equal status.

S: Stephen
Stephen's reply is so minimal as to seem almost rude. Why should this be
when in fact he does comply with Pat's request to tell her his name? It seems

that such a minimal answer may satisfy the request but does not satisfy the requester, who is put down, or shown insufficient respect, by it.

P: You haven't asked my name back

Pat then indicates that she does not consider that Stephen has fulfilled his conversational obligations, although strictly speaking, as we noted, he has complied with her request to give his name. Her 'You haven't asked my name back' is a genuinely indirect way of telling Stephen to ask her for her name. I call it 'genuinely indirect' because, although it takes the form of a statement when it is intended as a request, it also requires Stephen to work out what she wants from him. Her utterance also seems to convey an attitude—perhaps it is a reprimand. Will Stephen draw the right conclusion and will what Pat says have the effect she intends? Would the intention and effect have been any different if she had said 'You haven't asked me my name back'? And why, one might reasonably ask, didn't she simply give her name?

S: What's your name

Notice how inappropriate it would have been at this stage in the conversation for Stephen to ask Pat her name in the same way that she had asked his ('What's you name by the way'). If he had used exactly her words just three turns later in this short conversation, what sort of effect might it have had?

P: It's Pat

The *It* in Pat's 'It's' is anaphoric, a term linguists use to describe a word that refers back to an earlier item, in this case 'name'. This use of 'It's' establishes a cohesive link between her utterance and his—they are beginning to co-author the conversation. It also gives her utterance the typical information structure we find so often in utterances, that of proceeding from the known (the *It* of 'It's') to the unknown or new, the word 'Pat'.

Such simple observations about some of the pragmatic properties of this brief, trivial exchange show how subtle even the most apparently straightforward uses of language are. Pragmatics is about explaining how we produce and understand such everyday but apparently rather peculiar uses of language. The subsequent chapters of this book will try to do the necessary explaining.

Checking understanding (1)

Before we move on, perhaps you would like to try your hand at coming to some conclusions about what is going on in a simple conversation of the kind we have just examined. Try to come to some conclusions about the following short exchange, which I heard as I was listening to *Morning Edition* on Radio 5 one day:

2   A1: Mr Major's going to be at Wincanton today
    B1: Oh is he I didn't know that
    A2: No the horse not the Prime Minister
    B2: Oh the grey

The more you work on this conversation, the more you come to see that it is not so much what the sentences literally mean that matters when we talk as how they reveal the intentions and strategies of the speakers themselves. This point is very well made by Atkinson, Kilby and Roca, who define pragmatics as being to do with 'The distinction between what a speaker's words (literally) mean and what the speaker might mean by his words' (1988: 217).

In the rest of this chapter I am going to discuss some of the features of everyday language use which are of particular importance in pragmatics. When we get to the end of the chapter I shall be more systematic and make a number of observations about the properties of a single utterance, with the aim of signposting our way through the first few chapters of this book. Meanwhile, the first feature I want to discuss is appropriacy.

Appropriacy

Not very long ago my wife and I went out for lunch with two other couples, both a little older than we were and both slightly more important at work. We had a drink in the bar first and ordered our meal. In due course the waiter came back and announced that our lunch was ready, a communication which we all ignored. Four or five minutes later one of the more important members of the group said

3 I think we could go in now you know

whereupon we all duly stood up and began the awkward transition from bar to dining-room. The point is that in choice of words, in moment of speaking, and in status of speaker this utterance was absolutely appropriate to the situation.

Similar examples are easy to find. At one stage in my career I had a senior colleague who had the very bad habit of saying

4 Are we all here

at exactly the moment a meeting was due to start and only if he could see that we were not all there. But his utterance was perfectly attuned to the situation and always had the same effect, that of causing a younger member of our department to get up and go on a colleague hunt.

Or when I begin a lecture I usually call for attention by uttering loudly

5 Right, shall we begin

which I take to be the most appropriate utterance in the context. When I am feeling mischievous I sometimes begin pragmatics lectures by saying

6 May I speak English

This always causes a moment of consternation when the students think their lecturer really has gone bonkers at last. But this beginning enables me to make the neat point that 'May I speak English' is not the appropriate way to begin a pragmatics lecture in Britain. And to make the still neater point that when I say 'May I speak English' in a shop in Italy, the commonest response (I know, I have done the research) is

7   A little

This indicates that the addressee, frequently struggling with limited English, took me to be saying the more appropriate or expectable 'Do you speak English?'

And then there is the receptionist at the garage where I take my car, who can never remember my name and knows he should, so signals it every time I go with

8   What's your name again

And when I stayed for two nights in a bed-and-breakfast recently and had the same waitress each morning she used two different ways of asking me whether I'd like tea or coffee. You can surely guess which of the following utterances she used on the first morning and which she took to be more appropriate on the second:

9   Is it tea or coffee

9′ Would you like tea or coffee

And what is the most appropriate way of getting my fun-loving Australian friend out of the pub because I want to get home to my family before they've all gone to bed and left the milk bottles out in revenge formation on the doorstep where I'm bound to send them flying? I tried the rather feeble

10 How are you doing

to which my friend obligingly replied

11 Am I ready to go do you mean

Being rather a cowardly person, I of course protested that I wasn't, but I made it clear by bored stares at the wall and lots of posture shifts that I was getting itchy, so that it wasn't long before my friend said

12 You're in a hurry

and since she had initiated the conversation this time, I judged it okay to reply

13 No, well, yes I am

I cite these few examples because they are immediately recognizable as appropriate ways of using language to get business done. One of the features of language use that is of interest to pragmaticists is its appropriacy in relation to those who use it and those they address.

Non-literal or indirect meaning

As well as being appropriate to the contexts in which they occurred, many of the utterances in the last section were also indirect, in the sense that their literal meanings were not all the speakers intended them to convey. So

4   Are we all here

and

5   Right shall we begin

both purport to be questions in terms of the forms in which they are expressed, yet both are clearly intended to have other functions. Indeed, I would be rather cross if someone took 'Shall we begin?' as a real question and replied with a negative rejoinder. It would have been similarly inappropriate for my Australian friend to have replied 'I'm doing just fine' to my indirect hint that I was ready to go.

Sometimes the literal meaning is very far removed from the indirect meaning. Thus you would have to have seen *Fawlty Towers* to know that

14 He's from Barcelona

is a way of saying that someone is stupid, undeserving of sympathy, etc. But usually the indirectness is much more subtle than this, so that it takes a bit of working out to realize that

15 Radion removes dirt *and* odours

is an indirect way of saying that other washing powders are good at getting the dirt out but leave your clothes smelling foul. And when the BBC recently referred to

16 The campaign group called the Freedom Association

the listeners had to do quite a lot of work to come to the conclusion that the BBC was indicating indirectly that it did not necessarily share the philosophy of the Freedom Association and that its name might give a wrong impression. Similarly, the infamous headline in the *Sun* on the day after Black Wednesday when the pound left the ERM

17 Now we've ALL been screwed by the Cabinet

was an indirect reference to the relationship between a minister who had resigned shortly before, after having an extramarital affair, as well as an indirect way of saying that the Government had made a mess of things.

It is also remarkable that we are so clever at interpreting indirectness. Take the following conversation which Phyllis, our tea-lady, and I had recently:

18 Ph: Wasn't the wind dreadful in the night
    P: I didn't hear it
    Ph: Ee it was dreadful
    P: You know what they say

And she did: she understood the indirectness perfectly, and continued with

    Ph: I must have a guilty conscience

So we see that indirectness too is typical of real-world language use, and that literal or stated meaning is only one aspect of the meaning conveyed in an utterance.

Inference

One question we have to ask is how we get from a sentence that appears to have a literal meaning to an understanding of its indirect meaning. We obviously have to draw inferences or come to conclusions based on our best guesses as to what the speaker is intending to convey. So although we are not told that other washing powders leave our clothes smelling dirty, we can work out that this is a conclusion we are meant to draw from the stress on *and* in

15 Radion removes dirt *and* odours

In a similar way, 'called' in

16 The campaign group called the Freedom Association

triggers an inference. Why, we ask ourselves, did the BBC not simply say 'The campaign group, the Freedom Association'? 'Called', we decide, must be telling us something about the title 'the Freedom Association': that it is slightly suspect.

This suggests that communication is not merely a matter of a speaker encoding a thought in language and sending it as spoken message through space, or as a written message on paper, to a receiver who decodes it. This is clearly insufficient—the receiver must not only decode what is received but also draw an inference as to what is conveyed beyond what is stated.

Sometimes this inference is quite dramatic and much more interesting than the literal meaning itself, as when one of my colleagues said

19 I'm a man

Nothing remarkable in that, one might think, except that the speaker was a woman. Here the meaning she intended to convey was much more important than the literal meaning of her utterance.

Sometimes the inference just repairs a message that is ill-formed or in some way inadequate. So that in the building where I work there is a sign on the door of the gentlemen's toilet that reads

20 Female toilet on floor above

Think about it! Yes, well, everyone who goes up to the door seems to read the message without smiling, merely drawing the appropriate inference, which in fact replaces the literal meaning with a more appropriate meaning. If we were not able to draw such inferences, I shudder to think what might happen in our building.

In fact, it is interesting to notice how some speakers feel that, even when they are speaking metaphorically, a form of indirectness which always requires an addressee to draw an inference, they need to use the term 'literally' in their utterance. It is as though language really were a matter of literal meanings that could be encoded and dispatched by the speaker and received and decoded by the addressee. I heard a nice example of this on the *Today* programme on Radio 4 when a reporter said

21 The Conference trade has literally helped turn Brighton around

This means that every utterance may be subject to an inference so that the addressee can determine whether an utterance such as

22 I really like your new haircut

is sincere or ironical.

Sometimes there does not even seem to be much point in what people say, until one draws an inference. I was recently working on a short course with several colleagues, all spread out around various classrooms. For the first few days, the course members found it all a bit confusing. When one of them addressed me with the apparently redundant

23 Are you here Peter

as I was standing in my classroom door just before a class, I was able to draw an inference as to what she wanted to confirm, and thus did not take her for the loony she would otherwise have appeared to be.

Indeterminacy

Regarding some meanings as matters of inference has one important consequence. It implies that the utterances we hear are in some ways unclear, or, as linguists sometimes say, 'underdetermined'. By this we mean that an utterance might typically have one of several different possible meanings, and that the inferences we draw determine which of these possible meanings is the one the addressee thinks the speaker is intending. Good examples of underdetermined utterances in the previous section are

19 I'm a man

22 I really like your new haircut

and

23 Are you here Peter

In each of these cases we need to draw inferences which determine which of a number of different possible understandings is the right one.

In her book *Understanding Utterances*, Diane Blakemore (1992: 83) very interestingly draws our attention to how underdetermined the possessive is in English, and gives a long list of examples which, although they share the same grammatical form, are all determined quite differently. Her list includes

24 I have borrowed *Jane's car*
  I would hate to have *Simon's job*
  Yesterday's events really shocked the *country's president*
  Jane's father has bought her a car

There are many other structures besides possessives that are typically underdetermined. I remember that my daughter was very upset when she first noticed the sign 'Pet mince' outside our local butcher's shop. Indeed, butcher's signs are a rich source of such indeterminacy: I have often thought how fortunate it is that a *Family Butcher* does not do to families what a *Pork Butcher* does to pigs.

Sometimes the problem is to do with determining which word in a two-word phrase is the head word, so that although *a child actor* is a child who acts, the meaning of *a child psychiatrist* cannot be determined by analogy. Similarly, in *additive-free* the head word is *free*, whereas in *50% extra free*, this is not the case.

In my capacity as an external examiner at another institution, I recently found myself writing an examiner's letter which, on re-reading, I saw contained one particularly pompous sentence that might be understood in either of two quite different ways. The sentence was

25 There must therefore be a very good case for not allowing anyone to proceed to Year 3

The word that gave the trouble was clearly *anyone*—it was meant to mean 'a particular person' rather than 'every person'. A similar problem occurs

with *the team that won in mid-week at Everton* in the following sentence
which I heard on the *Today* programme:

26 Wimbledon are playing the team that won in mid-week at Everton

I once had an interesting intercultural experience of this sort. It was at the
time when I first went to live in Germany and was a couple of lessons into
my German course. Arming myself with a phrasebook and a good deal of
misplaced confidence, I took myself off to a bar for a drink. Although I
seemed to order my first beer with some success I was less successful with
the second, which involved consulting my phrasebook for the German word
for *another*. In English *another* is indeterminate between *another the same*
and *another different*, but in German these two notions are represented by
different expressions. This explains why, when I thought I was ordering
'another beer', the barman gave me a very dirty look and a beer that was
distinctly different from the previous one.

Sometimes the context helps us to determine the meaning. When most
people say

27 I've just finished a book

we take them to mean that they have just finished reading a book, but when
a university lecturer says 'I've just finished a book', he usually means that
he has just finished writing one. So knowing who the speaker is will help us
to determine what is meant. A colleague of mine once made what we thought
was a very funny joke when someone at lunch one day said that a particular member of his department had just finished a book, and my colleague
asked, 'Reading one or writing one?' This would only be a joke in a context
where the determination of *has just finished a book* could be problematical.
And in fact, another of Diane Blakemore's examples is

28 Should I read *your book*

where *your book* is clearly ambiguous between the book you own and the
book of which you are the author.

Although we may often think that what we say has one clear, determinate
meaning, the examples above show us just how indeterminate our utterances
actually are. Pragmatics is partly about trying to account in systematic ways
for our ability to determine what speakers intend even when their utterances
are so dramatically underdetermined.

Context

In the paragraph before last we discussed how context can help in determining the meaning of an utterance. Another way to think through this issue
is to think of all the contexts in which you might utter the same words. Take
the case of the utterance

29 I'm tired

If I say it late at night, it may count as a way of excusing myself and getting
off to bed before my wife. Or she may take it as a hint that I want her to
come to bed too. Either way it means that I want to go to bed. But if I say
I'm tired when the alarm clock goes off at ten to seven the next morning, it

probably means that I do not want to get out of bed, and perhaps might be interpreted by my wife as an invitation to her to get out of bed and make the coffee. In fact, we could think of as many meanings for *I'm tired* as we could think of contexts in which it might be uttered—or put another way, as many contexts for it as meanings that it might have. The same point could be made about

30 I've got a flat tyre

In a garage, this might be taken to mean that I need help; or if addressed to a friend with a car, that I need a lift; or as a response to a request for a lift from a friend without a car, that I can't give them a lift; or, indeed, a wide range of other things in all the other contexts in which you might imagine it being uttered.

Similarly

31 Can you open the door

is usually taken as a polite, indirect way of requesting someone to open a door for us. But imagine a non-typical context: you and I are robbing a bank and you are struggling with an oxyacetylene torch while I am keeping an anxious lookout. If I were to say 'Can you open the door' in such a context, it would obviously be a genuine question rather than an indirect request.

I found myself thinking very hard about the context when I had to give a lecture in a university in China on 4 June, the anniversary of the Tiananmen massacre. The title of my talk, which was about second-language acquisition, was 'Listening to Learners'. I began with this sentence

32 I suppose today it's especially important to be thinking carefully about what our students say to us

There was a perceptible tension as the audience struggled for a moment to determine whether *today* was a reference to 4 June specifically or to the more general contemporary language-teaching methodology scene. I let them consider which of the two contexts was most appropriate for a fraction of a second before going on to explain why listening to our learners is important in language-teaching. Had I referred to the Tiananmen context? For some people, perhaps yes; for others, perhaps no.

Sometimes it is interesting to try and guess the context of an utterance. Someone once said to me

33 Have you got a plastic bag

Can you guess the context? The same utterance may well have been addressed to you on some occasion in the past. I was once foolish enough to ask a lecture-theatre full of students to try and supply the context in which this utterance occurred. Someone shouted out, 'You'd just had a colostomy?' In fact the real context was much more interesting. It was seven o'clock one Saturday night in Warsaw at the time of military rule. I was with a Polish colleague who was looking after me and we were on our way to a party. I suggested that we should buy a bottle of wine, which caused her to say rather pityingly, 'You must be joking!' She explained that General Jaruszelski, who was in charge at the time, did not approve of drinking, and so had decreed that no alcohol was to be sold after 5 p.m. on Saturday afternoons, not even in the hotels where at every other time of the week hard currency could buy virtually anything alcoholic. So we hit upon the wheeze of playing the stupid foreigner in town. Entering the restaurant across the road, I asked whether they spoke English (no) or German (nein). So I explained that I would speak English and that my friend would translate: 'Translate please, Maria', I said, and she duly did. I then explained that I had had a meal in the restaurant two days before and had enjoyed a bottle of most excellent wine. Again Maria translated. As we were going to the birthday party of a very special friend, I was wondering whether it would be possible to have another bottle of their most excellent wine to take as a present. Maria translated again, and this time the lady behind the bar obligingly replied

33 Have you got a plastic bag

Luckily I had, so it was a case of 'Foreigners 1, General Jaruszelski 0'. But the reply is very interesting, because in the context in which it occurred it counted as an agreement to break the law, and could in theory have landed her (and perhaps us) in quite serious trouble.

   Another way in which we try to make the way we say things reflect context is in our use of politeness phenomena. We know that

34 Could I just borrow a tiny bit of paper

is a way of lessening our request, and much more likely to be acceded to than

35 Give me a sheet of paper

I recently received a long letter from a life assurance company, explaining in tortuous terms that they would be paying a lower bonus to policyholders. The last sentence of this letter was

36 I felt it important to write at some length on this rather important matter

which we all recognize instantly as an apology. In principle it might equally have been a congratulation or an appeal for a donation, but in fact we all know that it invokes a quite different context from either of these two theoretically possible ones. In this sense, we might almost argue that it is language which creates context and not context which determines the language we use.

   Because pragmaticists are interested in the meanings of utterances, they are also interested in the contexts in which utterances occur, since, as we have seen, the two are closely integrated.

Relevance

In the previous section we showed how understanding

32 I suppose today it's especially important to be thinking carefully about what our students say to us

depended on choosing the most relevant of two possible meanings. Deciding on the most appropriate reference for *today* is really a matter of deciding whether the reference to 4 June as the anniversary of the Tiananmen massacre or the reference to present times in general is the more relevant. Usually it is a fairly simple matter to decide on the most relevant way to take an utterance, so that in the case of

29 I'm tired

we can readily discount all but two or three meanings, on the grounds that none of the others could be relevant to the situation obtaining at the time of the utterance. And usually it is relatively easy to tell which of the remaining two or three meanings is the most relevant.

We know that relevance is important to understanding because there are mechanisms that enable us to check that we have achieved the most relevant understanding. For example, one day shortly after half-term in my son's first term at secondary school, he said

37 I'm enjoying school much more now

I was unclear about the reference of *now*. Did he mean that he was enjoying the second half of his first term at secondary school more than the first half, or did he mean that he preferred secondary school to primary school? Because I could see no way of determining which was the more relevant understanding, I had to ask him to clarify.

Relevance has been seen by Sperber and Wilson (1986) as the most important principle in accounting for the way we understand language. Since we take every utterance as relevant, we understand utterances in whatever way will make them as relevant as possible.

Misfires

There was the wonderful Admiral Stainforth who nominated the independent candidate Ross Perot for the American Presidency in 1992. When he began his nominating speech with the weedy shriek

38 Who am I? Why am I here?

he must have been astonished at the howls of laughter that greeted what seemed to his audience to be all too real questions. He had made a calculation that this ringing start to his oration would have a particular rhetorical effect, which unfortunately for him it did not have. It was a kind of pragmatic 'misfire'. Pragmatic misfires are very important because they tell us that there are expected norms for talk by showing us the effect when the norm is not achieved. If you think back over the last few hours, you will probably be aware that several of your utterances did not have quite the effects you would have wished—or at least so it seems when you judge from the reaction of those you were addressing.

A misfire I rather enjoyed occurred at a dinner, when someone said to an important professor sitting across the table from me

39 Will you have some more chocolate

None of us had realized up to then that when the chocolates had come round the first time he had somehow got missed out, but he made us all too aware of it with his petulant reply

40 I didn't even have any to begin with

What seemed to make him particularly angry was that *some more chocolate* presupposed that he had already had some 'to begin with', so that this presupposition was taken by the person to whom it was addressed as a considerable insult.

I once witnessed another misfire which I still do not fully understand. The customer in front of me in the sandwich shop one lunchtime handed over her money and said

41 Could I not have a twenty pence coin in the change please

It is obviously a bizarre utterance, but she and I were quite unprepared for the reaction of the shop assistant, who spun round and glared at her. What had she done wrong, I wonder?

And then there was one of the secretaries who works in the same building as me, who, in the days before the building became a no-smoking zone, put a big notice on her office door which read

42 Thank you for not smoking

This was taken rather amiss by one or two people who should have known better but who clearly did not like being ordered about by the secretary.

This reaction suggests that misfires are a kind of pragmatic failure which results from language being used in a way that is not appropriate to the context. Thus the first sentence of the letter which came with my council tax form would have been perfectly appropriate in some other context. The sentence was

43 Any English-speakers who have problems reading this form should contact Doreen McCarthy at the Adult Basic Education Service telephone: 265 5725

I did not contact Doreen McCarthy, although I had problems reading the form, which was written entirely in Urdu, Bengali, Hindi, Punjabi, and Cantonese. I did not contact her because I recognized the sentence as a misfire.

An interesting question arises as to whether you can have an intentional misfire. I was once at a meeting at the head office of a well-known cultural institution which specializes in employing people with fruity voices whose job is to make visitors feel uncomfortable. I had just arrived when a Fruity Voice came up to me and peered at my name badge. 'I'm afraid I don't know where Durham is,' she said. 'Is it in Northumberland?' I knew what was going to happen, but I could not resist the temptation to reply, 'Durham's in Durham.' I knew at the time that I would have to explain and apologize, and that we would both end up covered with embarrassment. As a pragmaticist I was well aware that my reply appeared to lack the information my interlocutor felt she was entitled to, and was in any case rather paradoxical in character. Was it a misfire or a calculated insult?

What have we said so far? We have listed a number of features of talk which are at the heart of pragmatics. They include the notions of appropriacy and relevance on the one hand and our liking for non-literal and indirect meaning on the other. We have seen that there is a crucial relationship between what we say and the context in which it is most relevant. This is made possible to some degree by the indeterminacy of language and the role of inference in language understanding. Although for convenience I have treated each of these features as distinct, it is already apparent that they are really a bundle which typically appear together. Take the case of the utterance

44 Now I've done it

which will be indelibly etched in my memory after one particular occasion when I heard it used. I was watching a group of American visitors on their first morning in China trying to eat fried eggs with chopsticks. Somehow one of them managed to snap a chopstick clean in half, and as he picked up the two broken pieces and proceeded to treat them as the next best thing to a knife and fork, he said despairingly to his colleagues

44 Now I've done it

His utterance seemed perfectly appropriate to a situation that could not have passed without some comment. It was certainly an indirect way of conveying whatever message it does convey. And it obviously requires an inference to be drawn to determine just how it is relevant in just whatever the context seems to be.

I am now going to try and round off this chapter in the more systematic way promised all those pages ago by looking at the pragmatic properties of a single utterance. I shall be suggesting that, although it is relatively easy to describe the pragmatic properties of utterances (as we have just been doing, in fact), it is much more difficult to know how to account for them or to explain how we understand underdetermined utterances more or less in the way the speaker intends.

The utterance

45 I'm here now

which Kaplan (1978) discusses briefly, looks superficially innocuous. But for a pragmaticist it has three very problematical properties.

Deixis The first of these is to do with an indeterminacy that can only be resolved when we look at the context, and particularly at three aspects of that context, *who* the speaker is and *where* and *when* the sentence is uttered. This indeterminacy stems from the speaker's use of the words *I*, *here*, and *now*. Although the meaning of the word *I* is perfectly clear and not at all problematical, the reference that is effected each time it is uttered clearly depends on who utters it. In this respect *I* is a quite different kind of description from *the Duke of Edinburgh*, which always refers to the same person. Just the same point could be made about *here*, whose meaning is clear enough but whose reference depends on the location of the speaker when the sentence is uttered, so that *here* might refer to *Durham* or *Durban* or *Marks and Spencer* or the speaker's bedroom. Similarly the reference of *now* is determined by the time at which the sentence is spoken. This property of a small set of words like *I*, *here*, and *now* that they refer to an aspect of the context in which they are uttered is called deixis.

Implicature The second problematical property of *I'm here now* stems not only from the natural indeterminacy of the utterance but also from the context, and from considering what inference ought to be drawn to make the utterance maximally relevant. Imagine the utterance being used by two different students talking to themselves on the day they arrive in Durham to begin their linguistics degree course. The first student comes from Southampton and uses *here* to refer to Durham; the second student comes from Singapore and has been looking forward to studying overseas for several years—for this student *here* refers to Britain. The point is that both references for *here* are equally consistent with any 'true' or literal meaning the sentence might be thought to have, but clearly knowing which is the right one is a matter of working out which understanding is the most relevant and might be thought to be the one being implied by the speaker. A similar point could be made about *now*, which for one speaker might refer to a particular date and for another might mean something more like 'at last'. Mrs Thatcher often used the word *now* to mean 'since 1979', but now (i.e. in the post-Thatcher period) not many people would use it in this sense. Thus one of the properties of language is that, in addition to conveying an invariant meaning, it also frequently conveys an implied meaning which the addressee must infer. This kind of meaning is called an implicature.

Utterances as speech acts The third problematical property of *I'm here now* stems not only from the natural indeterminacy of the utterance, and from the context and considering what inference ought to be drawn to make the utterance maximally relevant, but also from considerations of what it most appropriately counts as doing. So if I had heard that a relative had been injured and taken to hospital, I might race there as quickly as possible and say 'I'm here now', which would count perhaps as a comforting reassurance. On the other hand, if I get home from work and see my children larking about instead of getting on with their homework and say 'I'm here now', it counts as a stern warning. Or if I were to arrive late for a meeting and knew that I had kept my colleagues waiting, uttering 'I'm here now' would count as an apology. Because utterances not only convey an invariant meaning (the person speaking is in the location of the addressee at the time of speaking) but also count as *doing* something, be it reassuring, warning, apologizing, or whatever, we call them speech acts. After all, there isn't much point on saying 'I'm here now', which must be readily apparent to all and sundry anyway, unless you intend to do something by saying it.

Checking understanding (2)

In the following chapters we shall be looking at these three areas, deixis, implicature, and speech acts, in more detail. Meanwhile, you might like to think about one well-known famous utterance within the framework sketched out in this chapter. Consider President Kennedy's famous announcement in Berlin shortly after the Wall was erected, 'Ich bin ein Berliner', in which he intended to say (literally) that he was a Berliner:

46 Ich bin Berliner
    I   am Berliner
    (I'm a Berliner)

but because of his speech-writer's limited knowledge of German managed instead to say that he was a kind of cake:

46' Ich bin ein(e) Berliner (torte)
     I   am a   Berliner (cake)
     (I'm a cake)

Despite his mistake, his audience of course understood what he wanted to say and applauded loudly.

Can you identify the deictic property of this utterance, and any implicature(s) it contains, and what speech act is accomplished by it? In coming to these conclusions, take the context into account, try to work out what indirect meaning President Kennedy was trying to convey, and draw whatever inferences you need to to make proper sense of his utterance. In short, how do you get from an underdetermined utterance to the most relevant understanding of it?

Raising pragmatic awareness: using and understanding language

(1) This exercise works well if you do Step 1 individually and Steps 2 and 3 in your tutorial or with a group of friends.

1. Write a very short dialogue between two imaginary characters.
2. Dictate each utterance to your colleagues—as you dictate, they write down, not what you say but the contexts in which they imagine the utterance being spoken.
3. Ask each person to read out what they have written down, and discuss the pragmatics of the utterances in relation to the contexts which have been imagined for them.

(2) This exercise works best in a tutorial or with a group of friends. Choose an item from the list below and brainstorm all the contexts in which you could utter it:

I'm tired
I'm sorry
Is it me
I thought so
Don't

Why do you think a single proposition can function as so many different speech acts?

(3) Get together with a few friends. Each person should recall something surprising which someone once said to them. The other members of the group try to guess the context by asking Yes/No questions.

(4) This exercise works best in pairs. You and your partner each find three or four sentences from different newspaper stories, or captions for newspaper photographs, which invite the reader to draw an inference (e.g., 'The husband of the doctor who disappeared last week refused to comment. Meanwhile, the police continued digging in his garden'). When you have each found your sentences/captions, see whether your partner draws the same inferences as you and try to work out what triggers them. (*Acknowledgement*: this is Andrew Caink's idea.)

(5) This exercise works well in a tutorial group. Before the tutorial, cut out three or four magazine pictures and pin instructions to them which test

pragmatic skills. For example, if you cut out a picture of a romantic couple looking out over the sea at night, your instruction might be 'Ask these two for a cigarette/if they've lost a pen you've just found/where they get their hair done'; or if you cut out a picture of someone with a gun, the instruction might be 'Ask her/him for the gun'; or a picture of a toddler, 'Get this person to admire your shoes/call you Mummy'. Take the pictures and instructions to your tutorial and ask the other members of your group how they would carry out the instructions.

Further reading

Blakemore (1992: 3–23); Levinson (1983: 1–5); Mey (1993: 3–17).

2

Deixis: the relation of language to its point of origin

'Faith, sir, we are here today, and gone tomorrow'
(Aphra Behn, *The Lucky Chance*, IV)
'Here today, here tomorrow'
(advertisement for a computer supplier)

Keywords: deixis, point of origin, common ground, reference, indexicality, honorific, anaphoric, demonstrative, context, deictic centre, projection, grammaticalization.

This is a more theoretical chapter than the previous one, and relies on invented rather than live data. In it I make the point that the more speaker and addressee share common ground, the more they are able to effect reference.

2.1 *Reference resolved by context: the case of indexicals*

Consider the following:

1 I know you'll enjoy reading the chapter

2 When I say you have to read the chapter, I mean *you* have to read it and *you* have to read it and *you* have to read it

3 You never know whether to read every chapter or skip one or two

In (1) *you* picks out a particular but different person on each separate occasion when the sentence is read. On this occasion it is, yes, you, my friend, who is the referent (or person referred to). (And if by any chance there are two of you out there working together in a team reading the book aloud and saying nasty things about me, the author, then on this particular occasion *you* picks out and refers to both of you.)

Similarly, if in a lecture I were to deliver (2), the three stressed *you*s in the second part of the utterance would be accompanied by gestures and/or eye-contact of some kind. Each would pick out a different referent whose identity would be known only by those present at the time of my utterance.

Because *you* identifies a particular referent (or referents)—picks them out to refer to, if you like—we call these words 'indexical' and this function of language 'deictic', borrowing the Greek word meaning *pointing to* or *picking out*. Typically, (1) is considered an example of 'symbolic' deixis because, although a referent is picked out, this is not marked by any gestural behaviour. This is to be contrasted with the 'gestural' use of *you* in the second part of (2).

The lexical item *you* is almost always used deictically, and usually symbolically. But in

3   You never know whether to read every chapter or skip one or two

you has a much more general reference. In fact, being present when the sentence was uttered would not help you to identify a referent. Thus this generalized use of *you* is not deictic.

These three uses of *you* could be represented diagrammatically as in Fig. 2.1.:

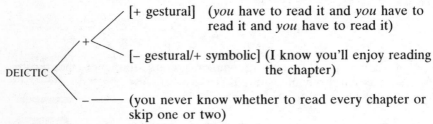

Fig. 2.1

Now consider the more problematical case of

4   You just have to read this chapter

Sometimes this use of *you* might be thought to pick out the addressee(s) and identify them as the referent, so that the use of *you* would be deictic. At other times it might be thought to be a general exhortation implying that the chapter was well worth reading, in which case the use of *you* would be non-deictic. The use of *you* is frequently problematical in intercultural communication where native speakers of English think they are using it non-deictically, but their non-native speaker addressees take it deictically to refer to themselves. Utterances like

5   You don't want to go to London

are guaranteed to bewilder in such encounters.

Checking understanding (1)

1. Try to think of utterances in which the following words might be used (a) gesturally, (b) symbolically in a deictic way, (c) non-deictically: *this, now, behind.*

2. Write five or six sentences containing either the word *that* or the word *then* which you could place on a cline from very obviously deictic to non-deictic.

At this stage let us consider a number of difficult questions:

1. How many deictic words are there in a language, and to what extent can these words be used both deictically and non-deictically?

Simple answer: Deictics are a closed class, i.e. there is a limited set of such words; some of them can be used non-deictically.

2. Is there any way of categorizing these words?

Simple answer: It is possible to categorize them according to semantic criteria such as person reference (e.g. *you*), place reference (e.g. *here*), and time reference (e.g. *now*).

3. Why should this small set of lexical items have this property?

Simple answer: Speakers will always find it useful to have a limited set of indeterminate lexical items (such as *you*) whose references are determined in the context of face-to-face interaction and which act as a shorthand for a potentially infinite number of descriptions (such as the names of all the people one would ever address).

Many pragmaticists would doubt whether any of these simple answers is truly adequate, but if we treat them as working hypotheses for the moment, this will enable us to establish a familiarity with a set of deictic terms.

Person deixis

We have already seen how *you* can be used both deictically (when the context is required to determine the reference) and non-deictically (when the reference is general rather than to particular, identifiable persons). *You* is also used in English in a much wider range of social contexts than would be represented by a single second-person reference term in most other languages. For example, most languages have at least two forms, an informal one for use when talking to friends and a more formal one used for showing respect to the person addressed, typically because they are older or more important than the speaker. In many languages the second-person plural form (*vous* in French) or the third-person plural form (*Sie* in German) has this honorific function, so that in German

6 Ich danke Ihnen
   I   thank them (dative)
   (Thank you)

is a formal way of thanking and at the same time showing respect to the person one is speaking to. In discussing this 'honorific' use of language, Levinson (1983: 90), following Comrie (1976), points out that deictics like *vous* and *Sie* are oriented to the referent (the person being referred to) rather than to the addressee (the person being addressed). This explains why it makes sense to describe the person we are talking to as *you* (plural) or *they* without appearing contradictory: we address our equals and refer to our superiors. To a native speaker of English this may seem exotic at first; but of course there are similar strategies in English, such as saying 'Shall we do x' or 'We could do y' to someone more important than yourself whom you are steering towards some course of action. Here the interrogative form and the use of the modal auxiliaries *shall* and *could* convey respect to the addressee. In Polish it would be usual for a ticket-collector, finding a passenger in the humiliating position of being ticketless on a train, to show respect by including him/herself in the reference as a sign of respect:

7   Nie mamy   biletu
    not have (1st pl.) ticket
    [We don't have a ticket]
    You haven't got a ticket?

In English this inclusion of self in a reference is usually sarcastic rather than respectful.

   In English the appearance of *you-all* (often used by teachers when talking to groups of students) and *yous* and the refusal of the old informal *thee* and *thou* forms entirely to die out in some areas suggests that speakers of English do indeed want to make distinctions that are impossible when there is only a single form available to them.

   Just as *you* (and the possessive forms *your* and *yours*) are typically deictic, so too are the first-person pronouns *I* and *we* and the possessives *my*, *mine*, *our* and *ours*. The minimalist approach, whereby most speakers of English make do with one second-person form, is also favoured with English first-person forms. In

8   What are we supposed to do

the deictic *we* would typically include the addressee in the reference if the speaker were one student asking another about an assignment, but exclude the addressee from the reference if two students were asking their tutor for instructions or advice. Many languages grammaticalize exactly this distinction between the 'inclusive' and 'exclusive' uses of *we*.

   The third-person pronouns, *he*, *it*, *she*, and *they*, are not usually considered deictic because they refer to objects or persons already mentioned in the discourse (antecedents). This kind of reference is called 'anaphoric'. A typical example of anaphoric reference would be *it* in (2), whose antecedent is *the chapter*:

2   When I say you have to read the chapter, I mean *you* have to read it
    and *you* have to read it and *you* have to read it

All pronouns require identification with some other point for their reference to be effected. In the case of third-person anaphors, the reference is determined in relation to an antecedent elsewhere in the discourse; in the case of deictics, the reference is determined in relation to the point of origin of the utterance.

Checking understanding (2)

Here are some problems to puzzle over:

1. Spend a few minutes trying to decide whether *we* and *our* can be used non-deictically.

2. Do you agree that all third-person pronouns are non-deictic? What do you make of *him* and *it* in *Let him have it, Chris*?

3. When the *fatwa* was pronounced on the author Salman Rushdie following the publication of his novel *The Satanic Verses*, he made a written statement apologizing for the distress his book had caused. Consider the following sentence taken from this apology: 'Living as we do in a world of so many faiths, this experience has served to remind us that we must all be conscious of the sensibilities of others.' Try to decide whether you think he meant to use *we* and *us* inclusively or exclusively (or even non-deictically).

Place deixis

Consider (4) again:

4 You just have to read this chapter

The reference of the demonstrative description *this chapter* can only be determined if the context indicates which of several potential possible chapters is being picked out. This makes it different from non-deictic descriptions like *the second chapter*. For most but not all speakers of English, there are two deictic proximal demonstratives, *this* (pl. *these*) and *that* (pl. *those*), which may be used either as pronouns or in combination with nouns. Again, English is rather minimalist in having only a two-member set of proximals, although for some speakers *yonder* is a third member of the set of terms denoting relative proximity to the speaker.

Other place deictics include

here, there, where (and the archaic *hither, hence, thither, thence, whither, whence*)
left, right
up, down, above, below, in front, behind
come, go, bring, take

The extent to which context is involved in determining the reference of these items is well illustrated by what happens when Literature students climb the stairs to the floor in the building where I work and to their surprise find the Linguistics Department office at the top of the stairs directly facing them. They then typically ask our secretary where the Literature office is. Sometimes she replies

9 Just along the corridor on your left

and sometimes

9' Just along the corridor on your right

This is not because she wants to be difficult (quite the contrary, in fact), but because she thinks (9) is more helpful for students who are standing in the doorway facing her directly with the Literature office down the corridor to their left (Fig. 2.2)

Fig. 2.2

and (9′) more helpful for students who look through her door over their right shoulders with the Literature secretary's office further along on the right-hand side of the corridor down which they are already facing (Fig. 2.3).

Fig. 2.3

Checking understanding (3) ─────────────────────────────

1. What is the difference between saying

10 I'm going to London

11 I'm coming to London

2. Is *somewhere else* deictic?

3. You are looking at a school photograph with Mark in the middle. If I described one of the other people as being

12 to the left of Mark

13 on the left of Mark

14 on Mark's left

in which cases would the use be deictic and why? (See Fig. 2.4.)

Fig. 2.4

Time deixis

Here is a list of some of the deictic items whose reference can only be determined in relation to the time of the utterance in which they occur:

this/last/next Monday/week/month/year
now, then, ago, later
yesterday, today, tomorrow

Although making such a list is relatively simple, the use of time deictics is not always so straightforward. For example, if I say to my son at the beginning of September

15 I hope you're going to do well this year

he knows that *this year* refers to the school year. If I say the same thing on 1 January, it refers to the calendar year. And if I say it on 20 October, his birthday, it refers to the year up until his next birthday. A related phenomenon occurs in the case of utterances including the deictic item *today*. If I say

16   Today's always a bad day

as I get out of bed on a Monday morning, *today* refers to *Monday*. But if I say

17   I'll see to it today

18   I filled up with petrol today

today refers to some unspecified moment in that portion of the day that remains unexpired (17) or has already passed (18). The use of *yesterday*, *today*, and *tomorrow* is also privileged over the use of the name term for the days, so that we cannot say

19   I'm going to finish this book on Thursday

if either today or tomorrow is Thursday. Again, English is rather minimalist in having only a three-member set of pre-emptive terms of this sort. Many languages have four or five, and some even have seven.

   Another very important time deictic is the tense system. In fact, almost every sentence makes reference to an event time. Often this event time can only be determined in relation to the time of the utterance. Thus when Alf Ramsay, the former manager of the England football team, said repeatedly in 1965 and 1966

20   England will win the World Cup

he was referring to an event which he thought would be accomplished in 1966. Now, it only makes sense to refer to that event with a past form such as

20′   England won the World Cup

or to make the sentence non-deictic by saying

20″   England won the World Cup in 1966

Checking understanding (4) ————————————————

Some weeks after his first wife died, Thomas Hardy wrote the poem 'After a Journey'. It included the line apparently addressed to his deceased wife

21   What have you found to say of our past

or, more accurately, it included this line and the word 'now'—but I am not telling you where he placed *now*.

1. How many grammatical positions can you find for *now* in this line?

2. Consider each position and decide whether *now* is used deictically or non-deictically, and if deictically whether it is used symbolically or gesturally.

3. Can you draw any conclusions about the relationship between where *now* is placed in the line and deictic usage in general?

4. Why do you think people say *bye now* and *bye then* when they part?

5. List all the examples of person, place, and time deixis you can think of.

2.2 *Deixis: further issues*

Deixis and inference

When we hear a deictic we typically make a number of assumptions about the context. In an utterance like

22 The postbox is on the left

the natural assumption is that the postbox is on the left in relation to the speaker. However, this unmarked centre can be suspended, as we saw in examples (9) and (9'). Here the use of *on your left* and *on your right* is deictic, since the same location is being indicated by two different descriptions and can only be determined by knowing the context, in this case the direction in which the addressee is facing. But the co-text associated with *left* and *right*, the lexical item *your*, advises the addressee that the spatial deictic centre has shifted from the unmarked norm (the location of the speaker) to a marked alternative (the location of the addressee). Sometimes a shift is accomplished without co-text, the context itself being sufficient to prompt the addressee to draw the inference that they rather than the speaker are the deictic centre. If I am the hider in a game of hide-and-seek, for example, I might decide to give the seeker a clue by calling out

23 Behind the tree

The seeker would draw the inference that I was behind the tree in relation to themselves rather than in relation to myself!

It is also very common for a speaker to update the deictic centre in more extended discourse. So that if I am giving you directions, I may punctuate them with expressions like 'after the traffic lights' or 'when you get to the post office'. These are signals to you to update the deictic centre and to interpret succeeding directions in relation to this new centre. We do the same with time when we say things like 'and then', 'even earlier', or 'after that', which serve to provide a new deictic centre in relation to which subsequent utterances are understood.

In

15 I hope you're going to do well this year

the three possible referents are determined by the three possible deictic centres or points of origin of the utterance. So that when an addressee knows the point of origin, they will be able to infer which reference is intended by the speaker.

Deictic change

We have already noticed how English has dispensed with the familiar second person *thou*, and that forms like *hence* and *yonder* are largely archaic. Many of the lexical items which are no longer used in face-to-face interaction have found a place in the interaction that goes on between a writer and a reader. *Hence* and *thence*, for example, like *now*, *then*, *earlier*, *in an earlier chapter*, *above*, *in the paragraph above*, *next*, *in the next section*, and the lexical item used in the first sentence of this paragraph, *already*, are frequently used to point a reader up and down a discourse. These deictics refer to parts of the discourse in relation to a deictic centre, the current place in the text.

This tempts us to draw some conclusions about the way that the deictic inventory adapts itself to the needs of language-users, and suggests that 'face-to-face' in our simple answer to Question 3 on page 21 is too narrow: 'Speakers will always find it useful to have a limited set of indeterminate lexical items whose references are determined in the context of face-to-face interaction, and which act as a shorthand for a potentially infinite number of descriptions.'

We might hypothesize that language is prototypically used in face-to-face interactions to encode aspects of the context that are available to interactants as a means of determining otherwise indeterminate references. But the spread of literacy and the use of the written form for even the most everyday communicative needs (such as communicating with the milkman) means that redundant face-to-face deictics such as *hence* find a new role in written communicative discourse. Is there perhaps a relationship between making do with a limited number of deictic items in face-to-face interactions and the extent to which a society uses a written code to communicate?

Deixis and cultural typology

The discussion of person deixis earlier in this chapter drew attention to the use of second-person honorific forms to encode the relative status of speaker and addressee. In deciding to use either *tu* or *vous*, a French speaker is in fact encoding the extent to which they and the addressee are of similar or different social status. This use of language therefore reinforces a social context that is acknowledged by the speaker as having an existence prior to the interaction.

In most European languages, speakers find it relatively difficult to refer to second-person addressees or to third persons. Such references are almost always more marked, and involve the speaker in a choice between a more complex set of linguistic alternatives than first-person references. However, this is not a universal linguistic phenomenon. There are certainly languages in which it is more difficult or more complex morphologically to talk about oneself than about others. Kelly (1984) shows how in Sara-Kaba, an unwritten language spoken in Chad, for example, speakers who refer to themselves in utterances typically have to use the first-person pronoun three times in a sentence. The relative difficulty of referring to oneself in Sara-Kaba, or to others in French, suggests that language is being used to invoke some aspect of social organization. Honorific uses of person deictics are therefore reflections of cultural typology. This is not very surprising: in cultures where there is a relatively greater distance between those with relatively more and those with relatively less power, we would expect face-to-face encounters to reflect this.

Most of these honorific references are relational in the sense that they encode social relations as they are perceived to exist in a particular interaction. Some are absolute, though. For example, the lexical item *wog* in British English encodes the status of the speaker and the status of the person referred to in an absolute way irrespective of the relative status of the inter-actants. Thus my wife, who comes from the country that used to be Yugoslavia, might be described by someone who should know better as a *wog*, a term denoting low status, but would not be able to refer to herself in this way without causing amusement. In British English it is possible, if despicable, to say of someone

24 She's a wog

but it is not possible, although it may cause amusement, for someone to say

25 I'm a wog

In this way language is used to reflect an external social context. Such uses of language seems to serve the purpose more of confirming an understood social structure than of resolving an indeterminacy.

Thus a speaker of French can use *tu* and *vous* and a speaker of English can use *Madam* and *Sir* either to reflect an existing social structure or to create one for the purposes of the interaction at hand. Why should language have these two functions? This is a paradox which we will return to in a later chapter.

The limits of indexicality

Most of this chapter has been about the deictic properties of a closed class of demonstratives that include determiners like *this* and *that*, personal pronouns and possessives, and some time and place adverbials. The social relation encoded in *tu* or *vous* raises a question about the extent to which language typically encodes a social relation, and whether non-demonstrative lexical items are also indexical.

Speakers must choose not only between *tu* and *vous* but also between an infinite number of possible ways of conveying the proposition or essential idea that underlies the actual utterance they will decide upon. Think for a moment about your reaction to the first example in this chapter:

1 I know you'll enjoy reading this chapter

Try to recall how you felt about the relationship that was assumed between yourself as reader and me as writer when you read it. You know that I was assuming a relationship between us, a kind of common ground, precisely because, as you think about it now, you may or may not be feeling happy with this assumed relationship. I don't suppose I would have conveyed the proposition in the same way if the addressee had been a member of the Royal Family—or even a member of my own family, come to that. This suggests that utterances themselves have indexical properties in that they invoke (i.e. they create or presuppose) a shared understanding of the speaker–addressee social relation. Could the same thing be true of lexical items, in the sense that the use of any particular lexical item assumes a common ground between speaker and addressee?

Recall

24 She's a wog

25 I'm a wog

Just the same arguments as we rehearsed before could be applied to sentences like

26   She's British

27   I'm British

The lexical item *British* can only be used by or to refer to a referent who meets certain eligibility conditions. Moreover, it is clear that there is not a single set of criterial properties which every referent described as *British* must display. The following examples all use the term *British* in a way that points up its indeterminacy:

28   My American friend thinks I'm very British
   British Summer Time
   I became a British subject when I came here in 1974
   I'm always careful to call myself British rather than English

In each of these sentences, the word *British* is used by the speaker in ways that assume the addressee's ability to pick out a relevant meaning. This suggests that indexicality cannot be limited to a small closed class of deictic items, but that everything we say assumes common ground between speaker and audience. This was already clear in the previous chapter, when we discussed some of the different ways in which the utterance 'I'm tired' is understood. The time has come to think more carefully about indexicality.

Checking understanding (5)

1. Try to work out prototypical (or best examples of) interactions in which the first three examples in this chapter might occur. Do this by deciding what sort of relationship between speaker/writer and addressee/audience is assumed:

1   I know you'll enjoy reading the chapter

2   When I say you have to read the chapter, I mean *you* have to read it and *you* have to read it and *you* have to read it

3   You never know whether to read every chapter or skip one or two

2. Heritage (1984) describes the way in which the word *nice* in

29   That's a nice one

exhibits indexicality when *that's* is used to refer to a range of different items. Think of a range of contexts in which it would be appropriate to say 'That's a nice one', and try to work out what you would expect an addressee to understand by *nice* in each case.

Common ground and indexicality

The deictic use of language we have been considering in this chapter has two clear properties: (a) it picks out a referent and (b) it relates that referent to a kind of common ground that exists between speaker and addressee. In the case of deixis, what is referred to and the point from which the reference is made are typically, although not necessarily, encoded in a single word: thus *you* picks out a referent and relates this referent to a particular point, typically the speaker's location at the time of utterance. This property of linking what is referred to to a background or context is what causes us to categorize deixis, and indexicality generally, as a pragmatic phenomenon: indexicality provides clear evidence that language is not an autonomous or self-contained phenomenon, but that aspects of context are organized into grammatical systems.

What, then, is the nature of this common ground in relation to which a referent is identified? One very important point is that there are far fewer options for elaborating the common ground than for elaborating the description of the referent. This is to be expected when we recall that the common ground is a phenomenon shared by speaker and hearer. Take one of the first sentences you read in this chapter:

30   And if by any chance there are two of you out there working together in a team reading the book aloud and saying nasty things about me, the author

It is readily apparent that the referential element of the deictic *out there* can be elaborated much more easily than the common ground element. Thus I might have written

31   out there in the real world

31'   out there at your desks

31"   out there in a library

I would have been much less likely to have written

32   ?out there miles away from me[1]

32'   ?out there in relation to me

The fixedness of the common ground is indicated in situations where we use different descriptions to refer to the same referent from different common-ground perspectives. Thus if at this stage in the chapter 'two of you out there' were to decide to write to me about some point, you might begin the letter like this:

33   There are two of us here who ...

My *two of you out there* and your *two of us here* pick out an identical referent. The different lexical items we each choose indicate the different points of origin of the two descriptions. When two people say to each other

34   I love you

each uses *I* to pick out the referent that the other picks out with *you*. Again, the referents are identical, but the deictic centres are different.

The fixedness of the deictic centre poses a particular problem when we want to quote what others have said to us. Imagine that my son says to my daughter

35   Why don't you want to come to the cinema with me, Eleanor

When she reports his utterance to me, she has a choice of several ways of representing its deictic properties. She might say any of the following:

---

[1] The use of ? before an example indicates that the example is awkward or unnatural.

36 Eddie said, 'Why don't you want to come to the cinema with me?'

36′ Eddie asked why I didn't want to come to the cinema with him

36″ Eddie complained that I didn't want to go to the cinema with him

In (36′) the deictic centre is partly projected from Eddie's original perspective to Eleanor's—she encodes this projection in her use of *I* and *him* and *didn't*, while her retention of *come* is still faithful to Eddie's utterance. Reported speech, and especially fully projected examples of reported speech like (36″), are important evidence of the existence of an unmarked deictic centre, which, as (35) and (36″) show, is that of the speaker's perspective even when the speaker is representing the speech of another person.

Our identification of this fixed deictic centre reveals an important pragmatic principle—that we are able both to assume shared knowledge and to foreground what is new in each particular utterance.

Because of the role of assumed knowledge in determining reference, deictic referents are typically denotations with limited descriptive power. Thus the pronouns *you* and *me* in (35) are semantically empty tokens, in the sense that they lack the descriptive power that the names of the people they refer to have. The pronoun *him* in (36′) is marked with the feature [+male], and significantly stands in anaphoric rather than deictic relation to its antecedent *Eddie*. Notice too that many place and time deictic adverbials are reductions of preposition phrases. Sometimes these reduced preposition phrases are deictic, while their non-reduced parents are both descriptions with more semantic content and, frequently, non-deictic:

Deictic	Non-deictic
up	up the stairs/hill (note *up the street* which may be either deictic or non-deictic)
down	down the pipe/rabbit-hole
above	above John/the waterline
below	below the belt/window
in front	in front of Mary/the children
behind	behind my back (but not *behind Rover*, *behind the tree*, which are deictic)

It is also significant that these are all noun-reduced preposition phrases (i.e. their nouns are gapped), and therefore more semantically reduced than preposition-reduced phrases such as (on today → today, to the right (hand side) → right). The deictic status of preposition-reduced adverbials is not altered by adding the gapped prepositions (i.e. by saying *on today* or *to the right*) and thus reconstituting them as whole phrases.

Grammaticalization and deixis

Leading on from the discussion of grammatical phenomena at the end of the previous section, in this section we illustrate Hanks's view that deictics 'constitute key points of juncture between grammar and context' (1992: 47).

Consider examples (20) and (20′) again:

20 England will win the World Cup

20′ England won the World Cup

Each of these statements encodes two moments in time, the time of the utterance and the time of the event. The first, the time of the utterance, is the deictic centre. This is the present, as we would expect. The second is the time of the event referred to—in the case of (20) some time in the future and in the case of (20′) some time in the past. The following sentence is slightly more complicated:

37 Because England had won the World Cup in 1966, they were granted an automatic place in the 1970 finals

In this sentence, we can distinguish three points in time, the time of utterance (present), the time of the first event referred to (longer ago in the past than the time of the second event), and the time of the second event referred to (a past time intermediate between the time of utterance and the time of the earlier event referred to). In this way the highly grammaticalized system of auxiliaries in English enables the speaker to refer from a present deictic centre to events at two points of distance in time, either in the past, as (37) illustrates, or, equally easily, in the future.

Of particular interest in (37) is the time of the second event, expressed by the use of the past tense. This is also the time of the other events which the speaker will refer to in the continuing discourse:

38 ...they were granted an automatic place in the 1970 finals, but were knocked out by Germany who came from behind to win

Example (38) shows that the 'second event' time in (37) is actually the time the speaker refers to in the continuing discourse, a kind of discourse time rather than event time. This suggests that even in a sentence like

39 I'm reading

which describes a present event, there are in fact three different time types encoded, even though they are all the present: the time of the utterance, the time of the event referred to, and the time the speaker refers to in the discourse. In case 'discourse time' is an unclear idea, imagine adding *now* to (39) to give

39′ I'm reading now

Clearly this use of *now* indicates that the speaker is referring to the present. This is even clearer when we consider the verb form known, significantly, as the present perfect. In

40 I've read most of the chapter now

we can distinguish the utterance time (present), the event time (past, indicated by *read*), and the discourse time that the speaker refers to (present, indicated by *now*).

Although these examples show that the unmarked temporal deictic centre is the present, this centre can be projected backwards as in utterances like

41 John tells me this isn't your first visit

42 What annoys me is that he will argue

In (41) and (42), events which are historically past are referred to as present (example 41) and future (example 42) because the deictic centre has been projected into the past. It can also be projected forward in utterances like

43 When you get to London . . .

44 If you went to London . . .

Here events which have yet to occur are referred to as present (example 43) and past (example 44) because the deictic centre has been projected into the future. We can tell that the deictic centre has been projected backwards in an example like (41) because it is impossible to say

45 *Yesterday John tells me this isn't your first visit[2]

45′ *John tells me this isn't your first visit yesterday

since *yesterday* always encodes a present deictic centre. Interestingly, (45) and (45′) are grammatical when embedded in an expanded sentence whose temporal deictic centre is unmistakably the present:

46 Yesterday John tells me this isn't your first visit/John tells me this isn't your first visit yesterday and now you tell me it is

One interesting example of fossilized projection of the temporal deictic centre from present to past occurs when a speaker refers to past cognitive events to do with understanding and retention of knowledge as though they were present. Thus in English, but not typically in other languages with comparable tense and aspect systems, speakers say *I forget* and *I (don't) understand* in response to utterances like

47 A: What's the name of that nice bread shop in Edinburgh
       B: I forget

48 A: Just boot the computer in the usual way and let the default programme take over
       B: I (don't) understand

This appears to be a kind of politeness strategy in which the speaker makes a past experience more immediate and thus more interesting for the addressee.

Summary   In this chapter we have seen how single lexical items such as *I*, *here* and *now* are part of a highly grammaticalized system and assume addressee knowledge of the speaker's identity (in the case of *I*), their spatial location (in the case of *here*) and temporal location (in the case of *now*) in order to identify referents in relation to this point of origin. Crucially, the references effected (i.e. to person, place, and time) can only be understood by an addressee who is able to reconstruct the speaker's viewpoint. When this reconstruction occurs, we have called the intersubjectivity attained 'common ground' or, in the earlier pages of the chapter, 'context'. Pragmatics is precisely about accounting for the ability of speakers and addressees to invoke a common context in relation to which a very wide range of language uses can be interpreted. This kind of interpretation is necessary because basic, literal meanings are radically underdetermined.

---

[2] An asterisk denotes an ungrammatical utterance.

In the health warning I put on this chapter in the first paragraph, I said that I wanted to use the chapter to make the point that 'the more speaker and addressee share common ground, the more they are able to effect reference'. One could go further still and claim that speaker and addressee will always attempt to find the common ground that will enable them to understand each others' utterances. Indexicals, and deictic indexicals in particular, are especially important to pragmaticists because they show how one kind of understanding, reference, is only possible when speaker and hearer share knowledge in common. Deictics display the prototypical property of all pragmatic language use—that of relying on speaker–hearer intersubjectivity for their interpretation. In the case of deictics this is more evident than in any other category of pragmatic phenomena. Hence their importance.

Raising pragmatic awareness: the relation of language to its point of origin

(1) Form a small group which includes at least one person with a good knowledge of a language other than English. Ask this person to translate utterances containing a range of deictic phenomena into their other language and explain any problems or differences to you. When the translator feels confident enough, ask her or him to translate each utterance literally, as if they were a computer, as well as naturally.

(2) This exercise works well in tutorial groups. Ask each member of the group to come with two consecutive sentences chosen from this book whose indexical properties they are prepared to discuss. It may help to ask each member of your group to score each indexical feature in their sentences on a five-point scale.

Further reading

Hanks (1992).

3

Implicit meaning

'Words are like leaves; and where they
  most abound,
Much fruit of sense beneath is rarely
  found.'
(Alexander Pope, *Essay on Criticism*)

Keywords: convey, entailment, conventional meaning, cooperative principle, implicature, maxim, inference, flout, hedge, metalingual gloss, intensifer, truth value, relevant, perspicuous, generalized, particularized, cancellability.

This chapter begins with a problem: how is it that a potential reader of Gerald Durrell's book *My Family and Other Animals* knows that the author is making fun of his family when the title does not say this? How is it that when you ask me how Manchester United did, and I reply

1 They won

you sometimes know that I am telling you that they did brilliantly (i.e. when they were playing in a European competition) and sometimes that they did rather poorly (i.e. when they were playing a non-league side in the FA Cup)? The meaning of *they won* is clear: the team referred to by *they* scored more goals than the team they were playing against. And yet this stated meaning is often less important than the other meaning that you understand from my utterance *and that I nowhere state*. How is it that we can convey meanings which we do not actually state?

   Take another example: the advertisement for instant tea, which, like the Coca-Cola advertisement, promotes its product with the legend

2 It's the taste

By itself this statement means very little, because we are not told what the taste is or does. And yet you and I understand it to mean that the taste is good. How can this be? And more puzzling still, when my daughter comes home from school and starts her destructive journey through the biscuit barrel, and I ask her why she did not eat her school dinner, and she replies

2 It's the taste

I understand her to mean exactly the opposite: that the taste is not good. How can the same sentence be understood to convey two meanings that are exactly the opposite of one another? This is the problem addressed in this chapter.

3.1 *Grice's theory of conversational implicature*

In order to solve this problem, we need first to draw a distinction between what the linguistic philosopher Paul Grice (1967a) called the 'natural' and the 'non-natural' meanings of utterances like *they won*. The natural meaning is that the team referred to by *they* scored at least one goal more than the team they were playing against. This kind of meaning is often called an entailment, a meaning that is present on every occasion when an expression occurs. So when you are talking about football, you can never say that a team 'won' without its entailing that they scored at least one goal more than their opponents. Unlike the entailment, the 'non-natural' meaning is variable, and on different occasions could be that the team referred to played particularly well or only rather modestly. This 'non-natural' meaning is only sometimes associated with the expression from which it may be derived, and is therefore not part of the *conventional* meaning of the expression.

Grice argued that speakers intend to be cooperative when they talk. One way of being cooperative is for a speaker to give as much information as is expected. So an addressee who knew that Manchester United were playing a top team in a European competition might be expecting the speaker to say that they had done reasonably well considering the circumstances. Since *they won* would be more than was expected, it would imply that Manchester United had done brilliantly. Conversely, an addressee who knew that Manchester United were playing a non-league side might be expecting the speaker to say that they had scored dozens of goals or that they had wiped the opposition out. Hearing only *they won*, less than might be expected, the hearer would draw the inference that they had played rather poorly. Because *they won* in the first context is more than the addressee was expecting and in the second less, in each case it gives rise to a non-conventional meaning. This kind of meaning was called an 'implicature' by Grice. He deliberately coined this word to cover any non-conventional meaning that is implied, i.e. conveyed indirectly or through hints, and understood implicitly without ever being explicitly stated.

Checking understanding (1) ————————————————

What implicatures are associated with the following utterances?
3   Some people believe in God
4   Damon Hill did well in his first season in Formula 1
5   I've got £100 in the bank
6   Linford Christie can run 100m in 9.9 seconds

Grice formalized his observation that when we talk we try to be cooperative by elevating this notion into what he called 'the Cooperative Principle'.

The Cooperative Principle: Make your conversational contribution such as is required, at the stage at which it occurs, by the accepted purpose or direction of the talk exchange in which you are engaged.

Within this Principle, Grice suggested four maxims:

Quantity
(i) Make your contribution as informative as is required (for the current purposes of the exchange).
(ii) Do not make your contribution more informative than is required.
Thus
7 Chelsea are having a good season
being all the information the speaker has, gives rise to the implicature
7' They aren't leading the championship
and
8 My job's OK
being a less enthusiastic way of talking about one's job than is expected, gives rise to the implicature that
8' The speaker is not happy in his/her work

Quality Try to make your contribution one that is true.
(i) Do not say what you believe to be false.
(ii) Do not say that for which you lack adequate evidence.
Thus
9 Smoking damages your health
being assumed to be well founded, gives rise to the implicature
9' The speaker believes/has evidence that it does
and
10 When will dinner be ready?
being assumed to be a sincere question, gives rise to the implicature
10' The speaker does not know, wants to know, and thinks the addressee knows.

Relation Be relevant.
Thus
11 You've got up to here now
gives rise to the most relevant implicatures, viz.
11' for *here*: page 38 (rather than Grice's third maxim, etc.)
11'' for *now*: at this stage in your pragmatics course (rather than today, since 1979, the twentieth century, etc.)

Manner Be perspicuous.
(i)   Avoid obscurity of expression.
(ii) Avoid ambiguity.
(iii) Be brief (avoid unnecessary prolixity).
(iv) Be orderly.
Thus
12 They washed and went to bed

being an orderly representation of the world, gives rise to the implicature

12′ in that order

and

13 Time flies

being assumed to be the expectable N + V structure rather than the less expectable V + N structure, gives rise to the implicature that

13′ the *tempus fugit* reading is intended (rather than that the addressee is an official at the insect Olympics and is being instructed to take a stopwatch and use it to time flies).

Checking understanding (2)

Grice observes that we are cooperative in other endeavours besides talk. Imagine two people working together on a single task such as cleaning a car, or building a wall, or changing a light-bulb. Can you think of any cooperative strategies they might use that are like those that apply in talk?

Flouting maxims

(7′), (8′), (9′), (10′), (11′ and 11″), (12′), and (13′) are all examples of implicatures that arise because the addressee assumes that the speaker is abiding by Grice's maxims. But the thought has probably already gone through your mind that speakers do not always abide by these maxims. For example, when I said

14 Durham's in Durham

to the intimidating lady (page 14), I was clearly not abiding by the maxim of Quantity in that the information I was giving did not appear, at least superficially, to be informative to the expected degree. I was considered rude precisely because I was obviously flouting one of the guidelines for holding a conversation.

Recently I just stopped myself in time from responding to a complaining student with

15 Well, it is a university

If I hadn't bitten my tongue in time, I would have flouted the maxim of Quantity by not providing any new information, and no doubt upset the student in the process by not contributing suitably to the interaction. Although (15) flouts a maxim, notice that there is still an implicature. The addressee will assume that, despite flouting a maxim, the speaker is essentially cooperative and must therefore be intending to convey a meaning. I cannot sensibly be intending to convey the entailment of

15 Well, it is a university

since this meaning is already known to the addressee. In fact, whenever a maxim is flouted there must be an implicature to save the utterance from simply appearing to be a faulty contribution to a conversation. In the case of (15), the addressee will try to work out what I am intending to convey in addition to the information that was already known to them (i.e. that we are in a university)—perhaps that there is no point in complaining since what the complainant has noticed is to be expected. This is the implicature, what is implicit in (15) but nowhere explicitly stated.

Checking understanding (3)

1. Is it possible to flout all of the maxims? Decide whether the following utterances are flouts, and, if so, of which maxims:

16 Easy read, *Finnegans Wake*

17 Me: Have you done your homework
Eleanor: Daddy you know you said we could have a dog

18 Ahead of current thinking (National Power advertisement)

19 In cordless technology we have the lead (Black and Decker advertisement)

20 The best 4 × 4 × far (Land Rover advertisement)

21 First and fourmost (Land Rover advertisement)

2. The following ways of using language have been considered flouts of Gricean maxims. Which maxim do you think each flouts?

tautology:

22 At the end of the day the Church can only afford to pay the number of people it can afford to pay (a bishop speaking on the *Sunday* programme on Radio 4 when asked whether there would be job cuts in the Church)

metaphor:

23 Money doesn't grow on trees but it blossoms at our branches (Lloyd's Bank advertisement)

overstatement:

24 Now we've ALL been screwed by the Cabinet (*Sun* headline)

understatement:

25 It was more a case of being economical with the truth

rhetorical question:

26 How many divisions has the Pope? (Stalin)

3. Are you now able to explain why

2 It's the taste

gives rise to the implicatures suggested at the beginning of the chapter?

Summary 1 There are guiding principles which govern cooperative talk. Knowing these principles (maxims) enables an addressee to draw inferences as to the implied meanings (implicatures) of utterances. Every utterance, whether it abides by or flouts the maxims, has both 'natural' meaning (entailment) and 'non-natural' meaning (implicature). Flouting a maxim is a particularly salient way of getting an addressee to draw an inference. Thus there is a trade-off between abiding by maxims (the prototypical way of conducting a conversation) and flouting maxims (the prototypical way of conveying implicit meaning).

Hedging maxims

Sometimes when we talk we simply make assertions like

9 Smoking damages your health

But if you listen carefully when people talk, you notice that speakers are frequently reluctant to make bald statements like (9), instead preferring an utterance like (27), which might be taken to indicate that the speaker does not want to engage in further argument:

27 All I know is smoking damages your health

In this utterance, the speaker is making the assertion that *smoking damages your health*. But by prefacing it with *all I know is*, the speaker simultaneously advises the addressee that the quantity of information being conveyed is limited. So the speaker makes an assertion and simultaneously advises the addressee of the extent to which they are observing the maxims—in this case, only to a limited degree. Thus the maxim of Quantity is 'hedged'—in the same sense that we can talk about 'hedging' a bet.

If the speaker had said

28 They say smoking damages your health

they say would be interpreted as a hedge on the maxim of Quality, and would serve as a warning to the addressee that the speaker's information might not be as well founded as would normally be expected. So *all I know* in (27) and *they say* in (28) have a metalingual function, that is, they serve as glosses or comments on the extent to which the speaker is abiding by the conversational maxims.

Do you remember Pat in Chapter 1 and how she hedged Relation when she said

29 What's your name by the way

Here *by the way* advises Stephen that what Pat has just said is not as relevant at the stage at which it occurs in the conversation as he is entitled to expect. When she was nine, my daughter went with a friend to see *Arsenic and Old Lace*. She described afterwards how, at one stage in the play, a character had said he thought it was his last glass of elderberry wine, making it clear by the way she related it that *last* was meant to be ambiguous. Then she added

30 It was dead funny—if you see what I mean

If you see what I mean hedges the maxim of Manner. Having said *It was dead funny*, she realized she had produced a second, unintended pun, this time on *dead*, and so added *if you see what I mean* to advise us of the obscurity.

We have seen how conversational maxims can be hedged with metalingual glosses. Speakers can also use metalingual glosses to assure their addressees that the maxims are being scrupulously complied with, as the following examples show:

31 Smoking damages your health and that's all there is to it (Quantity)

32 Smoking damages your health for sure (Quality)

33 The point is that smoking damages your health (Relation)

34 Put plainly, smoking damages your health (Manner)

One important point about these maxim hedges and intensifiers is that none of them adds truth value to the utterances to which they are attached. Thus examples (27)–(34) are true under just the same circumstances as counterpart sentences without maxim hedges would be. This confirms that the hedges and intensifiers are not part of what is said or conveyed by a speaker but a comment on the extent to which the speaker is abiding by the rules for talk. It seems, then, that when we talk we not only convey messages but frequently like to tell each other how informative, well founded, relevant, and perspicuous these messages are.

Checking understanding (4)

1. List at least three hedges and three intensifiers for each conversational maxim.

2. Which parts of the utterance have truth value and which maxims do you think are being hedged or intensified by which phrases in the following answer provided by Sir Humphrey in *Yes Minister*:

35 Well Minister, if you asked me for a straight answer, then I shall say that, as far as we can see, looking at it by and large, and taking one time with another, in terms of the averages of departments, then, in the final analysis, it is probably true to say that, at the end of the day, in general terms, you would probably find that, not to put too fine a point on it, there probably wasn't very much in it one way or the other, as far as one can see, at this stage.

Summary 2 Speakers frequently use highly grammaticalized hedges and intensifiers to inform their addressees of the extent to which they are abiding by the maxims. These hedges and intensifiers show that the guiding principles for talk suggested by Grice really do exist, and that speakers orient to these principles as they communicate.

Implicature and entailment

So far we have demonstrated that one kind of meaning, implicature, arises as a result of interactants' mutual knowledge of the conversational maxims. The non-natural, or non-conventional, status of this meaning is illustrated by utterances like

2 It's the taste

This is non-conventional in the sense that it gives rise to different implicatures in different contexts of use. This is really another way of recognizing that an implicature is the result of an addressee drawing an inductive inference as to the likeliest meaning in the given context. So when someone is trying to sell something, *It's the taste* will give rise to a quite different implicature from that inferred when we are discussing school dinners.

An inductive inference is a conclusion derived from a set of premises sufficient to justify it for so long as no additional premiss is added which would cause a different conclusion to be arrived at. Consider the following utterance

36 We have a child

The obvious inference to draw is that we have one and not more, since the Quantity maxim enjoins us to provide as much information as is required. But if an additional premiss is adduced (in fact we have two children), then the original inference is no longer valid. So if I am asked when buying a Family Railcard whether we have a child, I can reasonably say

37 We have a child, in fact we have two

But there are no circumstances under which I will ever be able to say

38 *We have a child, in fact we have none

This tells us that (36) entails at least one child and implies not more than one. Any attempt to deny the entailment, or conventional meaning, of (36) (*at least one*) must always result in a contradiction, since the speaker is saying x and not-x simultaneously. An implicature, on the other hand, is an inductive inference drawn by the speaker which will be valid on most occasions, but may be cancelled if an additional premiss inconsistent with the inference is added. Hence the implicature, or non-conventional, meaning of (36) (*no more than one*) may be denied.

Notice also that the direction of the entailment and the implicature cannot be derived algorithmically from example (36), but instead is determined by world knowledge. Hence

6′ Linford Christie can run 100m in 9.9 seconds [implicature: not less than 9.9], in fact he can run it in 9.8

is grammatical, whereas

6″ *Linford Christie can run 100m in 9.9 seconds [entailment: not more than 9.9], in fact he can run it in 10

is not.

Checking understanding (5)

Apply the *in fact* test to determine the entailment and the implicature in the following examples:

5 I've got £100 in the bank
39 Nick Faldo can do a round in 70
40 My daughter has five school dinners a week
41 My daughter eats five school dinners a week

Summary 3 We began with Grice's hypothesis that there are agreed guidelines for talk. We have now been able to show two distinct kinds of meaning, one of which, implicature, arises as a direct consequence of interactants accepting these cooperative strategies. Thus what is conveyed in an utterance will typically consist of what is said or entailed on the one hand and what is implied on the other. This is represented in Figs. 3.1(a) and (b).

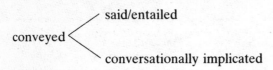

Fig. 3.1a

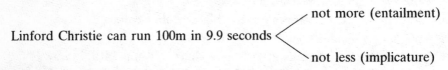

Fig. 3.1b

Entailments are conventional or semantic meanings which cannot by definition be cancelled without creating a contradiction; implicatures are inductive inferences which the hearer draws, and may therefore be cancelled: Fig. 3.1(c).

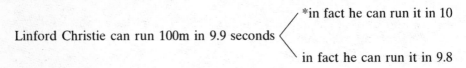

Fig. 3.1c

Particularized and generalized conversational implicature

Grice (1975) drew a distinction between what he termed 'generalized' and what he termed 'particularized' conversational implicature. Generalized conversational implicatures arise irrespective of the context in which they occur. So examples like

3   Some people believe in God
4   Damon Hill did well in his first season in Formula 1
5   I've got £100 in the bank

always give rise to the same implicatures no matter what the context. And these are clearly implicatures rather than entailments, since they can all be denied:

3' Some people believe in God [implicature: not all], in fact (virtually) everyone does

4' Damon Hill did well in his first season in Formula 1 [implicature: he did not win the Championship], in fact he won the Championship

(although perhaps it would be more appropriate to say

4" Nigel Mansell did well in his first season in Indy Car racing [implicature: he did not win the Championship], in fact he won the Championship)

5' I've got £100 in the bank [implicature: not more], in fact I've got £200

The issue in these examples is not what is the most relevant way to take them, since the same inferences will always be drawn whatever the particular context in which they occur. This is in contradistinction to the particularized implicatures that arise in the case of utterances like

1 They won

and

2 It's the taste

These are particularized implicatures because they are derived, not from the utterance alone, but from the utterance in context. As we have seen in the case of these two examples, particularized implicatures vary with the context.

The difference between generalized and particularized implicature will turn out to be a very important one for this reason: if all implicatures were particularized, one could reasonably argue that the single maxim of Relation, or Relevance, was sufficient to account for all implicature. The implicature would be what the addressee had to assume to render the utterance maximally relevant in its context. But generalized conversational implicature has little or nothing to do with the most relevant understanding of an utterance; it derives entirely from the guidelines for talk, and most often from the maxim of Quantity. This maxim enables an addressee to infer that when a speaker uses the quantifier *some*, it is because they are not in a position to use the quantifier *all*, and are therefore taken to be implying *not all*; or when a speaker uses the expression *did well*, it is because they are not in a position to say *won the Championship*, and are therefore taken to be implying *did not win the Championship*.

Summary 4 We can now add this further distinction to Figs. 3.1(a–c):

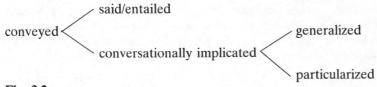

Fig. 3.2

Scalar implicature

Gazdar (1979) argues that these kinds of data show that we operate with scales, so that one scale would include *all* and *some* and another *won the*

Championship and *did well*. Choosing any item on a scale will imply that the items above it do not obtain. Other hypothesized scales include ⟨and...or⟩, ⟨certain...probable...possible⟩, and ⟨must...may...might⟩. This explains why we can resolve the sort of problem that arises if I say

42 You can get them in Harrods or Selfridges

In such a case, *or* might mean 'either Harrods or Selfridges but not both' or it might mean 'either Harrods or Selfridges or both'. This indeterminacy would be resolved if I said

42' You can get them in Harrods or Selfridges—I forget which

when I would clearly intend *or* to mean 'either Harrods or Selfridges but not both'. Similarly, if I said

42″ You can get them in Harrods or Selfridges—whichever is more convenient

I would clearly intend *or* to mean 'either Harrods or Selfridges or both'. These two meanings can be explained by appealing to the notion of scalar implicature. Because *or* is on a scale below *and*, a speaker selecting *or* would be implying *not and*. Thus 'either Harrods or Selfridges' is an entailment and 'but not both' is an implicature. In the case of (42″), this implicature is cancelled by adding 'whichever is more convenient'. This account of *or* saves us having to say that there are two different *or*s and that each needs its own dictionary entry. Thus we see how implicature enables us to give a simpler account of the semantic representation of *or*.

It is interesting to listen out for these scales when people talk. At a recent meeting I heard a student talked about in the following way:

43 He wasn't a poor candidate, but he was a weak candidate

It occurred to me that one could not have switched these descriptions around to produce

44   *He wasn't a weak candidate, but he was a poor candidate

although the following dramatic escalation is possible for a more mocking speaker:

45 He wasn't a weak candidate: he was a poor candidate

These examples show that when we are talking about candidates, there is a scale that includes ⟨poor...weak⟩, with *poor* being a stronger condemnation than *weak*.

These scales also apply to clause structure, so that the use of conjunctions such as *if* and *or* enable us to draw the conclusions that speakers cannot commit themselves to asserting the proposition(s) within the clauses so conjoined. Thus

46 If I've got £100 in the bank . . .

gives rise to the implicature *possibly I have £100 in the bank/possibly I do not have £100 in the bank*, as does

47 Either I've got £100 in the bank or I haven't

Generalized conversational implicatures are inferred irrespective of the context of the utterance, and result from the existence of the Quantity and Manner maxims. Particularized conversational implicatures are inferred in relation to a context, and result from the existence of the maxim of Relation.

Non-conversational implicature

Our children once chose a tube of toothpaste on the grounds that it had coloured stripes in it. The legend on the tube said

48 Actually fights decay

I was glad they chose the striped toothpaste because *actually fights decay* is such a perfect example of a conventional, or non-conversational, implicature. The lexical item 'actually' has a literal meaning or entailment—it means *in reality* or *in actuality*. But it also conveys a secondary, implied meaning, which is something like *although this is hard to credit*. This is an implicature because it is not part of the entailment of *actually*. It is conventional in the sense that (a) it does not derive from knowing the rules for talk (therefore it is not conversational) and (b) it is almost always associated with the particular lexical item (and thus a kind of natural meaning). Other examples of conventional implicatures include *but*, *even*, and *still*, as in

49 He was not a poor candidate, *but* he was a weak candidate

(entailment: *and*; conventional implicature: there is a contrast between the two conjoined propositions)

50 He stole *even* from the Queen
He stole *even* from the beggar

(entailment: *in addition/too/as well*; conventional implicature: what comes after *even* is a proposition at the end of a scale of probability)

51 Why some gentlemen *still* prefer bonds (headline in *The Times*)

(entailment: *now* (entailed) and *before* (presupposed); conventional implicature: while the proposition might have been expectable in the past, it is not now expectable).

There are also a large number of lexical items whose entailments are actually more difficult to determine with confidence than their conventional implicatures. These include *oh* as in

52 Oh what a pity
Oh how nice

(conventional implicature: the following proposition has only recently become apparent to me)

well as in

53 Well, we're not British Rail agents so I don't know the difference

(conventional implicature: the following proposition is not what the addressee is hoping to hear)

and *um* (conventional implicature: the following lexical item or proposition is taking some deciding on and may not fit its conversational or sentential context to the expected degree).

One feature of conventional implicatures which sets them apart from conversational implicatures is that, since they are 'conventionally' associated with particular lexical items, they are not readily cancellable. The cancellability problem is illustrated by the following examples:

48′ ?Actually fights decay, although this is not hard to credit

49′ ?He was not a poor candidate but he was a weak candidate, although no contrast is intended

50′ ?He stole even from the Queen/beggar, although there's nothing exceptional about that

51′ ?Why some gentlemen still prefer bonds, as is now expectable

52′ ?Oh how nice, and it didn't just occur to me

53′ ?Well we're not British Rail agents, so I don't know the difference, which will be what you were hoping to hear

Do attempts to cancel conventional implicatures give rise to contradictions (so conventional implicatures are entailment-like), or are they just very awkward?

Summary 5 We can now add conventional implicature to Fig. 3.2:

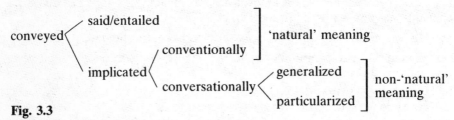

Fig. 3.3

Conventional implicatures are like entailments to the extent that they are conventional rather than inferred meanings in context; but they are unlike entailments (i.e. they are pragmatic) to the extent that they do not add truth-value to the sentences that contain them and the lexical items that give rise to them can be used in contexts which clearly disallow the implicature, as the following examples show:

54 What did you actually eat

(where *actually* does not imply that it is hard to credit that the addressee ate something)

55 A: I hope to meet a rich blonde
       B: Alexis is rich but she's not blonde

(where there is no contrast implied between being rich and blonde) and

56 I'm not even very sure of the date

(where *even* does not imply that not being sure of the date is at the end of a scale—but compare the following very similar example overheard in a conversation between two men in a theatre bar, which does seem to allow the conventional implicature:

57 And now she doesn't even know where she's parked the bloody car)

This is not quite the same account as Levinson's: 'Conventional implicatures are non-truth-conditional inferences that are *not* derived from superordinate pragmatic principles like the maxims, but are simply attached by convention to particular lexical items or expressions' (1983: 127).

His view, repeated in his discussion of presupposition, allows a conventional meaning to be inferred. The problem with this position is that it is very difficult to know what the premises would be from which the inference might be drawn when contextual knowledge is excluded.

Recognizing implicature

This section of the chapter will close with several examples of conventional and conversational implicatures, most of them from real utterances. This is to enable you to check that you are able to identify the implicatures that arise and/or the maxims that are hedged and/or flouted and the means by which an addressee infers implicated meaning.

Checking understanding (6) ——————————————

Conversational implicature as non-conventional:
1. In August/September 1992 a W.H. Smith advertisement featuring various items of stationery appeared on hoardings in Britain. The poster bore the legend:

58 We don't sell uniforms

This advertisement was followed by a series of 'We don't sell...' posters, which included an advertisement shortly before Christmas featuring videos of romantic films bearing the legend:

58′ We don't sell hankies

What are the implicatures in these two advertisements and how do they illustrate the non-conventional nature of conversational implicature?

2. How does the following invented example illustrate the non-conventional nature of conversational implicature:

59 A: Where's Sue
  B: There's a white car outside Bill's house

Checking understanding (7) ——————————————

Flouts: Which maxim is flouted by each of the following examples? How is the maxim flouted and what is the implicature or effect of the flout in each case?

60 A bad response could mean he is clapped out (from a *News of the World* article discussing the significance of the applause for John Major at a forthcoming Conservative Party conference)

61 Am I seeing double (question put to his friend by a potential customer standing in front of a Newcastle optician's shop displaying a billboard on which was written 'Appointment not always neccessary' (*sic*))

62 'Standard'—substandard I call them (comment made by a friend after lighting a series of disappointing fireworks bearing the 'Standard' brand-name)

63 Also available in white (comment scatched in the dirt on a white car)

Checking understanding (8)

Maxim hedges/intensifiers and truth value: How do the following differ?

64 It is a truth universally acknowledged that a single man in possession of a good fortune must be in want of a wife (Jane Austen, *Pride and Prejudice*)

64' It's true that a single man in possession of a good fortune must be in want of a wife (overheard as the question 'Do you think it's true that ...?' put by a student to her friend while chatting in the university library)

Checking understanding (9)

Implicature and stress: What is the difference between the following?

65 Radion removes dirt *and* odours (*Radion* advertisement)

65' Radion removes dirt and odours

Checking understanding (10)

Correcting an implicature: What is going on in the following utterance?

66 That was David Smeaton in, or rather more precisely on, Dartmoor (*Today*, Radio 4)

Checking understanding (11)

From conversational to conventional implicature:

67 A: Somebody told me it was cheaper to go by plane than by train. Is that right
B: Well we're not British Rail agents so I don't know the difference
A: I see

This is part of a conversation recorded in a travel agent. What does *I see* mean, and what does A mean when he says it?

Checking understanding (12)

Conventional and conversational implicatures: What is going on in the following examples?

68 A: What's the test score
B: England are following on
A: That's impossible

69 It's a humiliation to be sacked even from the Labour Party front bench (comment by a Conservative MP on the sacking of a Labour shadow minister, Radio 4 *Today*)

70 I have not even brought my wife into Horley Town Hall. That's what I think of Horley Town Hall (leader of Horley Council speaking on Radio 4)

71 *My Family and Other Animals* (Book title)

72 I never criticize anyone's handwriting

73 I never criticize anyone else's handwriting

Checking understanding (13)

Calculating implicatures: Since an implicature is an inference, it must be calculable, in the sense that we can work out the steps that a hearer must follow to arrive at it. First decide on the implicatures that arise in the following exchange, which you first came across in Chapter 1, and then work out how they are arrived at. Working for the second time with the same data should enable you to measure how much you have learnt.

74 A: Mr Major's at Wincanton today
  B: Oh is he. I didn't know that
  A: No, the horse, not the Prime Minister
  B: Oh the grey (Radio 5, *Morning Edition*)

Checking understanding (14)

A series of separate utterances taken from a single television broadcast are given below. They are transcribed so as to show the difference between what was actually said and what the accompanying Teletext subtitles showed on screen. Items printed in small capitals represent spoken text absent in the Teletext subtitles. What principles does the subtitler use to determine which features of the spoken language to omit from the subtitles?

01 NOW when you eventually married you tried to find them again didn't you?
02 her son and her daughter by her first marriage had BOTH left home
03 BUT sixty years ago the stigma of illegitimacy was strong
04 at the same time it's ALSO frightening
05 but NEVERTHELESS one in which attitudes to illegitimacy
06 I knew I wasn't their flesh and blood SORT OF THING
07 AND OF COURSE we used to get a few swear words IN BETWEEN
08 I remember a family THIS WAS when I was about nine I suppose
09 because she seemed a bit cold towards me I SUPPOSE
10 BECAUSE I MEAN they owned a car and everything
11 and I JUST simply walked down this lane
12 so he JUST took the case off me
13 AND THEN I MUST HAVE passed

14   and you could please yourself COULDN'T YOU SORT OF THING
15   so did you get on with his mother
16   two or three months ago I SHOULD THINK
17   I just said LIKE
18   and we didn't show it to that extent IF YOU KNOW WHAT I MEAN
19   OH yes YES
20   but I THINK it was when the children started to grow up
21   and the friendship grew from that WHICH WAS LOVELY
22   I grew up for another six or seven years before it REALLY hit me
23   so I thought WELL if Betty was there
24   WELL IT'S VERY GOOD OF YOU BUT I'm not sure if I want to go on
25   and said WELL I was QUITE sure that's what families were for
26   but ER I rang Gloria in the afternoon
27   we felt as if we'd known each other for a long time ODDLY ENOUGH
28   the WHOLE SORT OF end product REALLY
29   it was nice THOUGH WASN'T IT
30   it's still hard FOR ME to believe that it's happened

Summary 6 The Teletext data show how far we have come in this chapter.
We began with Grice's hypothesis that there are maxims for the conduct of
conversational interaction which can explain how implicit meanings are
understood. We have now shown that these maxims really exist and enable
us to account for the nature of one actually occurring talk type, the Teletext
subtitle, which systematically eliminates (a) grammaticalized maxim hedges
and intensifiers and (b) lexical items whose entailments can be recovered as
implicatures.

3.2 *Implicit meaning: further issues*

Keywords: implicature, explicature, relevance, inference, logical form,
maxim, compact structure, conjunction reduction, grammaticalization, social
meaning, resumptives, explanatory, lexical gap.

The first part of this chapter outlined Grice's theory of conversational implicature. In the second part we will test the adequacy of the theory and see to
what extent it is able to account for every implicature, and whether the four
hypothesized maxims are, on the one hand sufficient or, on the other, too
elaborate.

Implicature, explicature, and is the single principle of relevance sufficient?

So far we have used the term 'implicature' as a cover-all term for what
Sperber and Wilson (1986) in their work on Relevance Theory have been able
to break down further into two categories, which they call 'explicature' and
'implicature'. Thus an underdetermined utterance like *I see* in a context like

67   A: Well we're not British Rail agents so I don't know the difference
       B: I see

would require an explicature to elaborate its logical form. In the case of *I see* this would confirm the sentence type as an assertion, disambiguate the meaning of *I see*, and supply the assumed object to give an explicated form such as

67′ [I assert that] I see/understand that you are not British Rail agents so you don't know the difference

Notice that recovering even this explicated form requires inferences to be drawn. Even an utterance like *You're going to bed* could function as an order, an assertion, or a question: only an inference could explicate the intended function.

A second stage is then required to recover the implicature, that speaker B is not satisfied with speaker A's contribution to the interaction. This is represented as follows:

What is said	*Explicature*	*Implicature*
I see	I assert that I see = understand that you are not British Rail agents . . .	You must respond in a more cooperative way to satisfy me

Thus the explicature fleshes out the logical form of the original utterance whilst the implicature takes a new logical form. This is undoubtedly a useful distinction, and a powerful way of explaining how different hearers understand the same utterances to different extents, since it allows for the possibility that different hearers might complete neither, or only the first, or both stages of the inferencing process.

Checking understanding (15)

Distinguish what seem to you to be likely explicatures and implicatures for each of the following:

1 They won
2 It's the taste
9 Smoking damages your health
13 Time flies
63 Also available in white

The next stage is more controversial. Followers of Sperber and Wilson such as Carston (1988) and Blakemore (1992) claim that the Gricean category of generalized conversational implicatures are actually explicatures.

Blakemore, for example, argues that the *and then* reading of *and* is an explicature rather than an implicature. If we apply Blakemore's line of argument to

12 They washed and went to bed

in that order is an explicature, rather than an implicature resulting from the assumption that the speaker is abiding by the maxim of Manner, as was argued earlier. Similarly, determining that

13 Time flies

is an instance of the expectable $N_{subject} + V$ structure rather than the less expectable $V + N_{object}$ structure is to explicate the utterance. And assigning the structures likely to give most perspicuous readings to expressions like *child actor, child psychiatrist,* and *a break with tradition* results in explicatures. Carston (1988) argues that the scalar implicatures associated with the Quantity maxim are in fact explicatures. Under this account, what we have taken to be implicatures associated with the following utterances (given below in elaborated form) are to be reclassified as 'aspects of explicit content' because they are the representations of the sentences that function in 'the mental life' of the hearer (or, more simply, what the hearer takes the sentences to mean):

3   Some (but not all) people believe in God

4   Damon Hill did well in his first season in Formula 1 (but did not win the Championship)

5   I've got £100 (and not more) in the bank

6   Linford Christie can run 100m in 9.9 seconds (and not less)

It is not altogether clear that all these examples only elaborate the logical form, as suggested by Carston and Blakemore. And even granted that there are such entities as 'mental language sentences' (Carston 1988: 156), it is not clear why the logical form should be elaborated in this rather than in some other way, unless we accept the scalar Quantity implicatures that Carston rejects.

The position adopted by Carston and Blakemore is crucial to relevance theory, since their purpose is to argue that all implicatures may be accounted for by the single principle of relevance, which is given for every utterance. Language understanding may therefore be reduced to the single theorem: to understand an utterance is to prove its relevance. In order to argue this case, it is first necessary to deny the existence of generalized conversational implicatures which, as we have already noted, arise irrespective of context and are not relevance-determined at all. Treating them as explicatures, or elaborations of logical form occurring prior to the operation of identifying the most relevant way to take an utterance (implicature), appears to enable Sperber and Wilson to argue that a single overriding principle of relevance is sufficient to determine language understanding.

But the notion of scalar implicature enables us to explain a great deal of data in ways that are intuitively satisfying and require only a single rule. To treat them as explicatures returns us to having to supply a more elaborate logical form (for what real reason?) and to treat each case on an individual basis (surely a costly option). Perhaps this is the price that has to be paid for arguing that a single principle or maxim is sufficient.

Other less radical proposals have been made to reduce the number of principles to (Quality plus) two (Horn, 1984) and three (Harnish, 1976; Atlas and Levinson, 1981). Such proposals meet the economy of principles criterion—but are so few conversational maxims really sufficient? In fact, are four maxims enough?

The case for four, or even five, maxims

Perhaps it will be as well to begin by showing that at least four principles are required. One piece of evidence for Grice's original four maxims comes from maxim hedges. As we saw earlier, sentence adverbs such as *well, maybe, anyway* and *okay* (some uses) clearly hedge Quantity, Quality, Relation, and Manner, respectively. The same is true of their sentential equivalents such as *before I forget* (Relation hedge) and *if you see what I'm getting at* (hedge on Manner). Even more significant is the existence of pseudo-matrix sentence equivalents such as *all I know is that* (hedge on Quantity) and *they say* (hedge on Quality). These are significant because they have obviously developed from genuine matrix sentences with truth value (as examples 64 and 64' show). Their development therefore demonstrates how powerful an influence for change the four original maxims are. We can therefore be confident that there are four maxims when there are four metalingual ways of referring to each of them, and when these forms occur with such frequency in talk.

Once one accepts the principle that a maxim hedge is evidence of the existence of a maxim to be hedged, then one has to worry about the status of a series of sentence adverbs that add no truth value to the utterances in which they occur, but which do not appear to hedge any of Grice's four maxims. One very interesting example of such an adverb is *hopefully*. The German equivalent *hoffentlich* frequently occurs as a sentence adverb, as does *hopefully* in American English, and yet in British English it is often objected to. Thus objections are raised to utterances like

75 Hopefully this chapter is nearing its conclusion

The grounds for objecting are usually that chapters cannot be hopeful or, more accurately, doing things hopefully. But this objection is to miss the point that *hopefully* is used as an extra- rather than an intra-sentential adverb, and to fail to see that the grammar of the sentence is as represented in Fig. 3.4. This suggests that native speakers of English feel unhappy about *hopefully* used as a sentence adverb, to the extent that they will find a reason for objecting to it even when that reason turns out not to hold water. I suggest that a real reason for objecting to it would be that it attempts to hedge a non-existent maxim. But then what of speakers of American English, or indeed those speakers of British English, who do not object to *hopefully* as a sentence adverb? For them there is presumably some further maxim,

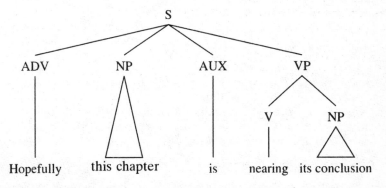

Fig. 3.4

which I have described elsewhere as the maxim of Involvement—*in giving an opinion, speak in a way consistent with your own opinion, sense of order, and conception of the world generally* (1989: 59). Other sentence adverbs that appear to be oriented to this principle include expressions of speaker opinion such as *happily*, *unfortunately*, and some but not all uses of *foolishly* and *wisely*. The fact that of these five sentence adverbs only *unfortunately* is firmly established in British English suggests that this is a marginally held maxim, which only comes into play when we are talking of things that are unfortunate or regrettable (thus *regrettably* too is acceptable to most speakers).

Summary 7 So you pays your money and you takes your choice: if you go for a single principle of relevance as sufficient to account for all the meanings that are inferred in understanding utterances, you have to treat Quantity-based scalar inferences as explicatures. If, on the other hand, you work from data to theory, you may well conclude that there is a wider range of non-truth-conditional metalingual glosses on utterances than can be covered by Grice's original four maxims.

Determiners and conversational implicature: a further case of scalar implicature?

There is a less than reassuring leaflet displayed in many hospital waiting-rooms in Britain which says in big letters on the front

76 What to do after a death

It's just as well it does not say

76′ What to do after death

since it would have no appropriate readers if it did. This reminds us that *after a death* implies after someone else's death, whilst *after death* has no implicature with respect to the death of any particular person. Why should this be?

  In a similar way, it is important to be clear about the difference between

77 They went to prison/school/market/church

77′ They went to a prison/school/market/church

and

77″ They went to the prison/school/market/church

Each gives rise to a quite different set of implicatures. Without a determiner, the implicature is that you go as an insider to do the business typically done there. When the determiner *a* occurs as in (77′), the implicature is that you are a visitor and that the prison/school/market/church is not one with which you are familiar. When the determiner *the* occurs (77″), the implicature is that the prison/school/market/church is one with which you are familiar.

  These examples are generalized implicatures which have nothing to do with the most relevant way to take the proposition on the occasion when it is uttered. If the implicatures are generalized, we would expect them to be related to the Quantity maxim in some way. Leech (1983: 91) argues that the Quantity maxim requires the use of the indefinite article when there is insufficient speaker–hearer shared knowledge to refer definitely. There is therefore a conversational implicature to this effect when the indefinite article is used. If this is right, *the* and *a/an/some* are on a scale. Could this scale have a third member [Ø] which implies that no reference, either specific or non-specific, is effected? This might account for the implicatures associated with (76, 76') and (77, 77', 77"). But how convincing an account is this?

Checking understanding (16)

Of course, not all implicatures associated with determiner phrases are generalized, as the following 'joke' which I recently heard in an after-dinner speech shows:

78 My father said it was time I went out and found a husband so I went out and found Jane's

Can you explain why this is a particularized implicature?

Compact structures and implicature

In the previous section we supposed a conversational account of the implicatures associated with (76, 76'), (77, 77' and 77").

A non-conversational account of the implied meaning which is different from any suggested so far in this chapter might proceed along these lines: the examples in (76') and (77) are compact structures in the sense that they are morphologically simpler. A compact structure will occur just where there is a more expectable meaning. So that the implicatures associated with *to prison* are more expectable than the implicatures associated with *to a prison* or *to the prison*. Thus the simplest structures are used for the likeliest or most frequent meanings. The question that naturally arises is whether such a cognitively elegant account obviates the need to invoke a theory of conversational implicature at all. What we have is simply a set of conventional implicatures which are assigned according to the principle that the most expectable meaning has the most compact morphological representation. The relative awkwardness of attempts to cancel these implicatures suggests that they are conventional rather than conversational:

79 ?I went to prison but I wasn't a prisoner

One further piece of evidence for this account is provided by

80 I went to Dartmoor

In the appropriate context, this would give rise to the implicature *as a prisoner*, which is conversational and cancellable, as (81') shows:

80' I went to Dartmoor but not as a prisoner

Checking understanding (17) ————————————

Compact structures and expectable meanings:

1. Take the case of <was>, which has an unmarked realization (/wəz/) and a marked realization (/wɒz/). Why do you think we find the following examples:

81 I was (/wəz/) in London yesterday (a past event)

82 I was (/wəz/) thinking of going to London (something I may do in the future)

83 I was (/wɒz/) thinking of going to London (a thought I had in the past)

2. Take the case of <some> which has an unmarked realization (/səm/) and a marked realization (/sʌm/). Why do you think we find the following examples:

84 I thought I saw some (/səm/) children playing in the street (non-specific reference)

85 Some (/sʌm/) people prefer winter to summer (specific reference)

86 Would you like some (/səm/) more cake (specific reference)

Another notable example of a compact structure is a sentence like

87 They went to the library and registered for a course

which favours the implicated interpretation that the registration took place in the library. It is much less clear that such an implicature arises in the case of

87′ They went to the library and they registered for a course

In fact, if any implicature arises, it is probably that the registration took place somewhere other than in the library.

Broadly, there are three candidate explanations for the interpretation of (87):

- (87) is a case of conjunction reduction with the second *they* ellipsed;
- (87) is not a logical conjunction (i.e. more than merely 'and' links the two sentences) and therefore not a reduced version of (87′) (as argued in Schmerling, 1972; 1975)
- irrespective of whether (87) is a logical conjunction or not, determining the meaning of *and*, perhaps = *and there* or *and then*, is a matter of explicature (Carston, 1988).

If (87) is a case of logical conjunction with the subject of the second sentence ellipsed (the first explanation), Ross's Coordinate Structure Constraint (Harman, 1974: 165–200), which states that no item may be extracted from one part of a coordinate structure, should apply. Yet it does not, as (87″) shows:

87″ What did they go to the library and register for

Under this explanation, the Coordinate Structure Constraint may be violated just where conjunction reduction results in an implicature not inferable from the original non-reduced sentence.

It is probably the very expectable nature of the meaning of (87) that has caused it traditionally to be accounted for under the maxim of Manner. The most 'perspicuous' reading of Grice is only a step away from the most 'expectable' meaning that we have been suggesting. One radical explanation not suggested elsewhere to my knowledge, would be to account for (87) and (87') in the same way as for (76) and (77) and argue that logical conjunctions may offer two Quantity-based scalar possibilities for expression ⟨conjunction without reduction...conjunction with reduction⟩. On this account, only the lower member of the scale, where it occurs, gives rise to the implicature that the two events are connected in some way. This implicature arises because the speaker is not in a position to state the two propositions as wholly separate.

According to the second explanation, (87) is a compact structure rather than a reduced logical conjunction with a meaning that is more expectable than the meaning of the non-compact (87'), possibly a conventional implicature. Thus there is some cognitively natural relationship between compact structure and expectable meaning, some principle of economy that matches likely meanings with less effortful descriptions.

The third explanation holds that *and* is underdetermined. Explicating (87) so that it matches our mental representation of what is conveyed will be preliminary to deriving any implicature (for example, they were fools) that is then entirely relevance-justified (they could have registered in a closer building). Notice how the explicature route is harder to justify for examples like

77 They went to prison

Although the mental representation is not problematical, it is hard to see how the logical form can be preserved in explicating the inferred meaning. Because interpreting (77) is not a matter of identifying the most relevant meaning, unless an explicature can be provided, this is a very problematical example for Relevance Theory.

Summary 8 The rather difficult section you have just read argues that, superficially, descriptions with determiners look as though they are on a scale ⟨the...a...Ø⟩. It would be good to argue in a parallel way that conjoined sentences are on a scale ⟨conjunction without reduction...conjunction with reduction⟩, although the traditional viewpoint is that understanding utterances like (87) requires a Manner-based inference. But there are grounds for doubting that this is the right account. For one thing, it would be convenient for there to be no exceptions to Ross's Coordinate Structure Constraint. To sustain this, one has to argue that examples like (87) are not logical conjunctions. The compact-structure solution is more naturally pragmatic, in the sense that it matches economy of form with preferred meaning, a principle which does operate in language use, as the Checking Understanding (17) shows. But this explanation lacks a proper theoretical framework of the kind that Grice's Theory of Conversational Implicature or Sperber and Wilson's Relevance Theory provides. Although superficially attractive, the third explanation, that these examples are explicatures, is problematical for Ø determiner phrases like *prison* in *to prison*, since the logical form cannot be preserved in finding an explicature to match the mental representation.

Checking understanding (18) ──────────────

1. What explicatures/implicatures can you find in the following examples?

88   It's good and loud

88′ It's good and it's loud

88″ It's good *and* it's loud

2. First underline the conjoined elements in the examples below—remember that only like structures are conjoined. Decide whether they are logical conjunctions. Now check that Ross's Coordinate Structure Constraint generally obtains by showing how extracting an item from the examples results in ungrammatical sentences:

89   My favourite breakfast is bacon and fried bread

90   You have seen tennis played at Wimbledon and I have seen football played in Newcastle

3. Underline the conjoined elements in the examples below. Decide whether they are logical conjunctions. Now try extracting an item from them:

91   I went to the store and bought some whisky (example from Schmerling, 1975)

92   I forgot my book and couldn't do my homework

Do (91) and (92) give rise to implicatures in a way that (89) and (90) do not?

───

Example (92) shows that by no means all reduced structures that give rise to implicatures allow extraction. Or, to take another example, no one doubts that if I say

93   The beer's nice and cold

there is an implicature that the beer is nice because cold (a because b), and if I say

94   He's big and cuddly

there is an implicature that he is cuddly because big (b because a). Yet neither example allows extraction:

93′ *What's the beer nice and

94′ *Cuddly, which he is big and

This suggests that pragmaticists need to look more carefully at all these examples, as Schmerling suggests. And probably you have already noticed that although (93) and (94) do not look like logical conjunctions, they also pose a problem for the explicature explanation: the *a because b/b because a* directionality requires the logical form of at least one of the examples to be substituted by a new form.

Grammaticalization: the case of maxim hedges

Most of the discussion so far in this second section of the chapter has 'actually' been about the relationship between implicature and grammaticality. And it's not quite over yet. Maxim hedges are a particular illustration of the process of grammaticalization: a number of structures are the raw material of hedges, in the sense that they are to some degree indeterminate between having truth value and being used metalingually. One example occurs in an utterance like

95 I believe smoking damages your health

This could be analysed as a clausal implicature in which the speaker, while not able to state simply *smoking damages your health*, does the next best thing and goes on record as stating it as their own (strongly held) belief. Alternatively, some speakers would use *I believe* as a hedge on Quality. A similar phenomenon occurs with utterances like

96 Smoking still damages your health (= continues to damage)

where *still* conveys the conventional implicature that smoking damaged health before. But once raised to the matrix sentence, *still* functions as a relevance intensifier and ceases to convey a conventional implicature:

96′ Still, smoking damages your health

Also works in the same way:

97 Smoking also damages your health (conventional implicature: it does something else)

97′ Also, smoking damages your health (intensifies Quantity, ceases to be a conventional implicature)

These examples show the close relationship between attachment at the highest level to the sentence (a syntactic property) on the one hand, and functioning as maxim hedges with a metalingual, truth-neutral function (a pragmatic property), on the other. As pragmatic meaning is necessarily non-propositional, either it must occur as an inference or its syntactic attachment must be outside the propositional structure of the sentence, i.e. it will occur as a sentence adverb, a tag, or a dummy matrix sentence, since it cannot logically have truth value.

Sometimes there is real difficulty determining just what is the grammar (i.e. within propositional structure or outside propositional structure) and hence the pragmatic status of such items. For example, what is your judgement about the status of *at least* in

98 Since the beginning of term at least

and in a sentence like

99 It appears to have truth value for some speakers at least

One further piece of evidence that this is an area of continuing grammaticalization is shown by what happens when the use of a hedged proposition by one speaker is reported by another. Imagine that the original speaker says

100 As far as my pragmatics essay is concerned, frankly, I don't give a damn

This might be reported as

100′ She said that as far as her pragmatics essay was concerned, frankly, she didn't give a damn

or as

100″ She made it quite clear that as far as her pragmatics essay was concerned, she didn't give a damn

Personally, I favour (100″) as a preferred reported speech version of (100). This tends to show that the process of grammaticalization is a continuing one, as syntactic structures are appropriated for pragmatic rather than propositional functions.

Now that we have spent so long discussing maxim hedges, you are in a position to compare the approach taken here with the rather different one suggested by Blakemore (1992: 95-8).

Implicature and social meaning

Consider the following three cases:

Case 1. Non-implicated social meaning   Hard as I try, I cannot get my children to say 'My friend and I'. They always say

101 Me and my friend saw this film

On some accounts this might be thought to be an example of so-called social deixis, because it tells you that the speaker is young. In fact the deictic label would be misleading, since we are not dealing with a demonstrative reference which can only be determined in relation to the point of origin of the utterance; indeed, one is precisely drawing an inference about the point of origin itself. But however one labels the indexicality of (101), it seems to me that the realization that this is the speech style of the young is an inference. Yet this inference is not derived from our knowledge of conversational maxims, since it is not a speaker-intended meaning but rather a conclusion we come to about the speaker themselves. It is not therefore an implicature.

Case 2. Resumptives   I once heard a rather anxious disc jockey on a North Sea ferry say

102   You have to guess from which country the tune comes from

He was trying to encourage a less than enthusiastic audience to take part in a little bit of the kind of fun and games that no one enjoys and everyone is reluctant to join in. The usual syntactic explanation for utterances like (102) is that when a constituent moves and leaves a trace, this trace is often filled with a 'resumptive' form (in this case, *from*) so as not to disturb the canonical word order. As I listened to the rather tentative plea of the disc jockey, it occurred to me that perhaps resumptives show a kind of pragmatic indeterminacy. He was not sure whether to say

102′ You have to guess from which country the tune comes (too formal)

or

102″ You have to guess which country the tune comes from (he did not feel relaxed enough for this)

In other words, I drew an inference as to what might be termed the 'social meaning' of his utterance. Since then I have been listening out for resumptives and have been surprised to find how often they seem to have a social meaning. For example, at a university committee meeting I attended, the secretary to the committee, an administrator rather than an academic, was asked to clarify how some proposed procedure might work. In the following utterance, her resumptive seemed to me to indicate that she was being tentative to avoid giving the impression of coercing academic members of staff:

103 We'll need to check out with members of staff the areas in which they might be interested in

If she had said the more formal

103′ We'll need to check out with members of staff the areas in which they might be interested

this would have sounded as though it was official policy rather than a suggestion that had still to be agreed. And if she had said

103″ We'll need to check out with members of staff the areas which they might be interested in

this might have sounded too familiar, and hence have given the impression that she was presuming herself to be an in-group member who could speak for colleagues rather than a representative of the administrative support system. And after his first match in charge of the England football team, Terry Venables, talking about the importance of making chances, said

104 ...which I thought we did that

The interesting issue is whether these inferences are like the inference drawn in the case of (101) or whether, despite the fact that the meaning conveyed is barely intended, it is in fact a conversational implicature. And if a conversational implicature, how is it calculated? As a Quantity-based implicature on a formality scale, or an indication that the speaker cannot decide on the more appropriate of two candidates to satisfy: Quality or perhaps Manner?

Case 3. Implicit meaning made explicit You will recognize the following examples from the Teletext set of utterances at the end of the first section of this chapter:

105 her son and her daughter by her first marriage had BOTH left home
106 at the same time it's ALSO frightening
107 and I JUST simply walked down this lane
108 so he JUST took the case off me
109 it's still hard FOR ME to believe that it's happened

In each of these cases, the item in small capitals is a lexical realization of what is implicated in the more economical subtitle version of the spoken utterance. The speaker is therefore more explicit than the subtitle representation of their utterances. In the subtitles, the meanings that are elaborated in the spoken versions are conveyed implicitly. The issue is whether there is a difference in the social meaning depending on which level of explicitness is chosen. Would hard-of-hearing viewers dependent on subtitles and those listening to the spoken text feel differently about the speakers, or feel that the speakers were in different relationships with each other?

This line of discussion raises the fundamental question of how explicit or how implicit to choose to be when we speak. When I give a lecture, do I say merely 'and' and imply *and then* or do I say 'and then'? My choice must be determined to some degree by my audience—if I am implicit I convey the notion that we belong to a shared world, but at the same time run the risk that the inferences I intend my audience to draw may in fact not be drawn.

In each of cases 1, 2 and 3, social meaning is conveyed. The inference may be an implicature (perhaps as in the case of 102–4) or not (as in the case of 101). Or social meaning may be conveyed by the extent to which a speaker chooses to be explicit (105–9).

Another very obvious area of social meaning is the occurrence of politeness phenomena. We will return to this issue in a later chapter. Meanwhile you might like to think about the status of the inference you would draw if you were standing on a station platform and two people approached you in succession and the first said

110   Got the time mate

and the second said

111   I'm sorry to bother you but you haven't by any chance got the time have you

If you drew inferences about the social status of each of these speakers, would these kinds of inference be more like those you draw in the case of (101) or (102/3)? (The example is from Brown and Levinson, 1978: 85; 1987: 80.)

Checking understanding (19) ——————————————

What conclusions do you draw about the extent to which the speaker decided to be implicit/explicit in the following description by a student of what he had been doing in his class ((.) indicates a brief pause approximately equivalent to the time it takes to say one syllable):

112   At the end of all the (.) we had to prepare a presentation about the class and although only one person presented her work in the end I think that was something that will help me (..) I mean when I compare my (.) the things I had written down with hers (.) what the girl said (.) I realized that I hadn't done so well and I . . .

And what sort of social relationship do you think this suggests he has with the person to whom he is talking? And what sort of person might he be?

Implicature as explanatory

Many linguists, pragmaticists among them, would deny that pragmatic phenomena have explanatory power. Pragmatics has been described as an 'epiphenomenon', a symptom which is entirely the consequence of the pre-existence of some other phenomenon, in this case the syntactic character of language. This final section of the chapter shows that pragmatics has explanatory power (a) in respect of language behaviour and (b) to the extent that it constrains the nature of the phenomenon that we call language.

The explanatory power of pragmatics in respect of language behaviour When we claim that pragmatic categories can be used to account for language behaviour, we are justifying the descriptive categories postulated by pragmaticists. At the end of the first part of this chapter we demonstrated how pragmatic categories such as maxim hedges have to be postulated to take account in the most elegant way of the processes that are involved in converting talk to subtitle. In this sense, pragmatic categories can be used to explain or account for language use or behaviour and to predict subsequent pragmatic 'grammars'.

The explanatory power of pragmatic categories in accounting for a lexical gap
Consider the following problem:

natural language can represent the existential quantifier [∃] of formal language (the language of logic) with words such as *a* and its plural form *some*, so that any description containing *a* or *some* refers to a single exemplar case or a number of exemplar cases included in the larger set of what is described;

natural language can represent the universal quantifier [∀] of formal language with words such as *all*, so that any description containing *all* refers to all the members of the set described;

natural language can represent the negation of the existential quantifier [~∃] with words such as *none*, so that any description containing *none* asserts that there are no cases (= not some) of what is described;

but natural language cannot represent the negation of the universal quantifier [~∀] with words such as *nall*, so that any description containing *nall* refers to 'not all' cases of what is described.

This phenomenon was first noted by Horn (1972), who observes that *nall (= not all) is in effect a Quantity-based implicature of *some* and that in natural language, in contradistinction to formal language, 'not all' is implied by the use of *some*. Since it is already an implicature, it is not lexicalized. The importance of this observation should not be overlooked—what Horn has shown is that a conversational maxim has determined what is lexicalized. Thus the explanation for this lexical gap is pragmatic. And there are other examples:

we find *sometimes* and we find *always*;
we find *never* but we do not find *nalways*, since 'not always' is an implicature of *sometimes*;

we find *permitted* and we find *obligatory*;
we find *forbidden* but we do not find *nobligatory* since 'not obligatory' is an implicature of *permitted*;

we find *or* and we find *both*;
we find *nor* but we do not find *noth*, since 'not both' is an implicature of *or* (as we established earlier).

This suggests that in this area of the lexicon it is the lexicon which is the epiphenomenon, and that pragmatic categories do have explanatory power, in fact the power to predict what may be lexicalized. Finally, it is worth noticing that relevance theory supports the epiphenomenal view of pragmatics because the claims it makes are entirely in the realm of interpretation, which is by its very nature epiphenomenal.

Summary 9 This chapter began by asking how we understand meanings that are nowhere explicitly stated but which are clearly conveyed. This led us to

Grice's theory of conversational maxims, and the inferences which we draw as a result of knowing that speakers are observing or flouting the maxims. These inferences and the implicit meanings that speakers convey are one and the same thing. One very important property of conversational implicatures is that they are cancellable, precisely because they are inferences rather than entailments—this also strongly suggests that they are inductive rather than deductive inferences.

We went on to note that these maxims are of two different kinds: those that are generalized and do not require a context for a hearer to recover the implicature and those that are particular to the context. If we pursue the generalized conversational implicature to its logical conclusion, we end up with what appears to be a paradox: that the very nature of what may be lexicalized is determined by systems that began life as principles that guide language use. And if we pursue the particularized conversational implicature to its logical conclusion, we end up suggesting that relevance is the single principle which determines utterance understanding: as Sperber and Wilson put it, 'It is relevance which is . . . given and context which is . . . a variable' (1986: 142).

Raising pragmatic awareness: implicit meaning

1. This exercise works best with a partner or in a small group. Consider the way in which the likely interpretation of each of the utterances in List A would be altered by the insertion of each of the maxim hedges in List B:

List A	*List B*
1 I don't know	well, anyway, honestly, actually,
2 Do you know the way	even, er, ee
3 She didn't say anything	
4 It's a good idea	
5 Tomorrow's Saturday	

Make up your own List A and List B in such a way as to provide better examples than these.

2. Working individually, cut four pictures out of a colour magazine and choose a different comment to attach to each. Each comment should flout a different maxim. Share your comments/pictures with friends or in your tutorial group.

3. Next time you attend a tutorial in a subject other than linguistics, take a sheet of paper and divide it down the middle. On the left-hand side record what is said in a short conversation between the tutor and a student and on the right-hand side what is meant. Decide what implicatures arise and why. Bring this to your linguistics tutorial to share with colleagues.

4. Work with two friends. Each of you should spend a few days listening out for a different conventional implicature such as 'actually', 'even', and 'but' in conversations. Agree a time to meet up and share your findings.

5. Work with television or radio interviews. Copy down several utterances that contain maxim hedges. Bring them to your next tutorial and write them on the board without the hedges. Your colleagues should try to guess the original hedges. (*Acknowledgement*: this is Andrew Caink's idea.)

6. Choose a simple comic-strip story and white out all the speech in the bubbles. Give it to the other members of your tutorial group and ask them to fill in the bubbles with maxim hedges only.

7. This exercise works best in a small group. Each member of the group takes one of the day's newspapers and identifies all the headlines which violate the Manner maxim. When you share your findings, try to arrange the violations on a cline from most to least extreme violation.

8. Each member of your tutorial group brings an utterance to the tutorial which they dictate. As each person dictates their utterance, everyone else writes down an imagined utterance spoken by the previous speaker which causes the dictated utterance to have an implicature. For example, you dictate 'The scissors are in the drawer' and I imagine the previous speaker might have said, 'Look at this new tie Roger's given me'. When the dictation is over, share the results. (*Acknowledgement*: this beautiful idea was thought up by Roger Maylor.)

Further reading

Blakemore (1992: 57–64, 95–8); Carston (1988); Grice (1967a); Harnish (1976); Kiparsky and Kiparsky (1971); Levinson (1983: 97–166); Ross (1967); Schmerling (1972; 1975).

4

Presupposition

'He that hath knowledge spareth his
words' (*Proverbs* 17: 27)

Keywords: background assumption, pragmatic presupposition, conventional
presupposition, inference/presupposition trigger, subordination, factive predicate, defeasibility, presupposition cancelling negation, logical negation,
metalinguistic negation, projection problem.

The previous chapter was about the conclusions an addressee comes to *after
hearing an utterance* as to the meaning the speaker intends to convey. This
chapter, in contrast, is about *the existing knowledge* that the speaker presupposes in the addressee and does not therefore need to assert. This presupposed knowledge is then taken, together with the entailed meaning of the
utterance and the addressee's knowledge of the world, as the conventional
basis on which an inference is drawn as to the implied meaning, or implicature, that the utterance conveys.

The first part of this chapter describes presuppositional phenomena. At
the level of description, the phenomena seem straightforward enough.
However there are many problems associated with presupposition. The
second part of the chapter draws attention to some of them.

4.1 *Presuppositions as shared assumptions*

The principle of economy

When someone says something to us, we typically make all sorts of assumptions about the background to their utterance which we presume to be
mutually known before the utterance ever occurred. Imagine someone says

1   Tell Madonna I'm at lunch

There would not be much point in saying this unless the speaker expected
Madonna to appear in the near future and assumed that the hearer knew
who Madonna was and was willing to pass the message on. Unless these
conditions are met, there is something wrong with saying (1)—which explains
why you and I have probably never said it to any of our friends. We can

therefore assume that these conditions on saying (1) are presupposed. Thus when someone says *Tell Madonna I'm at lunch*, they presuppose that Madonna is likely to appear soon and that the addressee knows who she is and will pass the message on. For the moment we will call this sort of background assumption a pragmatic presupposition, because it is clearly non-linguistic in nature.

It is very convenient that we can rely on presupposition, otherwise we would have to speak in a much more elaborate way. Instead of (1), we would have to say something like this: 'I'm expecting Madonna soon and since I know that you know what she looks like and I know that you are willing to pass on the message that I am at lunch, tell her that I'm at lunch.' It is obviously an advantage to be able to rely on shared presuppositions and thus be much more economical with words when we talk.

Checking understanding (1)

What is pragmatically presupposed in each of the following?

2   Could I not have a twenty pence coin in the change please

3   Thank you for not smoking (notice posted on a door)

Shared assumptions: definite descriptions, iteratives, questions

The pragmatic presuppositions discussed above are related to the context in which (1) is uttered. There is a further presupposition which is not related to the context of utterance, namely that there is such a person as 'Madonna'. In fact, whenever a proper name like *Madonna* or a definite description like *the image Madonna projects* is used, the existence of some referent that matches the description is presupposed. For the moment we are going to call this kind of presupposition a conventional presupposition, because it seems not to be context-determined and thus to be a kind of 'conventional' understanding which is provided by the definite description.

There is a sense in which both the pragmatic and the conventional presuppositions associated with

1   Tell Madonna I'm at lunch

precede (Madonna's) working out the implicature that the person who left the message is anxious to avoid her.

This is even clearer if you know that *Tell Madonna I'm at Lunch* is actually the title of a book: firstly, a potential reader decides that the pragmatic presuppositions or conditions on uttering the sentence do not obtain; this realization acts as an inference trigger, and on this basis the potential reader then recovers the implicature that the speaker is pretending to appear important enough (or, if male, strong-minded enough) to be able to get along quite well without spending time with Madonna.

So far we have seen that conventional presuppositions arise when a definite description occurs. So even when the pragmatic presuppositions associated with

1   Tell Madonna I'm at lunch

do not go through (i.e. when the expression is used as the title of a book), the conventional presupposition that there is such a person as Madonna certainly does. This might encourage us to schematize the two kinds of presupposition as in Fig. 4.1.

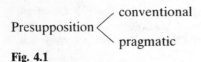

Presupposition
  conventional
  pragmatic

Fig. 4.1

So although indeterminate with respect to whether the speaker is referring to a book he owns or is the author of,

4   My book

certainly presupposes the existence of a book in any context in which the description is used.

   Other structures that give rise to presuppositions include iteratives such as

5   He's made another of his monumental blunders (Neil Kinnock talking about somebody else)

which presupposes that the person referred to had made monumental blunders before; and *wh*-questions such as

6   Who gave Pavel two mini-dinosaurs in a slime-filled egg?

which presupposes that someone gave Pavel two mini-dinosaurs in a slime-filled egg; and embedded *wh*-questions such as

7   I wonder what you are thinking

which presupposes that the addressee is thinking about something.

Checking understanding (2)

1. Identify the conventional presuppositions in the following first lines of Shakespeare plays:

8   In delivering my son from me, I bury a second husband (*All's Well That Ends Well*)

9   Come here my varlet, I'll unarm again (*Troilus and Cressida*)

10   When shall we three meet again, in thunder, lightning, or in rain? (*Macbeth*)

11   Who keeps the gate here? ho! (*Henry IV*, Part II)

12   Who's there (*Hamlet*)

13   I wonder how the king escaped our hands (*Henry VI*, Part III)

14   If music be the food of love, play on (*Twelfth Night*)

2. Identify the entailment(s), conventional presupposition(s), pragmatic presupposition(s), and implicature(s) in

15   Sue made another of her telephone calls

More shared assumptions

Other phenomena that have been claimed to give rise to conventional presuppositions include change of state predicates (*begin, continue, stop, play on* as in 14) and implicatives (*remember, forget, manage, happen*). Thus

16 I began jogging after a visit to the doctor

presupposes that I did not jog before; and

17 I continued jogging after my son became a faster runner than me

presupposes that I was jogging before my son became a faster runner than me; and

18 I stopped jogging after a visit to the doctor

presupposes that I used to jog before the visit to the doctor referred to.

There seems to be an equally close association between implicatives, such as *remember, forget, manage, happen*, and presuppositions, so that

19 The Prime Minister didn't remember/forgot to keep a record of her instructions at the time arms were exported to Iraq

presupposes that she should have kept a record; and

20 Her successor managed to win the election that followed

presupposes that winning the election was not easy; and

21 A similar thing happened to the American President in the case of Iran

presupposes that what occurred was a matter of chance.

You might want to argue that (19), (20), and (21) are really examples of conventional implicature. If you did, you would be in the very good company of Karttunen and Peters, who argue that if there is 'a rule of the language that associates a presupposition with a morpheme or grammatical construction' (1979: 11), then the supposed presupposition is a conventional implicature. In fact, all the presuppositional phenomena considered so far in this chapter, apart from the pragmatic presuppositions in (1)–(3), constitute strong *prima facie* evidence for the view that presuppositions are conventionally associated with morphemes and structures. The issue to which we will need to return in the second part of this chapter is precisely whether there is a rule of the language that associates these meanings with a morpheme or grammatical construction.

Checking understanding (3) ————————————————————

Look again at (16), (17), and (18). What other presuppositions can you identify in them?

Shared assumptions and subordination

In Checking Understanding (3) you will have identified the propositions contained in the temporal clauses *after I visited the doctor* and *after my son became a faster runner than me* as presuppositions. As well as temporal clauses introduced by *after* and *before*, temporal clauses introduced by *since*, *when*, and *while* give rise to presuppositions, as the following examples show:

22 Since you started this book, you must have paused several times for thought

(presupposition: you started this book);

23 When I started this book, I thought I would never finish it

(presupposition: I started this book);

24 Nero fiddled while Rome burnt

(presupposition: Rome burnt).

It is notable in all these examples that we have the structure shown in Fig. 4.2, with the main sentence (S_1) conveying the proposition that is asserted (i.e. Nero fiddled) and the embedded sentence (S_2) conveying the proposition that is presupposed (i.e. Rome burnt). Interestingly, there seems to be a similarity between the embedded sentence position and the sentence adverb position reserved for maxim hedges discussed in the last chapter.

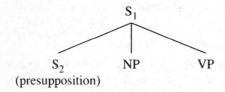

or

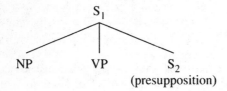

Fig. 4.2

The link between presupposition and subordination extends beyond temporal clauses. It is a moot point whether propositions that are so subordinated as to have become appositional are still being asserted or whether they are the raw material of, or have actually become, presuppositions. You will have to decide this for yourself. Specifically, you will have to decide whether the non-restrictive relatives *who were clever* and *who were cleverer still* in the following example are asserted or presupposed:

25 The Greeks, who were clever, invented geometry; but the Arabs, who were cleverer still, invented algebra

Notice that restrictive relatives never give rise to presuppositions, so that in (26) *who were clever* and *who were dim* restrict the class of Greek described and contribute to the truth value of the sentence:

26 The Greeks who were clever invented geometry, and the Greeks who were dim visited the oracle

And the embedded sentences in clefts are presupposed, so that in

27 It was the Scots who invented whisky

there is a presupposition that someone invented whisky.

In Chapter 3 we saw how real conditionals give rise to the implicature that the proposition contained within the conditional may or may not come about (see page 46). Unlike real conditionals, counterfactual conditionals *presuppose* that propositions mentioned in the *if*-clause did not occur and propositions denied in the *if*-clause did occur. Hence

28 If you had sent me a Christmas card last year, I would have sent you one this year

presupposes that you did not send me a Christmas card last year; and

28′ If you hadn't sent me a Christmas card last year, I would still have sent you one this year

presupposes that you sent me a Christmas card last year.

Unlike real conditionals, counterfactuals are used when the possibility of the existence or non-existence of the propositions mentioned in them cannot be entertained: the *if*-clause therefore *presupposes* that the proposition it contains has not occurred (affirmative sentences) or has occurred (negative sentences).

A most spectacular example of the relationship between subordination and presupposition was described by Kiparsky and Kiparsky, who detailed the properties of what they termed 'factive' predicates (1971). They show that a 'fact-S', like *the fact that Pat wanted to talk to Stephen*, will be presupposed in the highly restricted set of structures in which it may appear either as the subject or as the complement of a factive predicate. Thus all the following examples (in which the factive predicates are in italic) presuppose that Pat wanted to talk to Stephen:

29 The fact that Pat wanted to talk to Stephen *is odd*
The fact of Pat's wanting/having wanted to talk to Stephen *is significant*
That Pat wanted to talk to Stephen *is exciting*
Pat's wanting/having wanted to talk to Stephen *matters* to me
It*'s tragic* that Pat wants to talk to Stephen
His friends *regret* the fact that Pat wanted to talk to Stephen
Her friends *were*n't *aware of* Pat's wanting/having wanted to talk to Stephen

Thus *is odd, is significant, is exciting, matters, is tragic, regret* and *be aware* are all factive predicates. Apart from the extraposed *It's tragic that Pat wants to talk to Stephen*, none of these structures is possible with non-factive predicates like *seem* and *turn out*, whose subjects or complements are not presupposed. You can demonstrate this for yourself by trying *seem* and *turn out* in place of the factive predicates in the examples above. On the other hand, these non-factive predicates have their own set of structures which are ungrammatical for factives.

Checking understanding (4) ———————————

How many presuppositions can you identify in the following example and which morphemes or structures appear to trigger them?

30 One of the former Prime Ministers, who was barely tolerated by the Queen, regrets that she stopped taking notes when allowing exports to Iraq

Focus and presupposition

We have already seen that *wh*-questions give rise to presuppositions, so that

31 Why did Sue give Oxfam a donation

presupposes that Sue gave Oxfam a donation and asks for a reason. A non-*wh* question like

32 Did Sue give Oxfam a donation

does not trigger any presuppositions (except those that arise independently of the question—i.e. that *Sue* and *Oxfam* exist). But (32) does invite an addressee to respond in such a way as to treat at least some part of the question as presupposed by the answer. Fig. 4.3 shows how different proportions of possible answers to (32) are divided between presupposition (to the left) and focused, or 'new', information (to the right):

	Presupposition	*Focus*
33	She gave them	£100
33'	She gave them	her old clothes
33''	She gave	something to Save the Children
33'''	She	was out

Fig. 4.3

So if someone is in a pet shop and asks

34 Do you have any dogs going cheap

the reply

35 No, they're all expensive

treats their having dogs as presupposed and asserts that they are expensive (*No* denies that they are cheap); the reply

35' No, we only have cats

treats their having stock as presupposed and asserts that their stock is cats (*No* denies that they have [cheap] dogs); the reply

35″ No, they all go bow-wow

treats their having dogs as presupposed and asserts that they go bow-wow
(*No* denies that they go 'cheap'); and the reply

35‴ No, our birds go cheap

treats their having stock as presupposed and asserts that the stock which goes
'cheap' are birds (*No* denies that their dogs go 'cheap').

Stress and presupposition

I once heard the first line of *Twelfth Night*

14 If music be the food of love, play on

spoken with a very strong stress on *If*. This had the effect of turning the real
conditional (implicature: maybe music is the food of love, maybe music is not
the food of love) into a counterfactual conditional, with the accompanying
presupposition that music is not the food of love and the consequent implicature that the music being played at the time was not particularly tuneful.

The relationship of contrastive stress and presupposition is discussed by
Lakoff (1971: 333), who points out that

36 John called Mary a Republican, and then *she* insulted *him*

presupposes that calling someone a Republican is an insult just when the
stressed subject of the second conjunct (here *she*) and the object of the first
(here *Mary*) are co-referential, and when the stressed object of the second
conjunct (here *him*) and the subject of the first (here *John*) are also co-referential.

These examples are important because they show the speaker making
decisions about meaning at the level of phonetic realization, and are truly
pragmatic in the sense that the meaning conveyed is independent of the
meaning of the lexical items themselves. Thus

36′ John called Mary a Republican, and then *she* praised *him*

presupposes that to call someone a Republican is to praise them.

Negation and presupposition

It is sometimes claimed that presuppositions 'survive' negation, so that if you
negate

19 The Prime Minister didn't remember/forgot to keep a record of her
instructions at the time arms were exported to Iraq

20 Her successor managed to win the election that followed

and

21 A similar thing happened to the American President in the case of Iran

the same presuppositions arise. Thus

19′ The Prime Minister remembered/didn't forget to keep a record of her
instructions at the time arms were exported to Iraq

still presupposes that she should have kept a record, but now asserts that she did, so the presupposition survives and the assertion is reversed;

20′ Her successor didn't manage to win the election that followed

still presupposes that winning the election was not easy, but now asserts that he did not win it, so again the presupposition survives and the assertion is reversed.

21 A similar thing happened to the American President in the case of Iran

is more problematical because we do not usually find this use of *happen* negated. Nevertheless, if we say

21′ It didn't happen to the American President

we assume that, had it happened, it would have been a matter of chance.

And if you look again at (22)–(28), you will see that their presuppositions all survive negation too. Here the syntax enables us to model the negation showing how only the higher sentence predicate is negated, while the structure containing the presupposition remains unaffected (Fig.4.4).

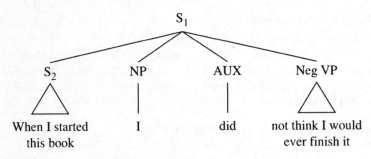

Fig. 4.4

Although not every example we have come across does 'survive' negation (e.g. 6 does not), the standard account of semantic presupposition is often expressed in these terms, so that a conventional presupposition is a proposition that is true if the sentence in which it occurs is true, and is also true if the sentence in which it occurs is false. So if I harbour murderous thoughts towards my neighbour who plays loud music, and say either that this is a matter of regret or that it is not a matter a regret, and whether in either case I actually regret or do not regret my feelings, that I harbour murderous thoughts is always presupposed:

37 I (do not) regret that I want to murder my neighbour

Treating the proposition that *I regret x* as A and the proposition that *I want to murder my neighbour* as B, this may be schematized as in Fig. 4.5.

Because conventional presuppositions are always true, they are sometimes thought of as entailments that survive negation.

A is true A is not true not-A is true not-A is not true	B is true

Fig. 4.5

Summary 1 We have described the assumptions that are taken for granted as the background to utterances as of two kinds, those that are necessary for the utterance to be appropriate, such as assuming that your addressee knows the identity of a person to whom you are instructing them to pass a message, and those that seem to be triggered by morphemes or structures. Among the second category we counted iteratives, and noticed how *another* (5), (15), *a second husband* (8), *again* (9), (10), and *former* (30) act as triggers and thus appear to confirm that these presuppositions, because they are a linguistic phenomenon, are 'conventional' and, like conventional implicatures, are not cancellable.

4.2 *Presupposition: a pragmatic phenomenon*

The first part of this chapter treated presupposition as 'conventional' because it was argued that presupposed assumptions are triggered by lexical (or structural) items. In fact, calling presuppositions 'conventional' in this way is something of an oversimplification, in which I rolled together two slightly different perspectives. The original view of presupposition, associated with the work of Strawson (1952), is of a 'semantic presupposition', an entailment that survives negation and is truth-conditional. This approach to presupposition is refined by Karttunen and Peters (1979), who argue that presupposition is conventional to the extent that it survives negation but pragmatic to the extent that it is non-truth-conditional.

In the second part of this chapter we will be considering whether all presuppositions should be treated as pragmatic, in the much wider sense in which the 'pragmatic' presuppositions of (1)–(3) are non-conventional background assumptions required to render the utterances in which they occur appropriate. We will do this by questioning Karttunen and Peters's assumption that there is 'a rule of the language that associates a presupposition with a morpheme or grammatical construction'.

Conventional presupposition: Counter-examples

Temporal clauses We begin with the well-known example
38 He suffered a series of illnesses before he was persuaded to make a will
which presupposes that he made a will, and
38′ He died before he made a will

which does not. Clearly what we know about the world—that when you die that's it—would not be consistent with assuming that later he made a will. This tempts us to conclude that the presupposition of (38) is an inference we draw as a result of bringing together a linguistic form and an understanding of the world. The pragmatic nature of this inference is confirmed by the fact that *he died before* does not necessarily pre-empt a presupposition, as (39) and (39′), which for most people both presuppose that he reached the hospital, show:

39 He suffered a lot of pain before he reached the hospital

39′ He died before he reached the hospital

Another problematical area for temporal clauses is the case of forward-looking examples. There is a parallel with *if* here: backward-looking conditionals are counterfactual, and give rise to a presupposition of non-existence in respect of the situation described in the *if*-clause; but forward-looking conditionals give rise to implicatures of possible existence in respect of the situation described in the *if*-clause. What about temporal clauses? Remembering that *when* and *if* share the same lexical form in some languages, when/if I say

40 When you get the chance, you should come to Durham

do I presuppose that you will get the chance? Or when/if I say

41 Come to Durham whenever it suits you

do I presuppose that it ever will suit you?

Gerunds and temporal clauses The gerund's status as a vehicle for conveying factivity is also very doubtful. Is the proposition that *she ate her cake* presupposed in the following examples?

42 She left before she ate her cake

42′ She left before eating her cake

42″ She left without eating her cake

In (42) and (42′) both the she-ate-her-cake and the she-did-not-eat-her-cake readings are possible, although the she-did-not-eat-her-cake reading is favoured. (Is it so usual as to be a presupposition, one might reasonably ask?) Because of the meaning of the lexical item *without*, (42″) can never presuppose that she ate her cake. The acceptability of the negative polarity items *any* and *at all* in the following examples also suggests that the presupposition supposedly associated with temporal clauses is in fact a matter of pragmatics, and depends upon a combination of structure and knowledge of the world:

43 She left before she ate any of her cake at all

43′ She left before eating any of her cake at all

43″ She left without eating any of her cake at all

Factives And if you do not believe I am as intolerant as I appeared to be when I wrote about my attitudes to my neighbour at the end of the first part of this chapter, you might say

44 Perhaps he regrets wanting to murder his neighbour

It is a moot point here whether it is presupposed that the person referred to wants to murder his neighbour. If some people feel that this is not presupposed, this seems to suggest that for those for whom it is presupposed, this is a matter of pragmatic knowledge and judgement rather than a reflex of a supposedly factive predicate. Nor is it contradictory to say things like

45 Although he hasn't taken his driving test yet, he's already regretting failing it

In the real world, factive predicates are often not accepted as such in everyday speech. I once heard Robert Runcie, the former Archbishop of Canterbury, say on television

46 I contest the fact that the Church is more divided

Although this may sound contradictory, we all know what he meant. This is a particularly interesting example because *contest* exhibits the syntactic behaviour of a 'factive' predicate in allowing all of (29'):

29' The fact that Pat wanted to talk to Stephen is contested/contestable
The fact of Pat's wanting/having wanted to talk to Stephen is contested/contestable
That Pat wanted to talk to Stephen is contested/contestable
Pat's wanting/having wanted to talk to Stephen is contested/contestable
I contest that Pat wants to talk to Stephen
His friends contest the fact that Pat wanted to talk to Stephen
Her friends weren't contesting Pat's wanting/having wanted to talk to Stephen

Yet semantically this 'factive' predicate casts doubt on whether the 'fact-S' sentence is a fact at all. Thus, although the Kiparsky and Kiparsky paper suggests two syntactic categorization frames, one for assumed knowledge and one for non-assumable knowledge, we see that the data do not pattern so neatly.

Definite descriptions In the days when Marxist ideology was in favour in some places, visitors to Britain from socialist countries often found it hard to accept that when they talked about

47 the bourgeois society

their British friends had no idea what they were talking about. Although the existence of a referent is presupposed by the use of the definite description, the referent was unidentifiable to most people who had not grown up with Marxist rhetoric. There is a clear distinction between example (47), where the referent is not yet known to some addressees and cannot be located, and a definite description like

48 Mind the table

where the referent may not be known to the addressee but the utterance is taken as an instruction to locate it (Hawkins 1978: 113)

Examples like (47) might be considered to have problematical status. Does it fail to give rise to a presupposition for some addressees so that the presupposition, when it arises, is a pragmatic phenomenon, as is being claimed here; or is there no presupposition to match (47), so that the sentence which contains the expression appears not to have a truth value? This second explanation is consistent with the semantic presupposition theory, and was widely held to be a correct view, with Russell's notorious example

49   the present King of France

being taken by many subsequent writers as a referring expression with no identifiable referent, thus rendering the sentence in which it occurs neither true nor false. (This was not Russell's view: for him the sentence was false.)

Change-of-state verbs   If a speaker were to say

50   At least we won't have to give up sex

they would typically be taken to be presupposing that they were practising sex (and implying that they enjoyed it). In fact just such assumed meanings, in this case triggered by a change-of-state predicate, are the stuff of 'humour' in sit-coms. Yet in fact I heard (50), not in a sit-com, but spoken by a Catholic priest contemplating unwelcome changes that he foresaw in the future, and seeing this one silver lining on the cloud. Clearly our knowledge of the world tells us that the presupposition does not go through in this case; and in fact the humour derives precisely from the fact that the utterance has a different pragmatic effect in the context of being spoken by a Catholic priest from the one it would usually have had.

Summary 2   The section you have just read shows how context and linguistic form interact to cause us not to identify the potential presuppositions that in most contexts are typically associated with the linguistic forms in question. We therefore see that it is safer to argue that presuppositions are pragmatic rather than conventional, even in the case of temporal clauses (38)–(41), gerunds (42)–(43), factives (44)–(46), definite descriptions (47)–(49), and change-of-state verbs (50).

Checking understanding (5)

Can you think up your own examples of temporal clauses, factives, definite descriptions, and change-of-state verbs which do not give rise to the presuppositions we might typically expect to find associated with them? As you do this, it may help you to remember that:

● temporal clauses are introduced by conjunctions such as *after*, *before*, *when* and *while*;

● Kiparsky and Kiparsky's list of factive predicates includes *grasp*, *realize*, *take into account*, *bear in mind*, *ignore*, *make clear*, *mind*, *care (about)*;

● definite descriptions are determined by the definite article, possessives, the demonstratives *this/these* and *that/those*;

● change-of-state verbs include *carry on*, *continue*, *cease*, *commence*, *begin*, *start*, *stop*, *leave off*, *go on*.

Presupposition and speaker choice

More generally, it is notable that there is a good deal of speaker choice in the area of presupposition. For example, speakers commonly decide whether to give lexical realization to what might otherwise be presupposed. We saw a similar phenomenon in the case of implicature, where the Teletext subtitler decided to delete the lexical realization from utterances where the same meaning could be conveyed as an implicature. I heard a good example of this on the radio, when what might have been presupposed was given lexical realization by the speaker who said

51 They returned to the place they had left

Being an iterative, *return* (or, strictly, the *re* of *return*, something less than a morpheme even) is typically held to give rise to the presupposition that those referred to in (51) had been in the place referred to before. The fact that the speaker chooses to make this explicit by lexical means argues for treating presupposition as pragmatic, since, if presupposition were conventional, this utterance would be tautologous to the point of unacceptability.

Another area of speaker choice occurs in the case of *some*, which gives rise to the presupposition of existence, and *any*, which does not. The presupposition-neutral status of *any* accounts for our inconsistent reaction to the road-sign

52 Sorry for any delay

posted at the end of roadworks. When we have not been held up, we think how courteous it is of the Ministry of Transport to apologize, especially when an apology is unnecessary. But when we have been held up, we find the road-sign infuriating precisely because it does not presuppose that there has been the delay which we have just experienced for ourselves. Under these circumstances,

52' Sorry for the delay

might be mollifying, but this sign is only very occasionally posted, presumably because it would be inappropriate to situations in which no delay had occurred and in which no referent for the definite description *the delay* could accordingly be identified.

Thus McCawley rightly observes that 'sentences with *any* do not commit the speaker to the proposition that the domain of the quantifier is not empty, whereas sentences with *every* and *all* do' (1981: 112). In saying this, he is claiming that, unlike *every* and *all*, the use of *any* does not presuppose that there are at least some examples of the description quantified by *any*. Thus (53) and (53') each presupposes that at least some ministers have a secret life, but (53″) does not:

53 Every minister who has a secret life risks reading about themselves in the newspapers

53' All ministers who have secret lives risk reading about themselves in the newspapers

53″ Any minister who has a secret life risks reading about themselves in the newspapers

Every, all, and *any,* along with *each,* are natural-language equivalents of the universal quantifier of formal logic. *A/an* and *some* are natural-language equivalents of the existential quantifier of formal logic, as we saw in Chapter 3. It seems hard to account for the fact that *any* does not presuppose the existence of examples of the description it quantifies and *some* does, when *some* is so frequently a suppleted form and *any* takes its place. It is notable that in both first- and second-language acquisition this is felt to be unexpected too, so that both small children acquiring English as a first language and second-language learners frequently produce utterances like

54 I've locked the door so someone doesn't get in

Such utterances are entirely logical if you take the view that only an idiot would lock a door unless there was the presupposition that someone might get in. Examples like (54) show that presupposition is a matter of speaker choice rather than formal requirement. This is a secondary argument for treating presupposition as pragmatic.

One noticeable difference in the use of *some* and *any* occurs in the department I work in, where my four American colleagues frequently privilege *some* over *any* in situations where my (British) preference would be for *any.* So when my American head of department asked for some information to take with him to a meeting recently, adding by way of explanation

55 in case I have to say something to somebody

I inferred (wrongly as it turned out) that he had someone in mind for a good telling off. Maybe the association of a presupposition of existence with the use of *some* is speaker- rather than form-related.

Defeasibility

'Defeasible' is the term pragmaticists use to mean cancellable. If a presupposition is a conventional meaning, it will not be defeasible since, by definition, no conventional meaning can be denied or cancelled without giving rise to a contradiction. Indeed, we have already seen that the standard definition of conventional presupposition is that it is an entailment that survives negation. But is it true that presuppositions are not defeasible?

Another category of predicate held to give rise to presuppositions are verbs of judging. So

56 I criticized Bill for mumbling

presupposes that Bill mumbled and asserts that mumbling is a bad thing; and

57 I accused Bill of mumbling

presupposes that mumbling is a bad thing and asserts that Bill did it. So according to the standard definition

56′ I didn't criticize Bill for mumbling

also presupposes that Bill mumbled; and

57′ I didn't accuse Bill of mumbling

also presupposes that mumbling is a bad thing. So far, so good.

Yet I can reasonably say

56″ I didn't criticize Bill for mumbling—not that he did anyway

which can hardly presuppose that Bill mumbled; and

57″ I didn't accuse Bill of mumbling—not that mumbling's (such) a bad thing

which can hardly presuppose that mumbling is a bad thing. Both these examples appear to cancel presuppositions. And not only can these presuppositions be cancelled, they can also be suspended, which again would not be possible if a presupposition was a conventional meaning. So

56‴ I didn't criticize Bill for mumbling—if that's what he was doing

causes the presupposition that Bill mumbled to be suspended; and

57‴ I didn't accuse Bill of mumbling—if mumbling's to be condemned

causes the presupposition that mumbling is a bad thing to be suspended.

Earlier in this part of the chapter we saw how a potential presupposition fails to arise if the context does not license it. In this section, we have seen how co-text can cause a potential presupposition not to arise or to be suspended. This suggests that the 'conventional' analysis of presupposition is wrong, and that a pragmatic analysis is to be preferred.

Checking understanding (6)

Consider the following examples from the first part of this chapter, and in each case add text which either cancels or suspends the presupposition:

7 I wonder what you are thinking

12 Who's there

16 I began jogging after a visit to the doctor

20 Her successor managed to win the election that followed

27 It was the Scots who invented whisky

28 If you had sent me a Christmas card last year, I would have sent you one this year

The status of presupposition cancelling negation

The status of presupposition cancelling negation has been and still is a very contentious issue in pragmatics. Essentially the issue is this: a negative particle can be used and the presupposition survive it, as in

20′ Her successor didn't manage to win the election that followed

(assertion: her successor did not win; presupposition: winning was difficult); or in

37 I (do not) regret that I want to murder my neighbour

(assertions: I regret/do not regret . . . ; presupposition: I want to murder my neighbour). But is this the same negative particle as the second negative particle in (56″) which prevents the potential presupposition that Bill mumbled from arising:

56″ I didn't criticize Bill for mumbling—not that he did anyway

A way out of this difficulty is to argue that the same negative particle is used with two different functions: one, which we might call logical or conventional, is to map one value onto another by means of introducing or eliminating the negative particle; the other, following Horn (1985), we can call metalinguistic. Metalinguistic negation is a device for objecting to some aspect of an utterance on any grounds except its conventional, semantic meaning. Thus in

27′ It wasn't the Scots who invented whisky, it was the Irish

the negative particle is used metalinguistically to object to the choice of *the Scots* rather than to deny that someone invented whisky.

We owe the insight that it is a metalinguistic use of the negative particle that occurs in cases where potential presuppositions fail to arise through negation to Burton-Roberts, who argues that metalinguistic negation is consistent with a pragmatic account of presupposition (1989: 218 ff.). (Metalinguistic negation also avoids the need for a three-value logic in a case like (56″), which, unless you allow the negation as a metalinguistic objection to the choice of 'mumbling', appears to be neither true nor false.)

Checking understanding (7)

Horn defines metalinguistic negation as 'a device for objecting to a previous utterance on any grounds whatsoever, including the conventional or conversational implicata it potentially induces, its morphology, its style or register, or its phonetic realization' (1989: 363). Identify the potential presuppositions that are being objected to metalinguistically in the suggested answers for Checking Understanding (6). Which of the suggested answers exhibit metalinguistic negation?

The projection problem

Another problem which has consumed a great deal of energy is the so-called 'projection problem'. It goes like this:

Step 1 Given that there are three classes of expression with different abilities to create presuppositions—those that are presupposition-creating such as factives,

37 I (do not) regret that I want to murder my neighbour

those that are not, including non-factives such as

58 I believe my neighbour is going deaf

and those that sometimes are and sometimes are not

59 I don't know that my wife fancies the milkman

Step 2 And given that examples like (37) may be embedded under predicates that do not create presuppositions, or only sometimes allow them (see
Fig. 4.6)

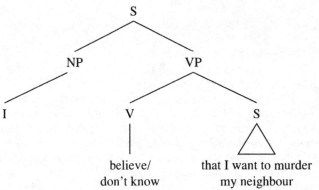

Fig. 4.6

Step 3 How do you determine whether the resulting sentences allow the
presuppositions associated with the embedded sentences?

In practice, given

60 I believe he regrets wanting to murder his neighbour

61 I don't know that he regrets wanting to murder his neighbour

in determining when (60) and (61) allow the presupposition that the person
referred to wants to murder his neighbour (and, for that matter, when 59
allows the presupposition that the speaker's wife fancies the milkman), do
you appeal to conventional or pragmatic criteria? There seems little doubt
that whether the potential presuppositions arise in these cases or not is a
property of speaker belief rather than structural form.

Conclusion

In the first part of this chapter we called one class of presupposition 'conventional' because it was possible to identify a morpheme, lexical item, or structure which appeared to act as a presupposition trigger. In addition, almost
all these identified examples appeared to pass an independent test of their
status: the ability to survive negation. In the second part of this chapter we
have seen that the number of counter-examples makes this account
untenable.

You might want to argue that the first part of the chapter appeared to sell
you a dummy and that, as well as being frustrating, this approach is pedago-
gically unsound. But I do not apologize, because there is an elegance about
the analysis presented in the first part of the chapter that has not been
captured by what is essentially a series of counter-examples to the thesis
presented in the second part. Thus the history of our treatment of presupposition over the last twenty-five years demonstrates the 'scientific' approach

of contemporary linguistics. We suggest a hypothesis that, in the face of a large number of counter-examples, is eventually shown not to be explanatorily adequate, even though we have yet to replace the first hypothesis with another of the same elegance and simplicity. In this chapter, I have tried to mirror this linguistic method.

More importantly, our discussion raises precisely the issue of where semantics ends and pragmatics begins. In Chapter 3 we argued that the definition of a pragmatic phenomenon is that it is non-conventional, in the sense that it is not determined by a linguistic item alone but by a combination of a linguistic item and what we know about the world. These two kinds of knowledge constitute premises from which an inference is drawn. From the first part of this chapter it might appear that conventional presupposition is not really a pragmatic phenomenon at all. In the second part of the chapter, we have shown that, despite its close association with linguistic form, what we earlier supposed to be a conventional presupposition is in fact a pragmatic phenomenon whose occurrence depends upon the speaker and hearer achieving a degree of intersubjectivity.

Raising pragmatic awareness: presupposition

1. Working by yourself, collect a few advertising slogans with interesting pragmatic properties (maxim flouts, implicatures, presuppositions, etc.) and bring these to your tutorial group to discuss.

2. Work with a partner. Choose any lyric with a strong story-line—Beatles songs work particularly well—and agree on three or four lines that you and your partner will work with. Then separate and each draw the scene depicted in the lyric in such a way as to represent all the presuppositions. Come back together to compare drawings and discuss the way you each represented the presuppositions. (*Acknowledgement*: this idea was thought up by Csilla Szabo.)

3. This exercise works best in a small group. Each person should think up a sentence containing a presupposition and dictate it to the group. As each sentence is dictated, you each write down a product which it could be used to advertise.

Further reading

Green (1989: 71-86). And if you want a testing read, Burton-Roberts (1989: chs. 6 and 10); Karttunen and Peters (1979); Levinson (1983: 167-225).

5

Speech acts: language as action

'It all depends what you mean by ...'
(CEM Joad's favoured means of answering
questions on BBC's 'The Brain's Trust')

Keywords: utterance, speech act, intention, proposition, sentence, truth
value, locutionary act, illocutionary act, perlocution, performative, felicity
condition, entailment, truth-conditional semantics, indirect speech act, form,
function, idiom theory, inference theory, short-circuited implicature, literal
meaning, meaningless segment.

At the end of the first chapter we saw how, depending on the context it which
it was uttered, *I'm here now* might be taken as a comforting reassurance, a
stern warning, or an apology. This chapter explores the property that utterances have of counting as actions, such as the actions of reassuring, warning,
or apologizing.

5.1 *Language as a representation of intention*

Language and action: understanding the phenomenon

Our butcher once asked why farmers have long ears and bald heads. When
I obligingly said I didn't know, he took the lobe of one of his ears between
thumb and forefinger and, pulling it downwards, said 'How much?' Next he
ran his hand through his hair, saying 'Cor' as he did so. This neat joke shows
how language and action can be co-incident. Of course there are times when
actions are preferred to words, such as when flagging down a bus or a taxi;
or times when either actions or language, or both, may be used, such as when
greeting someone in the street; or times when both language and actions are
required, as in the complicated ritual of introducing people to one another.
These examples show that there is no clear-cut boundary between using
actions to count as actions and using language to count as actions.

In fact, we usually think that we are doing something with words when we
talk. When my son was two years old he came into the bathroom one day
when I was bent double scrubbing out the bath and said in a particularly
jaunty and self-satisfied way

1   It's me again

This struck me as a rather peculiar utterance. Although the sentence was an accurate description of a state of affairs in the world, when we use *it's me again* as an utterance, it is usually to apologize for troubling someone a second time. This was not my son's intention on this occasion. I was not able to explain his utterance to myself until I recollected that on the previous occasion when he came into the bathroom as I was scrubbing out the bath, I had turned to him in exasperation and said

2   It's you again

He had evidently understood the semantics but not the pragmatics of my utterance and had assumed that to get in first with *it's me again* was the appropriate pragmatic strategy in the bath-scrubbing context we found ourselves in.

This simple example illustrates the difference between sentences like *it's me again* and *it's you again* and the use of such sentences as utterances. Knowing the literal meaning of the sentences is not enough to determine what they count as doing when they are used.

Checking understanding (1)

Although the following utterances all express the same proposition and are therefore true under just the same conditions, they are each used to perform a range of different acts. Try to list some of the situations in which each might be used and decide what speech act would be effected in each case.

3   Sorry

4   I'm sorry

5   I am sorry

Can you think of other examples of a single proposition being used for a variety of speech acts?

It is important to notice that three different aspects of meaning can be distinguished in the utterance

1   It's me again

First, it conveys the proposition that the speaker has returned to a place he/she was in on a previous occasion. In saying this we are regarding *it's me again* as a sentence with a truth value. (In fact, it is very difficult to think of any circumstances under which this sentence could be uttered without being true.)

Secondly, when this sentence is used as an utterance, it has the force of, or counts as, an apology. Thought of in this way, it does not make any real sense to ask if the sentence is true or not—rather the utterance represents the intention of the speaker to apologize.

Thirdly, the utterance will have effects or consequences that are not entirely foreseeable. Presumably, the speaker hopes it will mollify the addressee, but there will be occasions on which it has some other effect, such as making the addressee angry.

In *How To Do Things With Words* (1962) Austin called the first of these aspects of meaning the locutionary act (uttering a sentence with determinate sense, i.e. non-ambiguous meaning, and reference). He called the second the illocutionary act (performing an act by uttering a sentence). And he called the third (the effect the utterance might have) the perlocution.

Language and action: Austin's Theory of Speech Acts

The distinction between the meaning that sentences have as a result of our knowing whether they are true or false and the meaning that utterances have as a result of our understanding what they count as doing was first described in *How To Do Things With Words*. Austin drew attention to the 'performative' or action-accomplishing use of certain language formulas. A good example would be

6   Pass

as uttered by contestants in the television general knowledge contest, *Mastermind*. In this context, *Pass* is clearly a shorthand for the explicitly performative

6′   I (hereby) pass

Uttering *Pass* counts as forfeiting the right to supply an answer: it is not a statement (true or false) about the world. Moreover, it is only 'felicitous' to utter *Pass* under narrowly defined circumstances, such as when taking part in *Mastermind* or at particular moments in the bidding sequence of a game of bridge. Try walking down the street nodding at people and saying *Pass*, and it will only be a matter of time before someone sends for the van and you get taken away.

Checking understanding (2) ─────────────────────────────

7   I hereby pronounce you man and wife

counts as performing an action—we might say that it is explicitly performative.

8   I sneeze

is not. Make a list of as many explicitly performative utterances as you can think of and in each case think through the conditions under which it would be felicitous to utter them.

───

Yet, as Austin points out, utterances do not need to contain an explicitly performative verb to be performative. Take the case of promising. It would be distinctly odd for me to say to my wife

9   I hereby promise to pick you up at eight o'clock

Even

9′   I promise to pick you up at eight

would only be natural if I'd failed to honour such an agreement on a previous occasion. It would be much more natural to say

9″ I'll pick you up at eight

where the declarative form of the sentence and the proposition expressed are sufficient for it to count as a promise. Or I can intensify the Quality maxim:

9‴ I'll pick you up at eight, honestly

or I can use pitch prominence:

9⁗ I *will* pick you up at eight

Even saying

9′′′′′ Shall I pick you up at eight

or

9′′′′′′Would you like me to pick you up at eight

commits me to the promised action in the event of my offer being accepted. Only the first two of these seven ways of promising use the explicit performative verb *promise*. The last two examples are interrogative, and (9′′′′′′) even embeds what is promised within an interrogative sentence, yet all of them count as making a promise. That is to say, they all share a common set of felicity conditions, which include minimally

- that what I offer is in my power to deliver
- that it is desirable to the person to whom I make the promise
- that what is promised was not going to happen anyway.

Thus we see that non-explicit, even very implicit, ways of using language performatively are the norm. The implicit nature of many speech acts means that they are doubly pragmatic: they are pragmatic first because they convey meanings that are not entailments (illocutionary force), and at the same time they are typical of other pragmatic phenomena in that these meanings are frequently conveyed in non-natural or implicit ways (indirect illocutionary force).

This is well illustrated by the case of

1   It's me again

when used by speakers other than my son at the age of two. Typically this utterance counts as apologizing. But

2   It's you again

expresses irritation. Yet neither contains any explicit performative verb. One has the force of an apology, the other of an expression of annoyance, and both have literal meanings of a quite different kind.

More usefully, we might ask how *it's me again* comes to be understood as an apology when, as my son demonstrated in understanding only its semantics and not its pragmatics, this is far from being a natural assumption. Since the proposition conveyed in the utterance is already obvious without being uttered, the utterance flouts the maxim of Quality in the sense that if it were intended only to convey its literal meaning, it would lack sincerity or usefulness. It therefore conveys an implicature, perhaps an implicature that it shares with *it's you again*, namely that the person indicated (*me, you*) is imposing on (the territory of) the other party in the exchange. This implicature then enables the speech act, in the case of *it's me again* that of apologizing and in the case of *it's you again* that of expressing irritation, to be determined.

At this stage we need to be clear about some basic distinctions.

It is important to distinguish:	from:
sentences that describe states of affairs in the world	doing things with words

Thus

1 It's me again

could be thought of as describing a state of affairs in the world	or as an apology

It is important to distinguish:	from:
the truth or falsity of sentences	the felicity of utterances

Thus when President Kennedy said

10 Ich bin (ein) Berliner

it may not have been literally true	but it was felicitous.

It is important to distinguish:	from:
Truth as a source of meaning	Performative effect as a source of meaning

Thus it is reasonable to ask whether the meaning of

11 This is a no smoking zone

when addressed to someone smoking in a prohibited area, consists more

in knowing that it happens to be true as a description of the area referred to	or in understanding the intention of the speaker in uttering it and the effect that it is likely to have on the addressee

As Austin noted,

It is important to distinguish:	from:
The locutionary act (uttering a sentence with determinate sense (= unambiguous meaning) and reference	the illocutionary act (performing an act by uttering a sentence) and the perlocution (the effect the utterance might have)

Thus saying

12 I'm going on holiday next week

conveys the proposition that the speaker will be on holiday at the time indicated	and, when the addressee is the milkman, instructs him to suspend milk deliveries; if overheard by a thief, one of the effects might be to cause the speaker's house to be burgled

It is important to distinguish:	from:
Propositional content	Force

Thus in the following exchange with my daughter when aged six:

13 E: Daddy can I have the Oink
P: Good idea
E: Daddy just tell me the truth can I have the Oink

the proposition I express that	has the force of indicating that
taking *Oink* (a vulgar comic) is	taking *Oink* is not a good idea (as,
a good idea	unfortunately, Eleanor recognizes).

The left-hand column in this list of distinctions treats meaning in the manner of truth-conditional semantics—if you know when a sentence is true or false, then you know what it means. Thus, to take Tarski's classic example,

14 Schnee ist weiss

will be a true sentence if and only if snow is white. (I have followed the usual practice of using one language—here German—for the sentence and another—here English—to describe the state of affairs the sentence purports to describe so as to avoid a confusion between sentence and state of affairs in the world.)

Working down the left-hand column above, (14) is seen as a description of a state of affairs in the world whose meaning derives from recognizing the truth of the proposition it expresses. This way of understanding the meaning of (14) is to be contrasted with the speech act perspective set out in the right-hand column. Under this account

14 Schnee ist weiss

would be uttered for some purpose, such as giving information to a child or convincing a Saudi who had never seen snow, would be felicitous in such contexts (only), would be meaningful as an act of informing or convincing, and would be likely to have effects which would be only partly predictable.

Checking understanding (3) ——————————————————

How does speech act theory help you to understand the cartoon strip in Fig. 5.1?

Language and action: direct and indirect speech acts

We have already noticed that many speech acts are doubly pragmatic: they are pragmatic not only because they convey meanings that are not entailments or conventional meanings but also because these meanings are frequently conveyed in non-natural or implicit ways.

So when we say

1 It's me again

we are being indirect. In fact, we are stating one of the felicity conditions (imposing on someone else) that would make it appropriate to apologize.

And if I say to my wife

9′′′′′′ Would you like me to pick you up at eight

I am promising indirectly to pick her up by asking about one of the felicity conditions on doing it.

Fig. 5.1 Copyright House of Viz/John Brown Publishing. Reproduced with permission.

President Kennedy is promising to support Berlin all the way by stating one of the felicity conditions

10 Ich bin (ein) Berliner

that would usually have to obtain for someone to give themselves absolutely to Berlin.

And if I say

11 This is a no smoking zone

I am stating one of the felicity conditions that would need to obtain for me to be in a position to (attempt to) prevent someone from continuing to smoke.

When I say to the milkman

12 I'm going on holiday next week

I am stating one of the felicity conditions on suspending the milk delivery.

And when Mr Logic asks whether one of the felicity conditions for buying stamps is in place with the utterance

15 Do you sell postage stamps

he is assumed to be asking for a stamp.

All these examples show how it is sufficient for a speaker to state or ask about a felicity condition on an action to imply that they are performing the action.

Sentence types and direct and indirect speech acts

Imagine you had the misfortune to attend one of my pragmatics lectures and that, after half an hour in which I had been particularly difficult to follow, I said

16 I know this isn't very clear. Can anyone do any better

You might be very uncertain as to the illocutionary force associated with *Can anyone do any better*. If you were very bold, you might treat it as a genuine question and tell me that several of my colleagues had done better earlier in the week. If I held out a piece of chalk as I said it, you might take it as an invitation to come and have a try yourself. Or if you thought I was being sarcastic, you might take it ironically as an assertion that no one else could do any better.

The bold reading treats my utterance as a direct speech act in which the interrogative form is used to ask a question. The chalk-offering reading treats it as an indirect speech act in which I ask about one of the felicity conditions that would need to be in place to make it worthwhile inviting someone else to come and have a try. I am thus understood to be implying that someone should come and do just that. The ironical reading treats it as an indirect way of asserting that no one can do any better, which is inferred if you assume that I am asking what appears to be a Yes/No question to which the only possible answer is No.

This example shows us how a sentence with interrogative form can be taken not only as a question but also indirectly as an indirect request/invitation/order or as an indirect assertion.

English is fortunate in having one set of terms for sentence form:
- declarative (subject + verb order)
- imperative (no overt subject)
- interrogative (verb + subject order—with some exceptions)

and another matching set for utterance function:
- assertion
- order/request
- question.

This makes it easy to distinguish form and function when we discuss them. When form and function match, we call the effect a direct speech act, as in

17 Naturally, I hate music (declarative used as an assertion)

18 Please turn the music off (imperative used to give an order)

19 This comes as a surprise—why do you hate music (interrogative used to ask a question)

Notice how *naturally*, *please*, and *this comes as a surprise* can only be used with the type of utterance they occur with here: i.e. you cannot say *naturally, turn the music off* or *why please do you hate music*. We will be returning to this point shortly.

When form and function do not match, we call the effect an indirect speech act, as the following examples show:

20 I wonder when the train leaves (declarative form functioning as a question)

21 (to a child) You'd better eat your dinner fast (declarative form functioning as an order)

22 Have a good journey (imperative form functioning as an assertion = I hope you have a good journey)

23 Tell me why you say that (imperative form functioning as a question)

24 Who cares (interrogative form functioning as an assertion = No one cares)

25 Can you open the door for me (interrogative form functioning as a request)

Some of these examples are slightly awkward, but the point stands that every sentence type can be used for every utterance function. And in fact when we make a request/give an order, we almost always do it indirectly by using an interrogative sentence. This raises a very important question: is it appropriate to think of sentence forms as having prototypical functions or is it better to think of them more as we think of phonemes, as formally meaningless until they combine, in the case of phonemes with other phonemes to become morphemes, in the case of sentences with situations to become utterances? This is another issue to which we will return in the second part of the chapter.

Checking understanding (4) ————————————————————

1. What do you make of the following conversation I overheard at breakfast in a hotel between a middle-aged couple and a waitress?

26 Him (to waitress): Could we have some more coffee
(waitress goes away)
Her (to him): You should say may we
Him: Why
Her: Because it could mean are you able
Him: That's what I meant
Her: Of course you didn't

2. I stopped at a garage to fill up with petrol one evening on the way home and when I went to pay, the assistant said

27 Do you know about our offer on oil

What are you supposed to do when this happens?

3. We have a no smoking policy in our building. I have taken it upon myself to try and enforce this policy when I come across smokers polluting our corridor. What do you make of the following three brief encounters:

28 Me: You're in a no smoking zone
Female student: Am I
Me: The whole building's a no smoking zone
Female student: Thanks very much (extinguishing cigarette)

29 Me: This is a no smoking zone
Male student: Is it (getting up)
Me: Outside only I'm afraid
(student extinguishes cigarette)

30 Me: Excuse me you're in a no smoking zone
Mature, pipe-smoking, male student: Ah is it sorry (puts lighted pipe in pocket)

Syntactic reflexes of indirect speech acts

Earlier we made the point that *please* can occur (preverbally) in example (18)

18 Please turn the music off

but not in

17′ *Naturally, I please hate music

or in

19′ *This comes as a surprise—why do you please hate music

One might be tempted as a first reaction to suggest that this constraint is formal and that only imperative sentences with no overt subject allow (preverbal) *please*. But this is not correct, as

25′ Can you please open the door for me

shows. (25′) proves that preverbal *please* is grammatical just where the function is to order or request. This is even clearer when we free *please* from strict preverbal position. Thus

21′ You'd better please eat your dinner fast (more a threat than a request)

is more awkward than

21″ You'd better eat your dinner fast please (more a request than a threat)

If *please* is allowable at all with (17) and (19), it is only if they can be construed as requests:

17″ Please, I hate music (= request to stop playing the music)

19″ Please, why do you hate music (= request to explain)

Checking understanding (5)

1. Try using *naturally* as a sentence adverb in sentences with imperative (no overt subject) and interrogative (verb + subject) forms. If you can find examples, they will (almost) always be indirect speech acts which function as assertions.

2. Try using *this comes as a surprise + following structure* in such a way that *this* and the following structure are co-referential to introduce sentences with declarative (subject + verb) and imperative (no overt subject) forms. If you can find examples, they will (almost) always be indirect speech acts which function as questions.

The importance of these data cannot be overstated. What we are seeing is a syntactic reflex of a pragmatic phenomenon. In other words, what is grammatical is determined not within an autonomous syntax but in relation to the function of the utterance. These data demonstrate the need for a pragmatically sensitive syntax. And of course there are more data of this kind. For example, items like *at all* have negative polarity and cannot occur in a non-negative context, as (31) and (31′) show:

31 They don't care at all

31′ *They do care at all

By analogy, we would expect (32) to be grammatical and (32′) to be ungrammatical, but this is not borne out:

32 Don't they care at all

32′ Do they care at all

The most obvious explanation for the grammaticality of (32′) is that it is a rhetorical question and pragmatically equivalent to (31).

In fact, it is not only speech act data such as (31) and (32) which demonstrate that syntax is sensitive to pragmatic effects. Implicature too demonstrates the need for a pragmatically sensitive syntax. This is clear in a sentence which you read a few paragraphs back and which we will now treat as data:

33 If *please* is allowable at all with (17) and (19) . . .

Why is *at all* allowable in this sentence? Remember the clausal implicature that arises when a sentence is introduced by *if*: possibly S, possibly not-S. Here the negative polarity item is licensed by the implicature, which includes the possibility of a negative sentence, associated with *if*-sentences.

The case of *any* is similar. In the last chapter we saw how *any*, in contradistinction to *some*, does not presuppose the existence of the noun phrase it determines. As a consequence, *any* implies possibly *some*, possibly not-*some*.

Hence the negative polarity item *any* is grammatical, and in fact pre-empts the use of *some*, in sentences such as

34 Bring any whisky you see

since *you see* gives rise to the implicature *possibly you will see whisky/possibly you will not see whisky*.

Summary   In the first part of this chapter we have seen that language is used performatively. In fact, the performative nature of language is explicitly encoded in a limited number of lexical items, such as the verb *promise*. When we use this predicate, it counts as performing the action of promising. However, there are many other, implicit, ways of promising; indeed, all uses of language are performative. Thus sentences are grammatical objects which describe states of affairs in the world (snow is white) or in possible worlds (I'll pick you up at eight) and may be thought of as true or false. But when those sentences get used as utterances, it is not their truth value that determines what they mean so much as whether we understand what they are used to do.

As well as the formal properties of sentences (they may be interrogative, for example), they also have functional properties (when interrogative sentences are used as utterances, they are typically used to ask questions). However, not all interrogative sentences are used to ask questions; sometimes interrogative sentences are used indirectly to give orders (why don't you leave me alone) or to make assertions (who cares). This raises a very important issue only briefly touched on in the first part of the chapter, that of how we understand utterances whose intended meaning (e.g., no one cares) appears to be at odds with their literal meaning (e.g., who cares).

5.2 *Speech acts: the problem of literal meaning*

The first part of this chapter described one phenomenon, indirect speech acts, which raises a problematic issue: what is the status of the literal meaning of a sentence like (24)?

24 Who cares

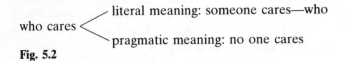

who cares ⟨ literal meaning: someone cares—who

pragmatic meaning: no one cares

Fig. 5.2

Idiom theory and indirect speech acts

One way of dealing with this problem would be to say that *who cares* is an idiom, meaning no one cares. This was a favoured solution at one time, and neatly bypasses the problem of literal meaning simply by claiming that *who cares* has idiomatic meaning (Sadock, 1974). Thus *can you x* is an idiomatic way of saying *do x*. One objection to this solution is that idioms are supposedly untranslatable, yet *can you x*, unlike true idioms such as *kick the bucket*, occurs widely across languages as an indirect way of making a request or giving an order. A still more serious objection to the idiom account is raised by examples like

35 Who likes fish

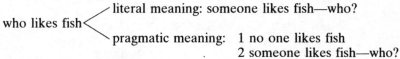

who likes fish ⟨ literal meaning: someone likes fish—who?
pragmatic meaning: 1 no one likes fish
                    2 someone likes fish—who?

Fig. 5.3

Thus *who likes fish* may be used either as an indirect speech act, to assert that no one likes fish, or as a direct speech act, to inquire as to the identity of those who do like fish. It is obviously unsatisfactory to have to claim that an expression is sometimes an idiom and sometimes not. And anyway, this would not be a sufficient account, since an inference theory of some kind would be needed so that a hearer could determine whether *who likes fish* was intended idiomatically or not.

Inference theory and indirect speech acts

The two possible ways to understand (35) raise the problem at the heart of speech act theory, that of how the illocutionary force of an utterance is determined. This is where implicature or relevance theory might help. When you hear someone say

35 Who likes fish

a Gricean implicature would enable you to determine whether a genuine question or a rhetorical question reading was more relevant. Alternatively, under relevance theory, you first recover the explicature, which is most easily expressed as a logical form integrated into a description, to give something like

35′ The speaker is asking who likes fish

An implicature might then be available, which would be an inference drawn from premises which would include the explicature and knowledge of the world prompted by the situation. This implicature would be relevance-oriented, and might take either of the forms suggested in Fig. 5.4.

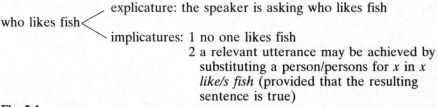

who likes fish ⟨ explicature: the speaker is asking who likes fish
implicatures: 1 no one likes fish
              2 a relevant utterance may be achieved by
                substituting a person/persons for *x* in *x*
                like/s fish (provided that the resulting
                sentence is true)

Fig. 5.4

Thus we could use either Gricean implicature or relevance theory to recover the intended meaning of

35 Who likes fish

and hence to determine the illocutionary force of the utterance (Fig. 5.5).

who likes fish

implicature 1 (no one likes fish) → illocutionary force: incontrovertable assertion

implicature 2 (a relevant utterance may be achieved by substituting a person/persons for x in x *like/s fish* provided that the resulting sentence is true) → illocutionary force: an offer of fish (in a restaurant), etc.

Fig. 5.5

Literal meaning and conventional meaning

However, both the Gricean implicature and the relevance theory mechanisms preserve the importance of the literal meaning of (35) as part of the calculation of the intended force of the utterance. To ask the question posed by Morgan in 'Two types of convention in indirect speech acts', is it really credible to suppose that in the case of utterances like

36 Can you pass the salt

so complicated a mechanism is required to arrive at the most relevant understanding (1978: 261-80)? Morgan argues that (36) is calculable but not calculated, and calls it a 'short-circuited implicature'. If you accept that (36) has become so conventionalized as not to require an inferencing procedure like that required to determine the force of (35), and you deny that *can you x* is an idiom, you are forced to the conclusion that there is no difference, or next to no difference, in conventional meaning between

36 Can you pass the salt

and

36′ Pass the salt

and that therefore the notion of literal meaning is unsustainable.

However logical this argument may be, we are obviously reluctant to abandon the notion that literal meaning is a stable, consistent component of sentences and utterances. Moreover, whatever its meaning status, there is clearly a difference between (36) and (36′), at least in terms of politeness. In the next section I am going to suggest a way out of this paradox which, so far as I know, is novel, and which I hope will be persuasive.

Checking understanding (6)

In the section you have just read, I have tried to show how pragmatic inferences (implicatures) have a role to play in helping to determine the speaker's intention (illocutionary force). Can you show how an implicature would help you to determine the force of the second utterances in each of the following dialogues? (37 and 39 are invented, 38 is real.)

37 Customer: I'd like to borrow money to buy a new car
   Manager: This is a Building Society

38 Patient: This is probably going to sound silly
   Doctor (interrupting): Not at all

39 A: And then as if that wasn't enough, my grandmother died on Christmas Day
   B: I don't know what to say

Literal meaning as a feature of sentences but not of utterances

In this section I am going to argue that sentences make a relatively arbitrary contribution to the understanding of utterances. In Chapter 1 we saw how the sentence

40 May I speak English

is frequently taken in some contexts (my experience is of shops in Italy) to be an utterance equivalent to the quite different sentence

41 Do you speak English

Thus in this context producing the sentence, i.e. actually saying *may I speak English*, counts as saying *do you speak English*. In this situation, the addressee can hardly have got as far as getting from utterance to explicature, never mind decided about the implicature and the status of the utterance as a supposed indirect speech act. It seems non-controversial to argue that the addressee's response relies more on knowledge of the situation than on the meaning of what is uttered. How can it be otherwise when the addressee does not understand (much) English?

I want to try and persuade you that, in understanding utterances in our mother tongue, we behave more than we suppose like non-native speakers faced with a language of which we have limited knowledge. We actually know much less of the meaning of our language than we think we do, precisely because what any token of our language means is much less determined than we tend to think it is. And, looked at alongside the knowledge we take into account in deriving implicatures, words and sentences make a relatively less important contribution to our understanding than we tend to think they do. This perhaps helps to explain why we have already had quite a lot of difficulty deciding just what words like *now*, *well*, and *oh* actually mean: in fact, I challenge you to go back to Chapter 1 and find a single example which the speaker intended to mean what he or she says literally.

Meaning is a relative phenomenon anyway. This is because lexical items have syntactic function as well as semantic content, and in each case the balance between syntactic function and lexical salience has implications for the extent to which their meaning is arbitrary. So we find a strong, non-arbitrary meaning attached to nominals, or naming words, like *substance* or *general*. And we can particularize them with determiners to give expanded phrases such as *a substance* and *the general*. But when these words acquire a secondary syntactic function, that of modifying other naming words as denominal adjectives, their lexical salience declines; so the meanings of *substantial* or *general* (adj.) are less concrete than the meanings of the nouns from which they are derived. And if you apply the productive morphology of English to mark a further derived syntactic function, the adverbial function of modifying adjectives or verbs, then the adverbs *substantially* or *generally* can be seen to be very much more arbitrary in meaning and much less lexically salient than their original nominal grandparents. In fact, we saw in Chapter 3 that when used as sentence adverbs, expressions like *substantially* and *generally* have lost their lexical salience to such a degree that they no longer contribute to the truth value of the utterances with which they are associated, and instead acquire a pragmatic function. In fact, their pragmatic function is the *raison d'être* of sentence adverbs.

This arbitrariness of meaning is especially obvious in the case of prepositions, which are notoriously difficult to translate across languages. Thus the single preposition *mit* would occur in German in contexts where English would use *by* (*mit dem Flugzeug*, 'by plane'), *of* (*voll mit*, 'full of'), and *with* (*mit einem Freund*, 'with a friend'). And, in fact, if you listen carefully to native speakers you will find that their choice of prepositions is often much more arbitrary than you might suppose. When I first noticed this consciously, I was listening to a bigwig from the British Council giving a talk about his work overseas. 'Is this fellow loopy? Should I tell him about care in the community?' I asked myself as I heard him say in rapid succession

42 a number of factors which seemed to militate towards an unbiased approach

43 the findings from the particular questionnaire

44 I hope some of you here will find some relevance for what I want to talk about

And then just afterwards I heard the trade union leader, Bill Morris, on the *Today* programme on Radio 4 say

45 There are 67 options and someone somewhere has to make sense into it

And just today, as I am rewriting the draft of this chapter, I have been to a function and heard a senior police officer say

46 The standard is very very high both on behalf of the pupils and of the teachers

and

47 I want to thank them for the entertainment they're going to provide to us

Although we may smile in a superior way and think we don't talk like this ourselves, actually we sometimes do; and the point is that it does not matter much because the choice of prepositions is relatively arbitrary anyway, as you may confirm for yourself by trying to justify your choice of *be in sympathy with*, *feel sympathy for*, *be sympathetic to/towards*, etc.

The last two paragraphs have taken us away from the problem of literal meaning in speech acts, but have made an important point in their own right, that the semantic component of language is much more arbitrary than we sometimes realize. So why is meaning arbitrary in this way, and how does this arbitrariness come about?

Of course, language is essentially arbitrary in the sense that the phonemes out of which morphemes and words are made are essentially meaningless segments. Thus none of the separate phonemes [ɑ], [p], [t] has meaning until they come together to make [ɑpt] or [pɑt], or [tɑp]. So phonemes are forms without meaningful function, whereas the combinations [ɑpt], [pɑt] and [tɑp] are forms with a function. Phonemes are like bricks, in the sense that they represent nothing but bricks until assembled as a wall or a house.

A phoneme is the smallest unit in language's 'visible spectrum', a 'visible spectrum' which includes at least the phoneme, morpheme, lexical item (word), sentence, utterance, discourse, and text. I do not think it is fanciful to see language as many times made, so that a sentence is to the lexical items which constitute it what a morpheme is to the phonemes which constitute it. Sentences may be regarded as syntactic structures or as semantic representations. As a syntactic structure, the sentence

35 Who likes fish

consists of a *wh*-proform as subject, with a predicate consisting of a tensed verb and a noun phrase. But it only attains the status of a sentence when these separate parts—*wh*-proform, verb, noun phrase—are grouped as constituents:

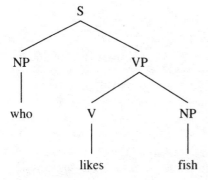

Fig. 5.6

In a similar way the three separate words—*who, likes, fish*—are separate forms whose function, to invite an addressee to complete the open proposition *x likes fish*, results not from their status as three separate forms, or bricks, but from their combination into a meaningful structure. That words have meaning is not in dispute, of course; but the argument I want to put to you is that their meaning comes from the combination of forms, phonemes or morphemes, that constitute them, and that they in their turn are forms that constitute a higher unit, a sentence, whose meaning is more and other than the meaning of its constituent segments. In fact, the meaning of a sentence is determined in relation to a state of affairs in a real or possible world, and may be expressed as a truth value—this is clearly not the way the meaning of a word or morpheme is determined.

Thus the constituent parts of a word (phonemes, morphemes) have a function in combination as a word, but words are forms when in their turn they are the constituent parts of sentences. And at the next level up, it will resolve our literal-meaning problem very neatly indeed to argue that sentences have a function as a combination of constituents, but are forms which combine with a set of felicity conditions and pragmatic presuppositions to give utterances. And in its turn an utterance has a function as a combination of a sentence and knowledge about the world. But when organized sequentially as a series of 'forms', utterances combine in regular ways to give a conversational sequence that has a function, such as is shown in my exchanges with would-be smokers discussed earlier in the chapter.

In this way we can have our cake and eat it because we are treating a sentence as two objects—as a combination of constituent forms which function as a sentence, and as a form which in combination with other propositions (felicity conditions or pragmatic presuppositions) constitutes an utterance. This point is well illustrated by utterances like

48 That was a wonderful meal

which is frequently false as a sentence but would typically be considered appropriate as an utterance (and would be unlikely to have the effect of deceiving). Similarly, the salutation which began a letter I once received from a would-be overseas student

49 My pleasant dear

is a perfectly grammatical expression but rather unconventional as a speech act (although in Arabic it would be fine). It is at the heart of language to be able to recognize this arbitrariness of meaning which is the result of seeing the simultaneous relation of an item both to the level below and to the level above in the 'visible spectrum' of language.

We are now ready to return to the specific problems of (35) and (36). Under the account of language suggested above, we can see that, when viewed as a combination of lexical items or syntactic constituents

35 Who likes fish

functions as a sentence expressing an open proposition. At the same time, this 'sentence' may also be thought of as a formal component of relatively arbitrary meaning, which, together with other premises, allows a hearer to infer the function of the utterance to which it contributes. These premises would be likely to include perceptions of aspects of the surrounding situation. If choosing from a menu in a restaurant were an aspect of the surrounding situation, one utterance function would be inferred; if talking about food people do not like was an aspect of the current situation, a different utterance function would be inferred.

In the case of

36 Can you pass the salt

we might want to argue that *can (you)* has more grammatical than lexical function, and that the salient proposition is contained within *(you) pass the salt*. This would be to treat *can (you)* as we might treat prepositions, which do not surprise us when they turn up in lexically unpredictable environments. Here *can you* turns up as a request: it is neither an idiom, which would be going too far, nor a literal meaning which requires the elaborate machinery of Gricean or relevance theory-inspired inference to determine its force; it is simply a formative which is more grammatical than lexical. So that the quarrelsome couple at breakfast, in arguing over whether *could* or *may* is to be preferred, are having the same sort of argument that might be had over *different to* and *different from*.

These arguments are tantamount to dissolving the difference between so-called 'direct' speech acts and so-called 'indirect' speech acts. This would be a welcome advance on postulating two classes of speech act, which seems to miss a generalization somewhere. Nor is this distinction syntactically motivated, since pre-verbal *please*, to take just one example, is blind to differences in the supposed direct or indirect status of speech acts, as we saw at the end of the first part of this chapter. Moreover, the literal-meaning hypothesis is at odds with the fundamental nature of human language: that meaning results from the combination of 'meaningless' segments.

Speech act choice

The explanation suggested here of how utterances are construed is not intended to obscure the fact that speakers do have choices to make in how to encode illocutionary force. It is intended rather as a more logical explanation of why sentences appear to have two levels of meaning, the literal (what our words mean) and the understood (what we mean by our words) (Atkinson, Kilby, and Roca, 1988: 217). As we noted above, there is certainly a difference between

36 Can you pass the salt

and

36′ Pass the salt

which will be explored in detail in our discussion of politeness in Chapter 7.

So, given the choice between ways of requesting that someone pass one the salt, the real issue is what societal and/or individual attitudes motivate the way chosen on any particular occasion. And what is the effect of the choice that a speaker makes?

Finally, speech acts might be seen as a prototypically pragmatic phenomenon, in the sense that they challenge the notion that there is a one-to-one correspondence between a form and its function. It is simply not possible to argue that interrogative sentences, to take one example, have a single function. In fact the function of an interrogative sentence when used as an utterance crucially depends on an essentially pragmatic phenomenon, how it is related to the world.

Raising pragmatic awareness: speech acts—language as action

1. You will need a partner for this exercise. Working separately, you and your partner each choose one short extract from a contemporary play and copy it out without the original punctuation. The best extracts are those

where two speakers are holding an emotional conversation over about ten very short turns. Exchange texts: you each invent your own punctuation, using either conventional symbols or any new ones that you need to invent to capture illocutionary force. When you have completed the exercise, explain your suggested punctuation to your partner.

2. Working individually, either listen out for or recall occasions when a speaker responds, as Mr Logic does, to the propositional content rather than the illocutionary force in the previous utterance. Television comedies and family arguments are good sources of data. Share and explain your examples in your tutorial group.

3. Choose an emotion such as anger or a behaviour such as showing tenderness or criticizing someone. During the next few days, see if you can provoke this emotion or behaviour in someone else. Report your strategies and your interlocutor's exact utterances to colleagues in your tutorial group.

4. Find a partner and choose a picture of a couple from a colour magazine. Each of you should take the role of one of the people in the picture. Decide who will speak first and what proposition he/she will convey. The speaker should then try several different ways of conveying the agreed meaning—each time, the person addressed gives it a score out of ten for effectiveness.

5. What is the relationship between language and touch? Out of class, note the occasions when language accompanies touch. Note down carefully what you observe and report it in your tutorial group.

6. How do people express disagreement? Out of class, listen out for disagreements. Note down what you overhear and report it in your tutorial group.

Further reading

Austin (1962; 1971); Grice (1968); Morgan (1978); Searle (1965; 1969; 1975).

6

Talk and context

'And like a downward smoke, the slender stream
Along the cliff to fall and pause and fall did seem'
(Alfred Tennyson *The Lotos-Eaters*)

Keywords: talk-in-interaction, sequential properties, dispreferred response, turn, outcome, conversation, adjacency pair, clarification, repetition, social structure, overlap, recycling, repair, transition-relevance place, projection, turn size, schism, lapse.

In the previous chapters the majority of the examples considered have been 'real' (or 'live') rather than invented. They have also typically been single utterances or very short exchanges, and have been used largely to exemplify varieties of pragmatic meaning such as implicature, presupposition, and illocutionary force. Rather than exemplify varieties of pragmatic meaning, in this chapter we examine talk, in fact extended talk, in its own right. This will enable us to see to what extent the kinds of pragmatic meaning we have become familiar with in the preceding chapters are appropriate and sufficient as an account of real talk. I thought of calling the chapter 'Real Talk' at one stage, because the units of talk are rarely single utterances or even exchanges as short as those examined so far. The expectation you hold as you begin this chapter, then, should perhaps be that the kinds of pragmatic meaning you are familiar with now will be useful in explaining how meaning is conveyed utterance by utterance, but that these accounts of utterance meaning may be inadequate as accounts of how extended talk works. Let us see.

The first part of this chapter is largely based on an extended conversation. The second, shorter part addresses the issue of the relationship of language and context which is highlighted by the first part.

6.1 *Talk-in-interaction*

In Chapter 3 we investigated the pragmatic meaning of *Well* and of *I see* in

1   A: Somebody told me it was cheaper to go by plane than by train. Is that right
    B: Well we're not British Rail agents so I don't know the difference
    A: I see

This exchange was adapted from a conversation in a travel agent's in a small town in the south of England in which A, an educated 35-year-old male, tries to obtain information from B, a 25-year-old female assistant. This is how the encounter begins:

2   A: can you help me I have to go to Edinburgh (.) somebody told me it
         was cheaper to go by plane than by train (.) is that right
     B: (1.5) well we're not British Rail agents so I don't know the difference
     A: oh I see

Below I draw your attention to a number of issues raised by this exchange (for convenience I have numbered them 1–12):

1. Who should speak first? And what is the effect of the customer seizing the initiative in this way?
   Notice that before we have even begun to consider the pragmatics of what is uttered, we are discussing the sequential ordering of the exchange.

2. A's opening is four units long with brief pauses approximately equivalent to the time it takes to say one syllable—indicated by (.)—between the second and third and the third and fourth units. This is a comparatively long and rather unusual turn in the sense that it contains four units. Do you think its effect could be to overwhelm B?
   Notice that we are again discussing the significance of the sequential properties of the exchange, irrespective of the content of the utterances that compose it. This seems to confirm the two-level status of the units of language as suggested in the previous chapter, since the sequential status of the utterance is being discussed irrespective of its illocutionary force.

3. A says *I have to go to Edinburgh*. He does not have to give a reason for asking for information, but giving a reason might be considered to be a politeness strategy. By their very nature, however, politeness strategies imply that there is something to be polite about, like troubling someone else for information. Do you think giving a reason for asking for information in this situation is a good strategy or not?
   Again, notice how, in discussing the way the information units of A's opening are structured, we are discussing the sequential properties of the interaction.

4. If it is appropriate for A to give a reason for asking for information, what advantages/disadvantages would there be in using a different formula, such as

I'm going to Edinburgh
I want to go to Edinburgh
I must go to Edinburgh

Unlike *must*, *I have to* gives rise to the conventional implicature that this decision was made for A by someone else. What conversational implicature arises as a result of *I have to*? Does A imply that he is an important person? Does he imply that it is not his fault that he is troubling B by making this enquiry? If the latter, does *have to* count as a kind of apology?

5. A is careful to be impersonal: he says *somebody told me* rather than *I was told* and *is that right* rather than *is he right*. By doing this he makes it easier

for B to reply that the information is wrong without suggesting that A, or someone known to A, is mistaken. Again, this is a politeness strategy.

6. What do you make of A's use of two past tenses, *someone told me it was*, rather than past + present (*someone told me it's*) or two present tenses (*I've heard it's*)? Again, this seems to be a politeness strategy, with the information being represented as historical rather than contemporary, and therefore easier for B to contradict without giving offence.

7. Notice A's choice of *right* rather than *true*. Again, A will lose less face if this information turns out to be false and B has to contradict it.

8. Taken altogether, this opening is marked by politeness strategies. These have the effect of making it easier for B to contradict A, but at the same time they place a distance between A and B. Perhaps these strategies are A's way of saying that he is male, middle-class, educated, a customer, and someone who expects to be served. Would he have done better to have been more familiar, to have gone to the opposite extreme, leant across the counter, taken B by the neck and said 'Give us a kiss love—is it cheaper to go to Edinburgh on the train or the plane'?

9. Can you account for the long pause before B begins to speak? Is this because she is overwhelmed, or because she is deciding whether or how to disappoint A?

10. In Chapter 3 we saw that *well* marks a dispreferred response. It is therefore in a sense conciliatory and counts as a kind of apology. B's response also contains two propositions, *we're not British Rail agents* and *I don't know the difference*. Which of these do you consider answers A's question better and responds more appropriately to his request for assistance? Which, if either, is syntactically or pragmatically subordinate? What do you learn about her position from her use of the powerful *we* in one proposition and *I* in the other? What effect is the powerful *we* intended to have on A? Given the illocutionary force, a refusal to comply with A's request for information, can you think of other utterances that would have conveyed this meaning equally successfully?

11. In Chapter 3 we also saw that there is a conventional implicature (*this is news*) associated with *oh*, and that *I see* implies that the preceding utterance is unsatisfactory. Do you think this kind of indirectness is A's best strategy at this stage?

Notice that, if *I see* is a dummy turn obliging B to retake her previous turn, we are again discussing the sequential properties of talk rather than the pragmatic meaning of the utterances that are its components.

12. In his opening, A presupposes that B has, and is willing to supply, information. B responds in such a way as to challenge this presupposition. We might expect the rest of this interaction to be about finding a formula that enables both A and B to save face or to proceed in such a way as to enable one or the other of them to come out with what they want at the expense of the other. Based on what you have seen so far, which of these outcomes would you put your money on? (This is a serious question—think carefully about it.)

In these twelve brief comments we have referred not only to pragmatic types of meaning such as implicature, presupposition, and illocutionary force, but also to the sequential meaning of talk, a property of conversation rather than of utterances, and to the way the use of talk invokes external status. Thus we immediately see that the ground covered in the preceding chapters serves us well in enabling us to understand utterances, but is not sufficient to account for the properties of 'talk-in-interaction' (Schegloff, 1987).

The conversational sequence so far goes something like this:

A: request for information (reason given)
B: refusal to supply information (reason given)
A: indication that this is not a sufficient response

Rather than try to guess what B might say by way of a next utterance, can you guess what B produces by way of a sequential contribution?

What B actually produces is not information but an offer to provide information. This is expressed in such a way that A must suggest the extent of information he thinks it would be reasonable or expectable for B to provide. B's turn is

3 B: I can tell you what it is to go to Edinburgh

Note B's use of *can* rather than *'ll*, which forces A's next sequential contribution. This comes in two parts, with the second part supplied after a one-second pause in which B was offered but declined the turn, thus obliging A to spell out the extent of information B is expected to give:

4 A: yes (1.0) by plane

B then confirms her agreement to the terms of the offer

5 B: by plane

and by breaking off forces A to take the turn again. A uses this turn to confirm that the terms are agreed, whereupon B reaches for the timetable. After a pause of nearly two seconds, A types, or characterizes, the sequence by expressing gratitude:

6 A: yeh (1.7) thanks very much

Thus the opening sequence of the encounter looks like this:

7 A: can you help me I have to go to Edinburgh (.) somebody told me it was cheaper to go by plane than by train (.) is that right
B: (1.5) well we're not British Rail agents so I don't know the difference
A: oh I see
B: I can tell you what it is to go to Edinburgh
A: yes (1.0) by plane
B: by plane
A: yeh (1.7) thanks very much

Another way of determining how this conversation is being directed is by examining the mechanism of the adjacency pair, which Schegloff and Sacks (1973) identified as two adjacent utterances produced by different speakers and ordered so that the first member of the pair requires an appropriate second member of a relevant type to be produced as a response. Typical examples of adjacency pairs are greeting–greeting, invitation–acceptance/refusal, apology–acceptance(/rejection). Thus the initiative rests with the speaker who provides the first member of an adjacency pair. From this perspective, the first five turns of this encounter exhibit the following adjacency pair properties:

7 A: initiates adjacency pair:
  B: responds
  A: forces B to recycle response = re-initiation of adjacency pair
  B: responds; and initiates adjacency pair
  A: responds

Thus we see how the initiative swings from A to B at this level, although at another level A has succeeded in getting B to agree to provide him with at least some of the information he is seeking, despite an initial refusal.

We might expect B to use her next few turns to tell A the cost of flying to Edinburgh. But what will happen after that? And do you still put your money on the outcome you predicted before?

It takes B thirteen seconds, during which time she is looking through the timetable, before she takes her turn. The next four turns consist of

8 B: (13.0) well there's a shuttle service (0.4) um (.) sixty pounds one way (2.5) er (2.3) when do you want to go
  A: I want to go at the weekend
  B: (0.3) what weekend
  A: next weekend

A opts to give the lexical realization *I want to go* rather than allow it to be presupposed. Is this a way of refusing to allow B to construct part of his turn for him? And if so, what does it convey? A's *at the weekend* is a deictic which would usually be taken to refer to the weekend following the time of utterance. But B does not process it in this way; she appears to reprimand A's failure to name a specific weekend by her choice of the potentially metalingual *what* (which questions the notion of weekend) rather than the preferred *which* (which would presuppose a set of weekends to choose from). Just as A had recycled his adjacency pair initiator in the opening of the encounter, so B recycles her adjacency pair initiator now in seeking clarification of what was already clear. A indicates his displeasure by the speed of his response, which consists of a deictic elaboration of his original turn.

In fact, they are at cross purposes, as the continuing sequence will show. For B, weekends are a list of dates in the timetable with different prices written beside them, so that her conception of 'weekend' is not deictic at all. For A, weekends are deictically stacked up ahead of the time of utterance. Thus from B's perspective *what weekend* is perfectly logical and refers to a timetable entry. But A has failed to reconstruct this perspective. So how do A and B stand now that A has mistakenly supposed B to have reprimanded him in refusing his deictic and has reprimanded her in return? His reprimand will seem unmotivated to B, just as A felt he had received a motiveless reprimand before.

Looked at sequentially, this part of the exchange has an expectable quality in the sense that it is used to deliver what was agreed, a price to fly to Edinburgh, and then to confirm the date of intended travel. However, it has one non-expectable element, the introduction of the 'shuttle service' sub-topic in the utterance *there's a shuttle service*. Although not taken up immediately by A, this feature provides A with a rationale for continuing the conversation.

Is your money still on the same outcome?

A needs to know what a shuttle service is. So as B converts A's *next weekend* to a date and matches it with the information in the timetable, he asks for clarification, thereby initiating a new adjacency pair in an area where B has specific knowledge which he must again request:

9   B: (0.3) what weekend
    A: next weekend (3.5) how does that work you just turn up for the
        shuttle service
    B: (0.8) that might be cheaper then (1.8) that's fifty
    A: fifty
    B: that's a saver (0.7) burit it's a standby[3]
    A: a standby

But B declines to clarify—is it because she is unwilling or lacks the necessary information? And how is A to know which? She continues her information search and produces a new, lower price, *fifty*. A repeats this as a kind of dummy turn to signal that he has received the information but is still waiting for his clarification request to be met. But instead of clarifying, B continues the mystification by typing it as *a saver* and indicating that there is a condition attached. A's *a standby* has the force of a clarification request merely by repetition of the mystifying term. By this time B has indicated that she holds a range of goods whose properties A is unaware of. What has A got which will enable him to take the goods which are available but still denied him? They must, like the information he sought in the first place, be valuable or they would have been provided by now. But A is making progress: the accessible part of the information sought at the outset, the cost of an air ticket, has now been acquired.

Do you want to hedge your initial bet?

The entire encounter is printed below. As you will see, there is a third speaker, the manager (M), a 45-year-old male. He remains at the back of the shop busying himself over a pile of papers until (lines 84–5), when he comes up to the counter. In the transcription, the beginning of each overlapping utterance is marked by a double slash (//) and the end by an asterisk (*); inaudible contributions are marked by double parentheses enclosing empty spaces, and pauses are indicated in tenths of a second—e.g. (1.5)—or syllables—(.) is equivalent to a pause of one-syllable length.

A: can you help me I have to go to Edinburgh (.) somebody told   1
    me it was cheaper to go by plane than by train (.) is that   2
    right   3
B: (1.5) well we're not British Rail agents so I don't know   4
    the difference   5
A: oh I see   6
B: I can tell you what it is to go to Edinburgh   7
A: yes (1.0) by plane   8
B: by plane   9
A: yeh (1.7) thanks very much   10
B: (13.0) well there's a shuttle service (0.4) um (.) sixty pounds one   11
    way (2.5) er (2.3) when do you want to go   12
A: I want to go at the weekend   13

---

[3] *Burit* = B's realization of *but it*.

B:	(0.3) what weekend	14
A:	next weekend (3.5) how does that work you just turn up for	15
	the shuttle service	16
B:	(0.8) that might be cheaper then (1.8) that's fifty	17
A:	fifty	18
B:	that's a saver (0.7) burit it's a standby	19
A:	a st//andby*	20
B:	//you ha*ve to book it in advance but um (.)	21
A:	are you guaranteed a seat	22
B:	(8.0) I don't think you are	23
A:	so you buy a ticket bef//ore but*	24
B:	//Ron* with the shuttle saver	25
M:	(0.8) yeh	26
B:	um (.) are they guaranteed seats	27
M:	(3.5) er	28
B:	this is a new one that Marie's just added in here (1.7) oh	29
	hang //on see*	30
M:	//British Airways*	31
B:	see see stop press (( ))	32
M:	(0.3) British Airways	33
B:	yeah	34
M:	er yeah the flight's a standby guarantee (..) yeah you you	35
	turn up and you've got to er (1.0) if they can't get on one	36
	flight they'll put you on the next any of the next two	37
A:	(0.2) and h//and*	38
B:	//(( ))*	39
A:	how often do they go	40
M:	every two hours	41
A:	every two hours (1.6) so you could wait four hours	42
B:	(1.0) yeh	43
A:	um hum (2.0) and that's fifty pounds one way	44
B:	yes	45
A:	(0.8) and have you got a timetable for	46
B:	not to give out no (0.7) I can tell you the times but I	47
	don't	48
A:	ye-es could you tell me how often they go Saturdays and	49
	coming back on Sundays	50
B:	(13.0) all right (0.3) Saturdays you're going out	51
A:	yeh	52
B:	(1.0) yeh	53
A:	yeh	54
B:	seven-forty nine-forty eleven-forty thirteen-forty	55
A:	(0.6) seven-forty eleven-forty	56
B:	(0.5) seven-forty	57
A:	nine-forty	58
B:	every two hours	59
A:	every two hours on on on forty minutes	60
B:	till (.) nineteen-forty	61
A:	yes (1.3) good	62

B:	and coming back they er (3.4) er (0.4) you're coming back	63
	Sunday aren't you	64
A:	Sunday please	65
B:	(2.8) nine-forty eleven-forty	66
A:	ah ha (.) so it's forty either way and it starts at seven-forty on	67
	Saturday from London and nine-forty from Edinburgh on Sunday	68
	(.) until what time on Sunday night	69
B:	same time nineteen-forty	70
A:	nineteen-forty (.) now what happens if you turn up for the nineteen-	71
	forty flight and they get you on any of the next two does that	72
	mean Monday (1.5) or do they guarantee to do something about	73
	it on Sunday night	74
B:	(2.0) I don't know (.) Ron what happens if he wants the last	75
	flight (3.7) will they do it like that or don't they allow	76
	that	77
M:	(1.0) what's that	78
B:	what happens if he wants the last fl//ight*	79
A:	//if I*want to come back	80
	on the//last flight on the Sunday night*	81
B:	//(( )) they don't put*on an extra plane do	82
	they	83
M:	(1.4) well theoretically if it's full they're supposed to	84
	put a back-up plane on	85
A:	um hum	86
M:	in theory (2.1) whether or not it works in practice I don't	87
	know	88
A:	(3.0) now if I buy a ticket from you then it costs I I pay	89
	you a hundred pounds //(.) n*	90
M:	//yes*	91
A:	then I go there and (0.6) n I'm in their hands	92
M:	that's right sir yes	93
A:	do you know what the rail return (.) weekend return to	94
	Edinburgh is by any chance	95
B:	we're not British Rail //agents*	96
A:	//you're* not a//gents I see*	97
M:	//but I'll*give you a	98
	rough idea	99
A:	ah ha thank you very much	100
M:	(12.0) sixty-eight pounds sixty	101
A:	sixty-eight sixty (0.6) good thank you very much (.) I //thin*	102
M:	//that's* from	103
	London sir	104
A:	that's from London (.) either way I've got to get myself (.)	105
M:	yeh	106
A:	to the right//place*	107
M:	//yes*	108
A:	yeh I'll think about it	109
M:	yeh	110
A:	thanks very much that's very helpful (.) bye-bye	111

Seen as a whole, the exchange enables us to reconstruct a wider social context. Because the travel agent is not a British Rail agent, the young female member of staff with low-status fronting responsibilities is trained not to provide information about rail travel. Such privileged information can only be given by the manager at his own discretion. A does not know this when he walks into the shop. But through his persistence, he reinforces the existing social structure in which real business is done by males of higher status over the head of the low-status female employee whose job it is to prevent such business from needing to be done. Thus each of the three interactants replicates a recognizable routine and creates again the society that was waiting to be remade. Thinking back to the initial politeness strategies of A, we see how this outcome was scripted as he began the encounter by establishing his status through distancing himself from B. When the distance between A and B is great enough and the information sought precious enough, M is called in. I have collected several examples of encounters of this kind, which show that it is typical for a higher-status manager, frequently, but not always, male, to be called in when a customer seeks something that is available but is beyond the authority of the low-status fronting employee to provide. Indeed, the situation is recognizable to us all, and remade many times in everyday life, as the stereotype of the secretary who guards the manager's door reminds us.

Within this overview, in which the social structure outside the interaction and remade by it has been sketched in, there are a number of notable features at the level of utterance and sequence that are worth commenting on. Line numbers are given for convenience.

101: A does get the information he was seeking. In fact, it takes A just over 4 minutes to obtain the information that it takes B 13 seconds and M 12 seconds to find. This shows that the information has a value—in fact 3 minutes and 40 seconds (4 mins 5 secs – 25 secs = 3 mins 40 secs) of negotiation.

25–35, 75–83: It is notable how difficult it is for B to engage M's attention. At 25, 27, 75, and 79 B raises her pitch, which is identified by Loveday (1984) as a typical subservience strategy for female speakers. It takes B two turns on each occasion to gain what passes for M's full attention. On the first occasion when his assistance is sought, he declines to approach the place where the negotiation is being conducted and remains a voice-throw away at the back of the shop.

46–8: If you were to listen to the tape of this exchange, you would recognize that the end-point of *and have you got a timetable for* is clearly a break-off by A and not an interruption by B. A breaks off his utterance with *for*, realized as [fə], not as [fɔ]. Thus *for* is not given the end-of-sentence realization [fɔ], although the turn is terminated at this point; instead the break-off is clearly signalled as occurring in the middle of a preposition phrase. By breaking off in this way, A forces B to take up the turn and respond to his request. B's response consists of a refusal to meet A's request (*not to give out no*), a pause, a conciliatory offer (*I can tell you the times*), and the beginning of a reinforcement of the original refusal (*but I don't*). The turn is broken off with *don't*, realised as [dəʊn], and not as [dəʊnt]. B's break-off is also signalled for what it is, not end-of-sentence but middle-of-constituent. It has just the same effect as A's had on B, that of forcing the other inter-actant to take up the turn. The turn has now become rather like the parcel in 'pass the parcel' with both speakers eager to avoid the floor: A plays for time as he seeks an opportunity to pursue his ultimate goal of getting a piece of specific information from B, and B hopes A will give up and go away.

55–8: The original tape reveals that B speaks very fast indeed at 55. 58 indicates that A had heard but had not processed 55 when he spoke at 56. To speak so fast that another party cannot process puts that party at an immediate disadvantage, although A's strategy for recouping the situation and giving himself adequate processing time is effective.

62, 67, 100, 102: A's two metapragmatic *ah-ha*'s and two metapragmatic *good*s acknowledge that he has secured goods of value: in 67, that he has understood a pattern that he had had problems with; in 100, that he has been promised the information he was seeking and had been denied until that point.

80: B invites M into the conversation as her informant, but A sees his chance and quickly manages to redirect the interaction from an A ↔ B to an A ↔ M exchange. Is this because he decides that man-to-man or customer-to-manager talk is more likely to secure the outcome he wants? Is it prompted by B referring to A in 75 and again in 79 heterogeneously by her use of *he*, as someone excluded from the homogeneous group that includes B and M but excludes A? A achieves this redirection by taking M's turn, through starting to speak before M responds to B's adjacency pair initiator. Although B did not have the information sought and for that reason brought M into the interaction again at this stage, she tries to stay in the conversation at 82 by providing a putative answer to her own question during what has now become A's turn. After this failed attempt to contribute to the interaction, she will have one more utterance only, the formulaic and no longer effective *we're not British Rail agents*.

89: The interaction takes a decisive turn when A, after a long pause, indicates with a non-deictic *now* that the encounter is moving to a new phase. The *then* in *if I buy a ticket from you then* implies an agreement, although A has still to discover the price of the alternative means of travel. The repair which replaces *it costs* with *I pay you* personalizes a matter—the exchange of money—which is usually not so directly mentioned, but elicits an overlapping *yes* from M followed in 93 by the deference marker *sir*. This is the moment at which A, with suitable politeness strategies, asks for the information he requires, this time by making reference to a felicity condition that can hardly be denied (whether M has the requisite knowledge) and expressing his request pessimistically (*by any chance*). M saves face with his offer to *give . . . a rough idea*.

102–4: As soon as M sees that he is not going to make the sale that he was offered at 89–90, he provides additional information without prompting, *that's from London*, and repeats the deference marker, *sir*. Suddenly the information held by the travel agent has become cheap, in fact free, as M attempts to secure a sale that no longer appears to be available.

In this description I have picked out some of the most obvious features of the interaction. There are many other interesting features that you might want to pursue for yourself, such as

- the relationship between the strategy of A, to request information and to confirm his understanding of what he is being told, and the sequential organization of the interaction;
- the way that B and M deal with the situation they find themselves in when asked for information they do not have or do not wish to provide;
- the use of non-deictic *you*;
- repetition;
- the stages of the interaction where indirectness is favoured over directness and the reasons for this.

Talk-in-interaction structure

This section describes some of the key principles of conversational sequencing—although you are no longer novices, since we have already met some of the terms which have entered the folklore of conversation analysis, such as turn, adjacency pair, overlap, recycling, clarification, break-off, repair, repetition. In a series of papers written between 1968 and 1980, Schegloff and a number of co-researchers established the basic mechanisms underlying talk-in-interaction. In what is widely acknowledged as a seminal paper, Sacks, Schegloff, and Jefferson (SS&J) (1974) discuss the way that turns are allocated in conversation. The four paragraphs and Checking Understanding tasks that follow are based closely on this paper.

SS&J show that a turn projects its own end, or 'transition-relevance place', and that the speaker may select a next speaker or allow self-selection of next speaker to take place in a way that minimizes gaps and overlaps. Because a turn's end is projected, next speakers have an opportunity to prepare their contributions.

Checking understanding (1) ————————————————————

Working with the interaction in the travel agent's:

1. find a turn whose end is projected and explain how this is effected;

2. find a place where the speaker selects next speaker;

3. find a place where next speaker self-selects;

4. find a place where there is a gap and account for it;

5. find a place where there is an overlap and account for it.

SS&J also describe a range of ways in which a next speaker is selected. These include the use of first-pair parts of adjacency pairs, the use of an address term, repair techniques such as one-word clarificatory questions, and repetitions of parts of a prior utterance with question intonation. Tags may also serve as an exit technique for a turn. Sometimes a next speaker is selected as the natural next speaker by virtue of being the understood recipient of some request, comment, or suggestion without overt selection.

Checking understanding (2) ———————————————

Working with the interaction in the travel agent's, find examples of:

1. a first-pair part of an adjacency pair;

2. the use of an address term;

3. a one-word or a short *wh*-phrase clarification request;

4. a clarification request involving repetition;

5. a tag used as an exit technique;

6. a place where there is a natural next-turn taker.

SS&J show how turn size may vary either because units such as sentences naturally vary in length or because a speaker may have a turn more than one unit long if no other speaker self-selects at a transition-relevance place (a point at which a new speaker would be possible). They show how, in a conversation involving four or more participants, schism may occur so that more than one conversation occurs simultaneously. And they show how conversation can become discontinuous so that lapses occur, although in the case where a next speaker has been selected only pauses, rather than gaps or lapses, are possible.

Checking understanding (3) ———————————————

Working with the interaction in the travel agent's:

1. find an example of a long single-unit turn;

2. find an example of a short single-unit turn;

3. find an example of a long turn resulting from lack of next speaker self-selection;

4. can you find examples of pauses and lapses?

SS&J also show how turns regularly have a three-part structure, consisting of orientation to preceding turn, business of present turn, and orientation to next turn.

Checking understanding (4) ———————————————

Find an example of a three-part turn in the interaction in the travel agent's.

Obviously enough, this is only a beginning, but a beginning that shows the systematic nature of conversation and provides a detailed metalanguage for describing it.

    Other important features of conversation include

- departures from the unmarked norm. For example, in the travel agent's, the whole middle sequence could be thought of as an insertion between the first and second parts of the conversation;
- the extent to which conversations are either unmarked exchanges between equals or are unequal encounters;
- repair: whether self-initiated and self-completed, other-initiated and self-completed, or other-initiated and other-completed;
- audience design, listener behaviour, and the co-authored nature of talk-in-interaction.

And then there are (the very small number of) metapragmatic folk terms, such as 'topic' and 'interruption'. In fact, metapragmatic folk terms are by no means universal, which seems to indicate different cross-cultural awarenesses. In Japanese, for example, there is no single word for 'interruption' but there is a word 'aizuchi', meaning to use the listener channel in ways that are supportive of the speaker by interjecting expressions like *I see*, *I agree*, *I pass*. In English there is no metapragmatic folk term for this phenomenon. There are some languages in which the verb form *interrupt* is in regular use but the nominal *interruption* is felt to be awkward—this is generally the case in Slavonic languages, for example. And even when two languages appear to have a common metapragmatic folk term, it is not necessarily being used to describe the same phenomenon in the two languages. So that what a member of another culture understands by 'pause' or 'topic' may not be the same as your understanding.

6.2 *Talk, convention, and context*

Talk-in-interaction and convention

This chapter has examined talk in its own right rather than as an illustration of types of pragmatic meaning. This examination has shown that, whilst categories of pragmatic meaning are important to our understanding of extended talk, the sequential properties of talk to which pragmatic varieties of meaning contribute are at least as important in any characterization of the nature of the talk-in-interaction.

Our description of pragmatic uses of language in the previous chapters has assumed that pragmatic meaning is non-conventional. In doing this, we have been studying pragmatics in the accepted way. But in fact we can see that the interaction in the travel agent's is conventional in many very obvious ways, and that the pragmatic meanings and sequential ordering of the contributions are much more obviously expectable than unconventional. This must make us question the established position that pragmatic meanings are non-conventional. In fact they are only non-conventional to the extent that they are not literal, truth-conditional or invariably associated with particular forms; but in the contexts in which they occur, they are typically conventional. Indeed, it makes about as much sense to think of pragmatic meanings as non-conventional (or even conventional) in their contexts as it does to think of any other linguistic level as non-conventional in its context: a fine hoo-ha there would be if we started to talk about non-conventional (or conventional) phonemes, or morphemes, or nouns, or truth-conditional meanings. The use of the term 'non-conventional' to describe pragmatic meaning can be seen as an unfortunate consequence of judging utterance meaning by the criterion of sentence meaning.

Each contribution to the encounter described in this chapter is a contribution to or a component of the developing talk-in-interaction and perfectly adapted to the role it plays in a whole conversation, both reflecting and creating the context which it invokes.

Implications: taking stock of pragmatic meaning

If you have been reading this book sequentially, you will have read a chapter about deixis which focused on the indexical properties of a limited set of morphemes (e.g. tense markers), lexical items (e.g. personal pronouns), and phrases (e.g. nouns determined by possessives and demonstratives). You will have read chapters about implicature and speech acts which focused on the pragmatic meanings associated with utterances. And you will have read a chapter about presupposition which focused on the shared understanding brought to utterances and linguistically encoded in them. And now at the level of talk-in-interaction we have seen how the most typical pragmatic category, the utterance, itself provides an insufficient account of the pragmatic meanings of talk-in-interaction.

The perception that an assemblage of pragmatic values in a form we call 'the utterance' is insufficient to account for the pragmatic meaning of utterances arranged sequentially in a form we call 'talk' enables us to confirm the difference between the function a category has as the sum of its components and the role it plays as a component in a larger category. This understanding of language is the key to resolving the apparent paradox of semantic, or 'conventional', and pragmatic, or 'non-conventional', meaning, as we have seen in the previous chapter.

This insight may be profitably applied to some of the issues that have been implicit in many places in our earlier discussions. For example, in Chapter 2 we noted that 'a speaker of French can use *tu* and *vous* and a speaker of English can use *Madam* and *Sir* either to reflect an existing social structure or to create one for the purposes of the interaction at hand'. We can now see that the use of *tu* or *vous* to reflect an existing social structure is really to use them to describe a state of affairs in the world, and is therefore a property of the sentence, whereas to use them to create a world for the purposes of the interaction at hand is a property of the utterance in which they occur. It is worth noting that the use of *tu* and *vous* as a property of the sentence is consistent with the notion that they are referent-oriented.

We have also noted that *I'm tired* can have as many meanings as it has contexts of use. It might mean *I want to go to bed*, *I want to go to bed alone*, *I want to go to bed with you (now)*, and *I don't want to get out of bed*, to suggest just four of the pragmatic meanings that in different contexts might be associated with it. Yet we still sense that it has a core or a literal meaning, although this meaning is not the meaning conveyed in any of the four examples just given. We now have an explanation for why this should be.

The core meaning of *I'm tired* is the meaning it has as a sentence; the real meanings of *I'm tired* are the meanings it has as a set of utterances. Thus one entailment, or sentence meaning, can have many different speaker meanings. And the speaker meanings are more precise and context-invoking than the less determined sentence meaning.

One small piece of evidence that the utterance and not the sentence is the conventional level comes from utterances like

10 B: I don't think you are

where the proposition *you are not (guaranteed a seat)* is hedged by *I think*, and the negation has been raised to a matrix sentence which contributes nothing to the truth value of the sentence as a whole. Part of the sentence grammar has been raised to a pragmatic position, and the sentence has been subsumed within the utterance so that it is no longer a separate component.

Talk and context

Chapter 3 began with a quotation from Pope's *Essay on Criticism*:

'Words are like leaves; and where they most abound,
Much fruit of sense beneath is rarely found.'

In the context of the discussion of implicature which it preceded, this quotation reminded us that less elaborated sentences often have implicit meanings when used as utterances. One might go further still and observe that it would be possible to say very little indeed in a situation where the context itself constituted all the necessary premises for inferring a meaning. Thus it is not done for you or me to speak when we are presented to royalty unless invited so to do. And when invited to speak, we use honorifics like *Sir*, *Ma'am* and *Your Royal Highness* to reflect that context at the level of the sentence. In the more usual way, with which we have been largely concerned in this book, meaning is conveyed by drawing an inference from two kinds of premise, the sentence we hear and our knowledge of the world. At the societal level, whole cultures will be placed at different positions on the continuum sketched in Fig. 6.1.

Premises drawn more from
knowledge of the world: ◄─────────────►
language used to reflect context

Premises drawn more from
utterances: language used
to create context

Fig. 6.1

This distinction between cultural types was elaborated by Hall (1976), who distinguished 'high-context' cultures, in which relatively little language is needed to establish a basis on which to proceed, and 'low-context' cultures, in which relatively more language is needed. Language functions both to reinforce externally perceived social structure (typical for high-context cultures) and to create new social structure for the purposes at hand (typical for low-context cultures). These two functions relate to what Hofstede (1980: 94) described as 'status consistency' and 'overall equality'. It is sometimes claimed that there is a set of properties which go with each cultural polarity, such that high-context cultures will be 'shame'-driven (an individual's behaviour is conditioned by the opinions of others), and characterized by deference and the maintenance of relative position, and low-context cultures will be 'guilt'-driven (individuals are accountable to themselves for their behaviour), and characterized by courtesy and the possibility of social mobility.

This is a macro-level approach to culture and more in the field of anthropology than linguistics, but not entirely irrelevant to our concerns, since the perception of the cultural type in which one finds oneself located will be reflected in and perhaps even created by language. Elsewhere (Grundy, 1994) I have quoted from a description of aspects of her own culture provided by a Japanese academic researching in Britain. To illustrate the point at the macro-level, I quote from her account of her own culture:

> In Japan, mostly husbands don't speak much at home. It is said that the words which husbands speak at home are only three: *meshi*, *furo*, and *neru*, meaning *meal* (I am going to eat—I'm hungry), *bath* (I'm going to take a bath), and *sleep* (I'm going to bed).

> There is an old saying that 'You have to know ten when you hear one'. In family life in Japan, 'Bring me that' or just 'That' is enough to ask Mother for something. Mother knows everything that Father needs or her children want.

At the micro-level, the immediate context of an utterance has always been important to pragmaticists. Grice never quite says that the relevance of an utterance is measured against a context. But he seems to imply that there is an external reality in relation to which implicatures are calculated when he says that 'the calculation that a particular conversational implicature is present requires . . . contextual and background information' (1967a: 57). Writing of context, Sperber and Wilson say that 'It is relevance which is treated as given and context which is treated as a variable' (1986: 142). Perhaps they are implying that context is taken as given in Grice and taken as to-be-found in their own formulation. Although there is a very important difference between these two positions, neither is as radical as that of many contemporary conversation analysts who, following the lead of Schegloff, are increasingly questioning the supposed status of an external social reality and suggesting that context is largely created through talk.

This is a recent perspective. Until the late 1980s there was no real challenge to the received view, summarized (but not accepted) by Zimmerman and Boden, that 'since social structure forms the presumptive context of activities of lesser scale, such as social interaction, it is ultimately the fundamental explanatory resource' (1991: 5). By 1992, Duranti and Goodwin were writing that 'context and talk are now argued to stand in a mutually reflexive relationship to each other, with talk, and the interpretive work it generates, shaping context as much as context shapes talk' (1992: 31).

One obvious difficulty in discussing the relationship of context/social structure and interaction is knowing how to formalize the influence of background knowledge on language use. Glover (1995) suggests the notion of a 'context prototype', or best example, for any speech event. Speakers create a context through their language behaviour which reflects their perception of a prototypical norm. Although the context prototype for the same activity is likely to exhibit cross-cultural variation, this seems to be a promising approach.

Another difficulty is that of demonstrating the relevance of context. Imagine a conversation with your doctor which begins with the doctor saying *How are you*: how do you know whether this is a casual opening (response: *Fine thanks! How are you*) or whether it is a professional enquiry (response: *Much the same I'm afraid*)? So that, although the existence of extra-interaction phenomena such as age, status, or setting is not in doubt, demonstrating that such aspects of context are relevant is much more problematical. Perhaps for this reason, it has even become fashionable to talk, as Schegloff does, of the non-consequentiality of context and of interactions in which context is 'just a context' (1992: 214).

The highly questionable contention that pragmatic meaning is non-conventional is linked to the belief that there is an external context which somehow helps us to make sense of pragmatic meaning. If, on the contrary, we could accept pragmatic meanings for what they are, it would be easier for us to understand their role in invoking context.

In the next three chapters, we attempt to progress beyond the largely utterance-level accounts of pragmatic meaning explored in the earlier chapters. The underlying question in the following chapters is: what is the systemic nature of language use? We will be considering three candidate systems: politeness theory, relevance theory, and activity-type theory. Each of these ways of accounting for language use might be thought potentially capable of accounting for all the context-creating, functional properties of utterances, talk-in-interaction, texts, and discourses. None will enable us to account for the meaning of an utterance in the way that a Quantity-based implicature will, because none attempts to account for pragmatic meaning; instead, each is a competing theory of language use. Politeness theory extends the notion of indexicality by showing how every utterance is uniquely designed for its audience; relevance theory is predicated on the notion that every utterance has a single most relevant pragmatic meaning; and activity type theory extends the notion of intentionality by showing how every utterance has a role in a goal-directed language game.

In the next three chapters we will investigate how far each of these candidate theories can account for the way language is used.

Raising pragmatic awareness: talk-in-interaction

1. Working as an individual, listen out for two consecutive utterances which are paired but where the second utterance is a slightly surprising rejoinder to the first. Bring your adjacency pair to your tutorial. Read only the first utterance of the pair and invite your colleagues to guess the second. Discuss the expected and the actual illocutionary forces associated with each adjacency pair.

2. While you are part of a conversation, watch out for interruptions. Note who interrupts, how they interrupt, and how the other speakers react. How do interruptions affect the conversational topic? Report your observations in your tutorial group.

3. While you are part of a conversation, listen out for clarification requests and repairs. Are repairs usually self- or other-initiated and self- or other-completed? Why do repairs occur? Report your observations in your tutorial group.

4. Observe from a distance two people who are deeply involved in a conversation. Record any moments of their interaction that are striking so that you can describe the non-linguistic features of talk-in-interaction which you observed in your tutorial group.

5. Eavesdrop on just five seconds of a conversation. Decide in advance that you will eavesdrop on five seconds from some predetermined moment (such as when someone next puts food in their mouth). Record exactly what is said, paying special attention to its sequential properties, and report your findings in your tutorial group.

6. Each member of your tutorial group should eavesdrop on the beginning of a talk sequence where the first speaker has a reason for talking. Does the speaker introduce the reason immediately or not? Compare your different observations in your tutorial group.

7. Work with a partner and together eavesdrop on a conversation. You should take one speaker and your partner the other: you should each listen carefully for the occurrence of fillers, hesitations, and pauses. Compare your observations.

8. How are conversations closed? Is the gist formulated? What sort of agreements are made? How are topics closed? Are they recycled? Do the same rules apply at the end of conversations as apply at the end of topics within conversations? Report your observations in your tutorial group.

Further reading

Mey (1993, chs. 11, 12); Sacks, Schegloff and Jefferson (1974).

Part II

Pragmatic usage

7

Politeness phenomena and the politeness status of language in use

Phyllis: He's a very polite-spoke man aren't you
Peter: It's not what they say at home

Keywords: distance, use, universal, usage, power, imposition, etiquette, (dis)agreement, redress, positive face, negative face, on-record, off-record, face threat, 'folk' view.

In Chapter 5, when we eavesdropped on the quarrelsome couple at breakfast, and in Chapter 6, when we eavesdropped on the encounter in the travel agent's, we appealed to the notion of politeness to account for parts of the data, and made the point that politeness strategies can be a way of encoding distance between speakers and their addressees. In this chapter we will be considering politeness phenomena as a means of characterizing the use of language to communicate. Politeness principles have been considered to have wide descriptive power in respect of language use (Lakoff, 1972; 1973), to be major determinants of linguistic behaviour (Leech, 1983), and to have universal status and linguistic manifestation (Brown and Levinson, 1978; 1987). Needless to say, these claims have not gone unchallenged.

Seen as the exercise of language choice to create a context intended to match an external context (specifically, what the speaker considers an appropriate means of addressing them), politeness phenomena are a paradigm example of pragmatic usage. Among the aspects of assumed external context that are particularly determinate of language choice in the domain of politeness are the power–distance relationship of the interactants and the extent to which a speaker imposes on or requires something of his/her addressee. In being 'polite', a speaker is attempting to create an implicated context (the speaker stands in relation x to the addressee in respect of act y) that matches the one assumed by the addressee.

Politeness phenomena are one manifestation of the wider concept of etiquette, or appropriate behaviour. In Chapter 6 we questioned the etiquette of speaker A, the customer, in repairing his utterance and substituting *I pay you* for *it costs*. The ground for this criticism of A is that *it costs* is more polite, or better adapted to its context, than *I pay you*. *I pay you* was a flout of the Queensberry Rules for polite behaviour whose below-the-belt status served the customer's purpose well, being the shortest route to a technical knock-out, but was not strictly in accordance with the rules for proper conduct. This suggests that there are conventions in linguistic etiquette just as there are in non-linguistic etiquette, and that linguistic politeness phenomena are predictable in relation to the contexts in which they occur.

In Chapter 4 we noted that presupposition encourages economical communication by taking for granted propositions which can be taken to be agreed and in many instances need not be stated. Politeness phenomena go in the opposite direction, as we saw in the introductory chapter with

1   Could I just borrow a tiny bit of paper

which is less economical but more likely to serve the speaker's purpose than

2   Give me a sheet of paper

Utterances frequently (although not invariably) exhibit such a trade-off between economy and the speaker's preference for a more spendthrift language strategy than is needed simply to communicate the relevant proposition. Of course, there will be situations when the strategy most likely to enable the speaker to satisfy his needs will be to utter (1), and other situations when (2) will be more productive; but it is very often the case that politeness phenomena depart from the principle of maximal economy of utterance, if by maximal economy we mean uttering only the proposition to be conveyed.

Being polite

Being on the receiving end of politeness affects each of us differently because polite utterances encode the relationship between the speaker and ourselves as addressee. Specifically, we would expect one person, perhaps someone we did not know all that well, to say to us

1   Could I just borrow a tiny bit of paper

and a different person, perhaps an older brother, to put it in the more direct way:

2   Give me a sheet of paper

If we do not see the relationship between ourselves and the person who addresses us as they do, we will be upset by the strategies they employ, since these strategies imply the nature of our relationship as they see it. This function of language, to imply the most appropriate speaker–addressee relationship, is what I take linguistic 'politeness' to be. You can test this for yourself by studying the following texts and ranking them on a scale from the one you would be happiest to receive yourself to the one which you would be least happy to receive.

Checking understanding (1) ───────────────────────

You might like to try this exercise with a friend or a colleague in your class: you should each read the five texts and rank them for acceptability, and then share your reasons.

Text A (a letter I received from a colleague in another department)
Dear Peter,
Thank you very much for agreeing to register our students on Tuesday. I know it must have made a very difficult day even more fraught but it was very helpful to me. I appreciate what you did and I feel indebted to you.

Text B (a letter from an airline replying to my complaints about poor service)
Dear Mr Grundy,
RE: LHR-BRU-WAW-BRU-LHR   13 and 19 December '93
We acknowledge receipt of your recent letter regarding the above. We were extremely concerned to learn of the problems you encountered, but trust you will appreciate that we are unable to comment before an investigation has been made. As soon as we are in possession of the facts, we will of course contact you further.
In the meantime, we would be grateful if you would kindly accept our most sincere apologies for the inconvenience caused.

Text C (extract from a letter my wife received from an employment agency)
At Alfred Marks, we place a high value on our temporary workers' opinions of the service we provide, and would, therefore, appreciate your comments.

Text D (sign displayed in the bar at the Royal Station Hotel, Newcastle)
Residents wishing to drink after 10.30 p.m. must produce their room key or residents card.

Text E (postcard advising customers of interruption to water supply)
INTERRUPTION OF WATER SUPPLY
Please note that your Water Supply will be turned
OFF on Sunday 11th November 1990
From 4.00 a.m. for up to 7 hours
During this period it would be inadvisable to draw hot water or to use any mechanical appliances connected to the supply. It is essential to ensure that all taps remain shut to avoid the risk of flooding when the supply is restored. For further advice please telephone . . .

In ranking the five texts for acceptability, you were making decisions about the way that propositions were conveyed. For example, in Text B there were a number of givens, typically noun phrases describing presupposed entities: *your recent letter regarding the above, the problems you encountered, the facts, the meantime, our most sincere apologies, the inconvenience caused.* In ranking this text, you were making decisions about how these were conveyed (e.g. the writer chose *the facts* rather than *what happened*) and what was said about each of them (*we would be grateful if you would kindly accept x*). In particular, you were measuring what was said and how it was said against your expectations of how the writer should be addressing you under the circumstances. 'Politeness' is the term we use to describe the extent to which actions, including the way things are said, match others' perceptions of how they should be performed.

This supremely pragmatic definition presupposes that every instance of communicated language exhibits politeness. So the small number of utterances that I shall comment on now must necessarily give only a very partial account of the huge range of politeness phenomena. I have selected just seven exemplar utterances almost at random, to give some idea of the nature of the ways in which politeness is manifested. Let us begin with the exchange between Phyllis, our tea-lady, and myself that occurs at the beginning of this chapter.

Example 1

3   Phyllis: He's a very polite-spoke man aren't you
    Peter: It's not what they say at home

Of particular interest in this exchange are Phyllis's switch to me as addressee, and my choice of *it's* in my response. Phyllis was talking about me to a third party in my presence, and therefore politeness required that I should be included in the conversation. Phyllis does this with the tag *aren't you*, which, strictly speaking, renders her utterance ungrammatical if viewed as a sentence. Since her utterance was a compliment, I felt obliged out of modesty to demur in some way, and chose *it's not what they say at home*. This kind of demur is a standard politeness strategy, comparable to the kind of thing I feel I have to say when you come to my house and you feel you have to say

4   What a lovely room

I then reply, equally untruthfully,

5   We've often thought of moving actually

What is interesting about my response to Phyllis's utterance is the choice of *it's* rather than *that's*. Had I said

3'   That's not what they say at home

that would have been taken to refer to the proposition that the person described is a very polite-spoke man and I would have implied that they say something different at home, thus contradicting Phyllis's opinion. But in saying *it*, I imply that at home they don't say what she says, and thus convey that she is kinder than my family. And at the same time I satisfy the requirements of modesty. This example illustrates the pervasive nature of politeness: even seemingly semantically empty categories including anaphors like *it* and *that* have a politeness function.

One last point about this exchange: notice that I reacted to Phyllis's compliment by demurring. Holmes (1986) has shown that men and women react differently to compliments, with men seeing them as threatening and women seeing them as expressions of solidarity. So if I had been a woman, my contribution would most probably have exhibited its politeness status in a different way.

Example 2   At the time of writing, our department has just acquired a spanking new photocopier. It works brilliantly but it takes some understanding. In its first week in our corridor, I happened to be passing when the Dean was using it. It seemed to me that politeness required that the Dean be acknowledged and that some reference to the new machine would be appropriate. This was our exchange:

6 Peter: It's brilliant this machine isn't it
   Dean: Yes it has a mind of its own
   Peter: That's also true

Taking a positive view of the world with an utterance like *it's brilliant this machine* is a generally recognized way of conveying respect to the addressee, and attaching the tag, *isn't it*, allows for the possibility of a second point of view. The Dean, who was finding the complexities of the machine more apparent than its brilliance, did indeed have a second point of view. Although superficially agreeing with me at the level of literal meaning, and signalling this with the overt agreement marker *yes*, his *it has a mind of its own* conventionally implicates something rather different. I inferred from his reply that he did not always think it was so brilliant, especially when he could not get it to do what he wanted it to do. *That's also true* confirms this implicature and continues the fiction that we are in agreement, matching the Dean's *yes* with my *also*. A lecturer who is not in agreement with the Dean is a fool, and of course the Dean too has an easier life if he can maintain a semblance of unity even where everyone holds their own opinions. So although I represent the machine as brilliant and he has another opinion, our politeness strategies minimize our disagreement.

One last point about this exchange: notice how I assumed that, as the less important person, I should speak first when I met the Dean in the corridor. Gu (1990) says that an inferior always speaks first in an encounter in China. Do you think there is a politeness norm in this area in the culture of which you are a native member?

Example 3 It may seem surprising when you first think about it, but politeness very often occurs where there is disagreement or difficulty. I once went to the garage in a tearing rage when their repair attempt on my car the day before had proved worse than ineffective. All the way there I was rehearsing how I was going to tear a strip off the foreman. When I got there, there were two customers in front of me, each of whom did to him exactly what I had been planning to do. When my turn came, he looked up at me with big doggy eyes and, running the back of his hand across his forehead, said

7 I need a cup of tea after that

I felt so sorry for him that my complaint collapsed into

8 You'll need a cup of coffee after me

and we both had a good laugh. I expressed my displeasure but, by making a joke of it, in a way that minimized the extent to which he was going to lose face.

Example 4 I wonder whether you hate sausages of dodgy provenance as much as I do? The other day, I couldn't see any bacon buns in the sandwich shop where I sometimes buy one at lunchtime. The exchange went like this:

9 Peter: Are there any bacon buns
   Assistant: Only sausage

If you listen carefully, you'll notice how frequently speakers try to avoid disagreement or overtly disappointing utterances. We frequently offer those we talk to something they have not asked for by way of redress rather than tell them we cannot satisfy their need. Here the offer itself as well as the implicit apology (*only*) have politeness status.

Example 5 At the beginning of this chapter, politeness phenomena were contrasted with presupposition when I suggested that presupposition tends to serve the principle of economy and politeness phenomena frequently go in the opposite direction. This is not always the case though. For example,

10 Can you pass the salt (implicature *now*)

is certainly more likely to meet the addressee's expectation of how they should be talked to than

10′ Can you pass the salt now

Here we see that an implicature, a meaning nowhere explicitly stated, serves a politeness function. This supports the claim that all language used communicatively has politeness status.

Checking understanding (2)

1. Following Brown and Levinson's (B&L) example (1978: 85; 1987: 80), in Chapter 3 you were asked to imagine you were on a station platform and two people approached you one after the other. The first said

11 Got the time mate

and the second said

12 I'm sorry to bother you but you haven't by any chance got the time have you

What assumptions would you make if you were addressed in these two ways and why would you make them?

2. Imagine I say to my ten-year-old daughter

13 Just eat it up

and she says to me

14 Aren't you going to eat it

We each intend our utterance to get the other to eat their dinner. Why would we use different strategies to achieve the same effect?

3. Imagine you have a five-year-old daughter called Honey and you want to spend a morning shopping without a small child in tow. How would you ask Honey's best friend's mother to look after Honey for the morning? Why not write down your suggested strategy before consulting the key (page 199):

15

Now imagine you have a five-month-old baby called Howler and you want to dump her on your neighbour overnight since you've been invited to stay with a friend who hates babies. How would you ask your neighbour to look after Howler overnight? Again, write down your suggested strategy:

16

What are the differences between the way you would make the two requests and what reasons can you suggest for these differences?

Brown and Levinson's model

The most fully elaborated work on linguistic politeness is B&L's 'Universals in language usage: politeness phenomena' (1978), reissued with a new introduction and revised bibliography as *Politeness: some universals in language usage* (1987). Working with data gathered from Tamil speakers in southern India, Tzeltal speakers in Mexico, and speakers of American and British English, they provide a systematic description of cross-linguistic politeness phenomena which is used to support an explanatory model capable of accounting for any instance of politeness. Their claim is that broadly comparable linguistic strategies are available in each language, but that there are local differences in what triggers their use.

B&L suggest that all human beings have 'face', a property broadly comparable to self-esteem. In most encounters, our face is put at risk. Asking someone for a sheet of paper, or telling them they cannot have a drink after a certain hour, or complaining about the quality of their work on one's car, or asking them the time, to give just four examples of situations cited in this chapter, all threaten the face of the person to whom they are directed. So when we perform such actions, they are typically accompanied with redressive language designed to compensate the threat to face. So we may ask someone just to 'lend' us 'a tiny bit' of paper, or pretend that our prohibition on drinking is a general rule directed towards someone else, or make a joke of our complaint, or ask the time in a way that stresses our solidarity with the addressee. These are all examples of politeness, the use of redressive language designed to compensate for what B&L call 'face-threatening behaviour'.

In fact, 'face' comes in two varieties, which B&L call 'positive face' and 'negative face'. Positive face is a person's wish to be well thought of. Its particular manifestations may include the desire to have what we admire admired by others, the desire to be understood by others, and the desire to be treated as a friend and confidant. Thus a complaint about the quality of someone's work threatens his/her positive face. Negative face is our wish not to be imposed on by others, and to be allowed to go about our business unimpeded with our rights to free and self-determined action intact. Thus telling someone they cannot have a drink after a certain time is a threat to their negative face.

In dealing with each other, our utterances may be oriented to the positive or to the negative face of those we interact with. In

11   Got the time mate

the kinship-claiming *mate* and the informality of elliptical *got* show that the utterance is oriented to the positive face of the addressee, who is being treated as a friend. It is therefore an example of what B&L call 'positive politeness'. But in

1   Could I just borrow a tiny bit of paper

the remote *could*, the minimizing *just* and *a tiny bit*, and the euphemistic *borrow* are all oriented to the addressee's negative face, and seek to compensate for and play down the imposition and potential loss of face that having to give someone a piece of your paper involves. It is an example of 'negative politeness'.

Checking understanding (3) ————————————————

Go back to the five texts you studied earlier and try to identify as many positive and negative politeness strategies as you can in them.

When we have a face-threatening act to perform, according to B&L's model, we have to choose from three superordinate strategies: do the act on-record, do the act off-record, and don't do the act at all. By 'on-record' they mean without attempting to hide what we are doing, and by 'off-record' they mean in such a way as to pretend to hide it. Thus if I were to say

17 Oh no, I've left my money at home

this would be an off-record way of hinting that you might lend me some. In theory you could ask if I was hinting that you should lend me some money and I could deny that I was and claim that I was merely making an observation—in this sense, I am acting off-record.

Checking understanding (4) ————————————————

Can you find any examples of off-record strategies in the five texts you studied earlier?

Of the three superordinate strategies, the first, perform the face-threatening act on-record is the most usual. In fact, there are three subordinate on-record strategies, making a total of five available strategies when we have a face-threatening act to perform:

Do the act on-record baldly, without redress [1]
       "   "   with positive politeness redress [2]
       "   "   with negative politeness redress [3]
Do the act off-record [4]
Don't do the act [5]

An illustration may help. Let me tell you about a real-world problem I'm wrestling with as I write this chapter. We have a neighbour who lives across the road from us who has just bought a very old car which he keeps parking outside our gate. When he does this, it invariably drops oil all over the road right outside our house. This is not only unsightly but in due course is bound to get walked on to our carpets. I am wondering what to do. I know that speaking to him about it constitutes a face-threatening act: the question is, how should I perform it? I could do it baldly without redress and say

18 Don't park your leaky old banger outside our house any more

or I could try positive politeness:

18′ Bill my old mate, I know you want me to have the benefit of admiring your new car from my front room, but how about moving it across the road and giving yourself the pleasure

or I could try negative politeness:

18″ I'm sorry to ask, but could you possibly park your car in front of your own house in future

or I could try an off-record strategy like

18′′′ Is your car all right outside our house

or I could do what I've been doing up to now and chicken out, being content to harbour vandalistic fantasies instead. When I do pluck up the courage, I'll probably combine (18″) and (18‴) to produce a hybrid like

18′′′′ I'm sorry to ask you Bill, but I don't suppose you want us to have the pleasure of admiring your new car from our front room for ever. It's just that we've nowhere to park when it's outside our house.

In picking one of these five linguistic strategies I work with an equation in which any distance differential and any power differential and any imposition are computed:

Distance + Power + Imposition = degree of face-threat to be compensated by appropriate linguistic strategy

Earlier we saw politeness strategies (11–16) which were the result of each of these three factors being particularly strong. When Bill and I talk, there is no power relationship between us, since we work in quite different jobs and are more or less the same age. There may be some distance differential depending on how we each see our own and the other's place in the world and the degree of mutual familiarity and solidarity we each feel. But clearly, in dealing with this problem, the most important factor in the equation that adds up to x degrees of face-threat is imposition—there is a significant imposition involved in being told where we should or should not park on a public road.

The most important point about B&L's five strategies is that they are ranked from [1], which has no linguistically encoded compensation, through a sequence of escalating politeness strategies to [5], where the face threat is too great to be compensated for by any language formula so that the most appropriate politeness strategy is not to do the act. A speaker will only choose a high-numbered strategy where the face-threat is felt to be high, since being 'too polite' implies that one is asking a lot of someone. My problem with Bill's car is a simple one: either it's just too face-threatening to try and tell someone where to park, so I won't try, or, because he is a neighbour and a sort of friend, I can make a joke of it (positive politeness) and at the same time apologize for the coercion (negative politeness), as in (18′′′′). What would you do in my position?

Example 6 One source of humour in television sit-coms is the use of politeness strategies that are not the result of expected computations of power, distance and imposition. Very occasionally this happens in real life. I remember a wonderful occasion in my first teaching job when the headmaster and I took a group of 25 boys camping. This was a very rare event for the headmaster, who was perhaps trying to relive his own youth and whose memories of camping dated mainly from the war years. To the great amusement of the boys, he began by setting a working party to digging a latrine (of which he was destined to be the sole user) and another working party to scavenging for timber to make a campfire. A third group assisted in the preparation of the evening meal, a monster stew into which the headmaster threw everything he could lay his hands on, including, towards the end of the preparation period, several rather earthy potatoes that he couldn't be bothered to peel. When the meal was eventually served, there was an apprehensive circle of boys with enamel plates swimming in doubtful stew watching to see what the headmaster would do. The headmaster served himself last, by which time all the cutlery had been taken. 'Have any of you chaps seen a fork?' he asked, whereupon a rather cheeky thirteen-year-old chimed in with

19 I'd try a spade if I were you sir

I can't say that the headmaster smiled. The humour resulted from the very great power differential which was being ignored in the positive-face-oriented joke, and the public ridiculing of hours of painstaking cooking which threatened the headmaster's negative face. Laughter, on this occasion, and frequently in sit-coms, is one way of marking the incongruous politeness status of an utterance.

Checking understanding (5)

In (19) the speaker used a positive politeness strategy, joking, in a situation which did not allow positive politeness. B&L (1978: 107, 136; 1987: 102, 131) give a list of positive and negative politeness strategies (which may not be entirely unproblematical):

Positive politeness	Negative politeness
Notice/attend to hearer's wants	Be conventionally indirect
Exaggerate interest/approval	Question, hedge
Intensify interest	Be pessimistic
Use in-group identity markers	Minimize imposition
Seek agreement	Give deference
Avoid disagreement	Apologize
Presuppose/assert common ground	Impersonalize
Joke	State the imposition as a general rule
Assert knowledge of hearer's wants	Nominalize
Offer, promise	Go on record as incurring a debt
Be optimistic	
Give (or ask for) reasons	
Assume/assert reciprocity	
Include speaker and hearer in the activity	
Give gifts to hearer (goods, sympathy, etc.)	

Recall two or three occasions when the politeness behaviour you observed was particularly striking and try to work out why this was, referring where appropriate to strategies listed by B&L.

The universal character of politeness

One challenging line of criticism of B&L's model is that the politeness usage they describe is not universal. Thus Matsumoto (1988) argues that in

Japanese the structures associated with negative politeness strategies in B&L's model do not have a negative politeness function but instead are a social register. Gu (1990) argues that the model is unsuited to Chinese usage, in which politeness phenomena still reflect to some degree the etymology of the word for *politeness*, one of whose constituent morphemes (*li*) denotes social order. Like Matsumoto's and Gu's, most other criticisms of the B&L model on these grounds post-date the 1987 reissue of their work. Even so, it is striking that B&L soften the title from 'universals . . .' to 'some universals . .'.

Of course, we would not expect identical computations of appropriate politeness formulas across cultures any more than we would across varying situations in a single culture. Just as we employ different strategies to get different people to do things for us, so asking for assistance when (for example) your car breaks down will impose to different degrees in different societies (Nwoye, 1992). It is important, therefore, to separate culturally variable estimates of power, distance and imposition, which we would expect to occur, from the strategies and linguistic manifestations of strategies which a universal account of politeness would need to capture.

Much of Matsumoto's criticism centres on the way that deference is manifested in Japanese honorifics. She claims, in my opinion rightly, that B&L's formulation does not account for such data. But her perspective raises the issue, not of whether politeness phenomena are universal, but rather of whether B&L are right to treat deference as a politeness strategy: 'it is far from clear that deference can be equated with the speaker's respecting an individual's right to non-imposition' (1988: 409). In fact, we probably need to distinguish two uses of deference:

● the situation where it is given expectably and unexceptionally as an automatic acknowledgement of external social status and thus reinforces an existing culture (which seems to me not to be a politeness strategy at all);
● and deference which is given expectably but exceptionally in a particular situation as a redressive strategy.

In the first situation, the speaker is attempting to produce a context-reflecting utterance acceptable to the addressee as addressee, and in the second to produce a context-creating utterance acceptable to the addressee in the situation shared by speaker and addressee. The problem, of course, is in distinguishing between situations where speakers have no option in their choice of *tu/vous*-type alternatives and situations where they do, and can thus use honorifics as politeness markers to invoke a new context. Perhaps an illustration would help.

Example 7 I once took part in a debate with a Conservative Member of Parliament many years my senior in which I probably said some hard things about his speech. After the debate I bought a round of drinks. When it came to asking him what he would like, this is how the exchange went:

20 Peter: And for you sir
       MP: Oh so it's 'sir' now is it

Mine was clearly a politeness strategy that misfired as I tried to create a context to match my addressee's perception of how he should be addressed.

Matsumoto (1988) gives examples of four ways that you might ask someone in Japan if they were going to have lunch, each displaying deference at an appropriate level. One could hardly imagine a Japanese professor, addressed with the elaborate deference that professors customarily receive in Japan, challenging the speaker in the way that the MP challenged me. As stated above, we need to distinguish cross-culturally variable estimates of power, distance, and imposition from the strategies and linguistic representations which a universal account of politeness would need to capture.

In fact, objectors to B&L's account frequently cite exotic-sounding examples of apparent deference which are claimed as evidence that some notion of social order or societal interdependence, rather than positive and negative face, underlies politeness. A typical example is provided by Gu (1990), who cites the etymology of *bai* (to prostrate oneself at the foot of another) as in *baidu* (to read) as evidence that knowing one's place underlies Chinese politeness. Without being a native member of Chinese society it is very difficult to say anything definitive about this claim, but I rather doubt it. To me it would be like claiming that the Greek word *polis*, meaning 'city', from which 'politeness' is derived, somehow determines the principles of politeness in the many societies whose word for politeness is derived from the Greek original. Or take the case of

21 Can you pass the salt

This request is frequently represented by

22 Can you give me the salt

in non-native speaker English, usually because this is a literal translation from the mother tongue. Surely this does not mean that deference is a motivating principle in the mother-culture politeness systems of such speakers' mother cultures. What I am suggesting is that the 'prostrating oneself' element of *baidu* is as conventional and inert as a politeness strategy as the notion that a salt-passer or giver is a person of power dispensing alms to others of inferior status. And in fact the untenability of this putative account is confirmed by the pragmatic grammaticalness of (22) amongst equals, such as family members or close friends.

Whether B&L have found a formula that is universal is always open to discussion. But what is really important about their work is that their approach is potentially capable of accounting not only for pragmatic uses of language but maybe also even for the more abstract notion of pragmatic usage, i.e. it might form the basis of a pragmatic grammar. They point out that, whilst 'usage principles of the Gricean sort do generally obtain', politeness is not equally distributed: 'it is not as if there were some basic modicum of politeness owed by each to all' (1987: 4–5). It is just this distinction that allows us to argue that Gricean principles can be used to account for the pragmatic meaning of particular utterances, since we are all equally enabled to measure utterances in terms of their compliance with such usage principles. And at the same time we can argue that the wider system of politeness, because it is central to 'the linguistic expression of social relationships' (B&L, 1987: 49), is a preferred candidate system in any account of the systematic nature of language use. (I should admit that this is to make a much grander claim for politeness as an explanatory key to language use than B&L do.)

Redefining the folk term

Much of our thinking about politeness is bedevilled by the fact that 'polite-ness' is a folk term. In Britain 'politeness' is typically used to describe negative politeness, which is presumed to be 'a good thing'. A typical folk view of politeness is implied in Phyllis's use of *very polite-spoke* in the exchange with which this chapter begins. I guess a strong connotation of *very polite-spoke* is RP speech, and that such a folk view of politeness as the speech style of the over-classes is strongly indicative of value for the speaker. Thus the value-neutral way in which 'politeness' is used as a term of pragmatic description applicable to all communicative instances of language use is easily confused with the quite different, but all too pervasive, attitude to politeness in society at large. This is why, in our earlier discussion, I delib-erately highlighted the much more important status of *it's* in our exchange and ignored the folk view implied by the use of *very polite-spoke*. From a pragmaticist's point of view, as we said earlier, 'politeness' is the term we use to describe the relationship between how something is said and the addressee's judgement as to how it should be said. Under this definition, a theory of politeness is potentially capable of accounting for pragmatic uses of language, but will always risk being confused with a prescriptive approach to linguistic etiquette. Indeed, Gu's description of address modes in Chinese (1990: 250), in which non-familial addressees are styled *grandpa* or *aunt* as a mark of respect, are essentially descriptions of prescriptions rather than descriptions of context-creating politeness phenomena.

Language in use

The title of this chapter presupposes that language in use has politeness status, a point made again in the previous paragraph. This is not a conven-tional view, although it seems to me very defensible. The conventional view is of politeness as a 'bolt-on' redressive element typically found in interac-tional but not in transactional discourse. This may be seen as an echo of the folk view of politeness as somehow extrinsic to the meanings we convey.

The conventional position is clearly put by Kasper:

> Conversational behaviour that is consistent with the requirements of transac-tional discourse will thus be characterized by close observance of the Cooperative Principle. Interactional discourse, by contrast, has as its primary goal the establishment and maintenance of social relationships. (1990: 205)

As Kasper goes on to point out, this is to claim that observing maxims of Quality and Manner will have priority over satisfying face-wants in transac-tional discourse, while the opposite will obtain in interactional discourse. But to make this claim is to miss the point that face-wants are satisfied precisely by giving priority to veracity and clarity in certain situations, including trans-actional discourse such as you find in a book like this. Thus in conversation it is preferred to begin with a safe topic such as the weather when talking in the street to someone with whom you are slightly acquainted, but not when talking on the telephone, where time costs money. Both strategies are politely adapted to their contexts, including in particular to addressees' expectations of how talk should be directed to them. For this reason, an adequately formulated theory of linguistic politeness which can account for the extent to which the things we say match our addressees' perceptions of how they should be said would be a strong candidate theory of pragmatic usage.

Raising pragmatic awareness

1. Working individually, eavesdrop on two or three conversations and write down what people say when they smile. Try to identify the politeness status of what is said. Share your findings with friends or other members of your tutorial group. Finally, invent a further eavesdropping task with a politeness dimension for members of your tutorial group to try.

2. Cut a picture out of a colour magazine which contains two people who are clearly together. Write down five or six different ways in which one of the people might convey one of the following propositions to the other:

- one person inviting the other out;
- one person asking the other the time;
- one person accusing the other of telling a lie;
- one person telling the other he/she smells.

Bring your picture and possible utterances to the tutorial and ask your colleagues to decide which way of expressing the proposition would be most appropriate for the people concerned.

3. This exercise works best in a small group. Pick a nation and decide how that nation is stereotypically seen by yourselves. Then try to associate this stereotype with typical politeness strategies. If you can get this exercise to work, do the same thing with an intra-cultural group such as the young or the old within your own culture, or with some ethnic- or gender-determined group. If possible, follow this up by careful observation of a representative of the group you were stereotyping to see whether your stereotype is at all reflected in your subject. To what extent is stereotyping one person's view of another person's pragmatics? (*Acknowledgement*: this is Kelly Glover's idea.)

4. Listen out for the way people reflect their own status in talk. Make a careful note of what you hear and report it to your next tutorial group.

Further reading

Brown and Levinson (1978; 1987), especially the introduction to 1987; Leech (1983: 79–84); Matsumoto (1988; 1989); *Journal of Pragmatics* 14/2 (special issue on politeness); *Journal of Pragmatics* 21/5 (special issue on politeness across cultures).

8

Relevance theory and degrees of understanding

'nor ever as guessing'
(Gerard Manley Hopkins
The Wreck of the Deutschland)

Keywords: relevance, utterance, understanding, cognitive, implicature, explicature, inference, logical form, implicated premise, implicated conclusion, contextual resource, garden-path utterance, understanding failure, understanding test.

It is typically assumed that a grammar is neutral between speaker and hearer since it represents knowledge of language rather than productive or receptive skills. Pragmatics has usually been assumed to be about understanding rather than producing utterances, although the question of how we acquire productive pragmatic L1 and L2 competence is increasingly being researched. Yet although pragmatics is understanding oriented, before relevance theory (RT) there was no developed cognitive account of pragmatic understanding.

It seems obvious that a theory of language understanding must also account for degrees of understanding, and even for failures of understanding, especially as we are frequently aware of the different degrees to which we and those we talk to understand each other. This chapter is about the extent to which RT is a candidate theory of pragmatic usage by virtue of its ability to show why utterances are understood to different degrees by different hearers.

8.1 *Relevance theory and understanding*

Sperber and Wilson's (S&W) theory (1986) may be seen as reducible to the theorem that to understand an utterance is to prove its relevance. In this section of the chapter we will examine six features of RT which are particularly important in describing the way we understand what we hear.

Implicature and explicature We first discussed explicature in Chapter 3. An explicature is an elaborated logical form and an implicature is a new logical form, both of which are taken to represent meanings conveyed by the speaker. Thus an explicature would be needed to determine whether *my book* refers to the book I own or the book I am the author of. The notion of logical form, which was problematical enough before, is further problematized by RT, which treats it as an explicature based on an inference. Because an inference is required to determine this elaborated logical form, on occasion a hearer might presumably not be able to determine the explicature. If a hearer fails to determine this, they will not be able to use the explicature as a premise in calculating implicatures. The new level of explicature proposed by S&W provides an intermediate level between what is said and implicatures, and thus the model provides for the possibility of a failure to understand on a graded scale at three levels (said, explicature, implicature) rather than just two levels (said, implicated).

Implicated premises and implicated conclusions S&W show that deriving an implicature from an explicature is frequently a two-step process which requires a first implicature, which S&W call an implicated premise, before the consequent implicature, or implicated conclusion, can be inferred. Imagine you and a friend were to have the following exchange

1   You: What do you think of *Middlemarch*
    Friend: I just love long books

You would first have to recognize that your friend was implying that *Middlemarch* was a long book (the implicated premise) and then draw a further inference (the implicated conclusion) as to exactly what *I just love* was intended to convey (i.e. is the utterance sincere or ironical?). Here then is a further level at which an implied meaning might fail to be recovered. So you might recover both implicated premise and implicated conclusion, or implicated premise only, or neither.

Speaker judgement and hearer resources S&W say: 'the speaker must make some assumptions about the hearer's cognitive abilities and contextual resources, which will necessarily be reflected in the way she communicates, and in particular in what she chooses to make explicit or what she chooses to leave implicit' (1986: 218). Of course, this is not a new idea; but it was not so clearly stated before, and reminds us that if the speaker overestimates the hearer's resources, then implicit meanings may not be recovered.

Recovering meanings and processing opportunity S&W say: 'The organization of the individual's encyclopaedic memory, and the mental activity in which he is engaged, limit the class of potential contexts from which an actual context can be chosen at any given time' (1986: 138). This reminds us that pressure of time, complexity of structure, etc., limit our ability to recover contexts, and that an implicated meaning may fail to be recovered for these reasons.

Accessibility The most accessible interpretation is the most relevant since 'A phenomenon is relevant to an individual to the extent that the effort required to process it optimally is small' (1986: 153). Of course, there are degrees of accessibility, and the means chosen to convey meanings may have different accessibility ratings for different addressees.

Garden-path utterances RT predicts that in garden-path utterances a hearer will not escape being led up the garden path and encouraged to understand an inappropriate meaning, since 'The principle of relevance does not normally warrant the selection of more than one interpretation for a single ostensible stimulus' (1986: 167) and 'The first hypothesis consistent with the principle of relevance (is) the best' (168). The 'first hypothesis consistent with the principle of relevance' is not necessarily the first hypothesis that suggests itself, so that if a hearer were to know that a garden-path understanding was in the offing, they might conceivably find a 'second' hypothesis 'consistent with the principle of relevance'. But if the speaker does not intend the hearer to recognize that they have recovered a garden-path meaning, at least at first pass, the principle of relevance should, and does, lead an addressee to recover an inappropriate implicature even if led to it deliberately by the speaker.

We have enumerated six features of RT potentially capable of explaining degrees of understanding of or even failures to understand implicated meanings: explicature, implicated premises and conclusions, overestimate of hearer resources, processing opportunity, accessibility to hearer, and speaker-intended inappropriate understanding. Their credibility as accounts of the understanding mechanism can only be proved by showing that failures to understand can be attributed to them.

Checking understanding (1)

In the conversation in the travel agent's discussed in Chapter 6, a misunderstanding occurred when the customer and the assistant were discussing which weekend the customer wanted to travel on:

B: (13.0) well there's a shuttle service (0.4) um (.) sixty pounds one way (2.5) er (2.3) when do you want to go
A: I want to go at the weekend
B: (0.3) what weekend
A: next weekend (3.5) how does that work you just turn up for the shuttle service
B: (0.8) that might be cheaper then (1.8) that's fifty

Can this understanding failure be explained by any of the mechanisms described above?

8.2 *Applying relevance theory*

Degrees of understanding

There is an obvious practical difficulty finding data which provide incontrovertible evidence of understanding failure. Some years ago I hit on the idea of taking an example of language that was a natural 'understanding test', and presenting it to an audience who might be expected not to pass the test. The experiment is reported elsewhere (Grundy, 1991) so only a brief outline is given here.

The understanding test consisted of an extended joke-telling routine from the television programme *The Two Ronnies*, in which one of the presenters, Ronnie Corbett, sits in a chair and tells the studio audience a joke. The sequence typically lasts for about three minutes and contains a series of intermediate jokes as the joke-teller builds up to the main joke. I chose a joke because, in the characterization of Harvey Sacks, jokes exhibit 'supposed supposable unknownness to recipients' (i.e. the audience should not have heard the joke before) (1974: 341) and constitute an 'understanding test' (346). A joke is an 'understanding test' in the sense that there is some supposed audience who would not pass it, although if the test were failed by the real audience the joke would lose its point. Jokes therefore have in-group status, and may be expected not to be understood by out-groups. The experimental audience selected to listen to Ronnie Corbett's joke were a group of non-native-speaker university teachers of English with near native-speaker competence but limited experience of the British culture of which the joke-teller is a native member. They could tell where the comic effects were created because the studio audience indicated this with laughter whose intensity varied with the 'quality' of the joke. My experimental audience were left to work alone for an hour with a tape of the joke-telling sequence and twenty questions, ordered so as to track the progress of the joke and designed to determine whether or not the audience had passed the understanding test. They found the task predictably difficult. In the following sections, I will try to show that the understanding processes suggested by RT and listed above provide a plausible account of the understanding failure of the experimental audience.

Implicature and explicature 'We will call an explicitly communicated assumption an explicature. Any assumption communicated, but not explicitly so, is implicitly communicated: it is an implicature' (S&W 1986: 182).

Consider the following fragment from the joke-telling routine:

2   Tonight's story was actually handed down to me by my dear old grandfather (pause)

Part of the explicating process is to disambiguate *handed down*, which appears to be used here as a phrasal verb meaning 'bequeathed'. This explication is presumably based on the inference that when *handed down* occurs in close proximity to someone referred to as a 'dear old grandfather', the phrasal verb reading is the most relevant. Thus one implicature of the explicated utterance is that the joke-teller's grandfather is no longer alive. But the joke-teller continues after a pause just long enough to make his audience think the sentence is complete and therefore confirm to themselves that the explicature and implicature are the right ones

3   the other night as he was clearing out our attic

Knowing that the joke-teller's grandfather is still alive causes us to revise the original explicature and substitute the new explicated meaning that *handed down* is not a phrasal verb at all but a regular verb followed by an adverb. The really subtle point is that unless you got the inappropriate explicature the first time (i.e. the phrasal verb determination), you could not get the joke, which consists in denying an implied meaning. My experimental audience were predictably at a loss to know why the audience laughed after *attic*.

Checking understanding (2)

Can you apply the explicature → implicature process of understanding to the part of the joke where the joke-teller says

4 /you can go up if you like Terry but it looks far too dangerous for me so off he goes and/ ooh sorry I nearly got stuck there

(The text between slashes is spoken in a camp manner because the joke-teller is representing Terry's friend as a homosexual stereotype.)

Implicated premises and implicated conclusions 'We will distinguish between two kinds of implicatures: implicated premises and implicated conclusions' (S&W 1986: 195).

In considering the following fragment, my experimental audience were asked to decide whether the joke-teller was a successful entertainer:

5 It was a scrapbook really of all the ecstatic rave reviews of my past performances (pause) I let go of it at one point and it nearly floated out the window

Although the first part of this sequence up to the pause implies that the joke-teller was a successful entertainer, the second part requires the implicated premises that scrapbooks containing large numbers of rave reviews are heavy, that this scrapbook is not heavy, and that therefore it did not contain (m)any rave reviews. Without these two implicated premises, the implicated conclusion that the joke-teller was an unsuccessful entertainer is not recoverable. Predictably, my experimental audience did not succeed in recovering the implicated premises necessary to understand the joke, presumably because they were satisfied that the first part of the sequence up to the pause had conveyed what the joke-teller actually intended them to think. Perhaps if the joke-teller had triggered the need to look for an implicature directly by saying immediately after the pause 'all one of them', for example, the experimental audience would have been able to recover the implicature that the joke-teller was an unsuccessful entertainer.

Checking understanding (3)

Can you identify an implicated premise and an implicated conclusion in the italicized part of the following description of the joke-teller's grandfather taken from the joke-telling sequence?

6 he's a remarkable man really (pause) ninety-two and still doing all the things he was doing when he was twenty-one (pause) you know you can imagine my shock the other night when I peeped through the crack in his bedroom door *and I saw two sets of false teeth in his glass*

Speaker judgement and hearer resources 'The speaker must make some assumptions about the hearer's cognitive abilities and contextual resources, which will necessarily be reflected in the way she communicates, and in particular in what she chooses to make explicit or what she chooses to leave implicit' (S&W 1986: 218) and 'A speaker who intends an utterance to be interpreted in a particular way must also expect the hearer to be able to supply a context which allows that interpretation to be recovered' (S&W 1986: 16).

My experimental audience were asked to explain why the real audience laughed when they heard

7   On with the joke which concerns these two Rugby players who were both spending the summer holidays at Scarborough (pause) for a bet

Because my audience were not able to supply the kind of context that enables you and me (to understand that a joke-teller might pretend) to wonder why someone would spend their summer holidays at Scarborough, they were unable to understand the joke.

Recovering meanings and processing opportunity 'The organization of the individual's encyclopaedic memory, and the mental activity in which he is engaged, limit the class of potential contexts from which an actual context can be chosen at any given time' (S&W 1986: 138).

At one stage the joke-teller says

8   I was watching the late-night film you know about Ivan the Terrible and his wife Blodwen the Extremely Disappointed

How is an experimental audience who have heard of Ivan the Terrible to know that there is no such person as Blodwen the Extremely Disappointed? If I knew who Blodwen the Extremely Disappointed was, they might reason, then I could understand why the joke-teller had said she was Ivan the Terrible's wife. How is the experimental audience to supply a context in which the reference is not, as they may suppose, to *the* Ivan the Terrible but to an imaginary Ivan who is terribly disappointing in bed?

Accessibility 'A phenomenon is relevant to an individual to the extent that the effort required to process it optimally is small' (S&W 1986: 153).

Talking about a tooth that had been giving him problems, the joke-teller says

9   It was still plaguing me this morning at rehearsals so I thought it's no use I'll have to have it out so I went along to the BBC emergency dental service they have no appointment necessary you just go up to one of the scene boys and tell them to get a move on and that's the end of it

Clearly quite a lot of processing effort is required to draw the inference that the tooth was knocked out by a scene-shifter who felt insulted by the joke-teller. But since any other conclusion would require more effort, the regular audience therefore assumes that this is the relevant inference. However, the experimental audience had problems with this utterance—clearly for them the effort required to process it was too great for the implicature to be recovered. One can speculate as to why this should have been—perhaps the reference to *the BBC emergency dental service* was taken at face value and therefore what followed seemed especially difficult to prove relevant.

Checking understanding (4) ————————————————————

Why do you think the following part of the joke, which is about the joke-teller's au pair girl, might pose processing problems so that the full significance of what is being conveyed might be difficult to recover?

10 She's just come over to learn the language and she's doing very well (pause) this morning she said to me I hope you'll be forgiving me my extremely bad language but I'm afraid my grandmaster needs touching up

Garden-path utterances 'The principle of relevance does not normally warrant the selection of more than one interpretation for a single ostensible stimulus' and 'The first hypothesis consistent with the principle of relevance (is) the best' (S&W 1986: 167, 168).

Jokes frequently allow 'more than one interpretation for a single ostensible stimulus'. Indeed, it is often necessary for there to be more than one interpretation. This joke, for example, is about a man who is thrown off a fairground wheel. His friend rushes up to him in horror, and the joke ends in the following way:

11 Terry he said Terry he said are you hurt (pause) the friend lifts himself on one elbow and said well of course I'm hurt he said I went round three times and you never waved once

The joke turns precisely on the interpretation of *hurt* to mean physically hurt when the friend asks *are you hurt* and to mean emotionally hurt in Terry's reply. Thus the audience must understand *hurt* differently from the way Terry takes it for the joke to work.

In a related way, jokes typically work by allowing the audience to derive an implicature and then denying that this was a meaning the joke-teller intended to convey. This is how the joke-teller talks about his au pair girl:

12 she's been doing a bit of work for us this weekend at home (pause) and (pause)

The first pause acts as a trigger which encourages the audience to draw the inference that *doing a bit of work for us this weekend at home* is not an entirely innocent statement. This inference is then confirmed by the second pause after *and*. Having led his audience up the garden path in this way, the joke-teller then denies that this implicature is well founded and insists that the purpose of her stay is to learn the language:

13 no she's just come over it's true she's just come over to learn the language

So it turns out that 'the first hypothesis consistent with the principle of relevance', that there is something going on between the joke-teller and his au pair girl, is inappropriate, or at least it is a contrivance of the joke-teller. The experimental audience were not able to derive the implicature at the pauses, perhaps through lack of contextual resources, perhaps because pauses give rise to 'weak implicatures' (S&W 1986: 222). Thus they were not able to construct 'the first hypothesis', were consequentially unable to understand the significance of *no* and *it's true* as denials of that hypothesis, and could not therefore understand the joke.

The understanding process

The last example shows how lack of contextual resources might prevent an audience from being led up the garden-path in the way intended by the joke-teller. It therefore shows how two of the relevance theory-inspired accounts of how utterances are understood are at work at the same time. And of course this is the usual situation. For example, in

2   tonight's story was actually handed down to me by my dear old grandfather (pause)
3   the other night as he was clearing out our attic

we showed how *handed down* must first be explicated for the joke-teller's intended effect to be realized. But this makes several assumptions: that the hearer has the necessary contextual resources and stores sufficient information about the syntactic and semantic entries for *hand down*; that there is sufficient opportunity for processing the item; that it is sufficiently salient for the processing cost to be small, and that the hearer is able to recognize that he or she has been the victim of a garden-path utterance in which the first 'relevant' meaning accessed turns out not to be the right one. This utterance, therefore, shows how a range of different processing mechanisms are involved in recovering intended meaning, and that a failure in any of them will lead to an understanding failure.

Checking understanding (5)

At one stage the joke-teller says he was in bed reading the *Radio Times*

14   and admiring a photo of Patrick Moore (pause) and wondering what it must be like to put your suit on with a shovel

Can you invoke some or all of the six mechanisms discussed above to account for why this utterance might pose an understanding test, indicating, where appropriate, which sort of audience would be expected to find processing the utterance particularly problematical?

Conclusion

In this, as in the previous chapter, we have been considering candidate theories of pragmatic usage. In the case of politeness, we argued that every use of language has politeness status, and that therefore to find a way of characterizing politeness is to find a way of characterizing all language use. In this chapter we have shown how relevance theory accounts for the process of language understanding since relevance is given and understanding utterances is a matter of proving their relevance. As proving the relevance of an utterance is determined by the accessibility of its relevance to the addressee, understandability status should in principle be a means of characterizing language use.

Raising pragmatic awareness

1. This exercise works best in a small group. Each person should think up a sentence. Write all the sentences up in random order on the board. Try to

see how each sentence could be relevant in the context provided by the previous sentences. As you do this, think about the problems anyone would have in working out the connections for themselves and the contextual resources required. Try inserting additional sentences to reduce the processing effort required of the reader.

2. In your tutorial group, choose any of the keywords at the beginning of this chapter and write an entry for your chosen word for a dictionary of pragmatics. Compare your proposed entry with those of colleagues.

Further reading

Blakemore (1992); Grundy (1991); Sperber and Wilson (1986).

9

Speech events

'Suit the action to the word, the word to
the action' (*Hamlet*, III.ii.17)

Keywords: speech event, recognizable routine, speech act, interrogative,
expectation, genre, activity type, goal, strategy, knowledge of language, E-
language, I-language.

In this chapter we show how speech acts play a role in the wider context of
speech events, and how the routine of a speech event is a candidate system
which might account for pragmatic usage. The term 'speech event' is used to
refer to a sequence of utterances that follow an expectable pattern and
constitute a recognizable routine.

The role of utterances in speech events

In Chapter 5 we saw how sentence types such as interrogatives are frequently
used to do things other than ask questions. Read through the list of interrogatives below, which we have already met in earlier chapters, and as you
read each, think about just what it is used to do, if possible in some context
you can imagine for it other than the one in which it was presented to you:

1 What's your name by the way
2 Are we all here
3 Right, shall we begin
4 May I speak English
5 What's your name again
6 Is it tea or coffee
7 Would you like tea or coffee
8 How are you doing
9 Are you here Peter
10 Have you got a plastic bag
11 Will you have some more chocolate
12 Why do farmers have long ears and bald heads
13 Shall I pick you up at eight

14 Do you sell postage stamps

15 Do you know about our offer on oil

16 Have you got a timetable for

What is important about all these indirect speech acts is that they play a recognizable role in a larger context. So (12), for example, is recognizable as the first turn in a joke inviting the standard response *I don't know* and (15) is recognizable as an offer to tell, inviting the standard response, *no*, with a particular intonation contour. In the case of (2), spoken by a senior colleague when a meeting was due to start, we saw that the most appropriate response was non-verbal—indeed to provide an answer such as 'No, we're not' would be accurate but useless. All that one can safely say about these utterances is that, since they are open propositions, each invites some sort of response. But the functions of the utterances and the nature of the responses depend on the speech events of which they are a part. They are expectable just to the extent that they have roles in recognizable routines.

This is not to deny the possibility of routines taking unexpectable directions, as happened on the occasion when I responded in an unexpected way to (15) (page 96) or when Mr Logic responded in his absurd but 'logical' way to the expectable response to his utterance *Do you sell postage stamps* (page 93). Typically, unexpectedness occurs when some non-predicted speech event is created. For example, the utterance *what's it for* usually occurs when someone sees an object or instrument whose function they do not know. In the following exchange it has a different function:

17 A: What is it

   B: A kittle

   A: A kittle?

   B: Yes a kittle

   A: What's it for

You have probably already guessed that *what's it for* is a strategy aimed at getting B to provide sufficient information for A to understand *a kittle*. Since B is a non-native speaker of English describing a picture to her English teacher, A's question constitutes a novel but expectable strategy which satisfies a pedagogic purpose and duly brings about a problem-resolving response. The next two turns are

18 B: It's for boil water

   A: Oh a kettle

Anybody listening to this exchange would be able to 'type' the speech event as an unequal encounter, such as a pedagogic instruction sequence, involving a native and a non-native speaker, and would define *what's it for* in terms of its function in the speech event, which is to enable A to determine what B is describing.

Genres

Another way of making the point just made would be to say that speech events are genres. This is clearest when we look at the properties of a recognized genre such as a recipe. Consider this example:

19   Scampi Provençale

Method	*Ingredients*
1. Fry the onion and garlic gently in the butter or margarine until cooked but not browned.	1 onion, chopped 1 clove of garlic, chopped 25g (1oz) butter or margarine
2. Add tomatoes, wine, seasoning, sugar and parsley, stir well and simmer gently for 10 minutes.	1 375g (15oz) tin tomatoes, drained 4 15ml (table) spoon dry white wine seasoning
3. Drain the scampi well, add to the sauce and continue simmering for about 5 minutes, or until they are just heated through.	pinch sugar 1 15ml (table) spoon parsley, chopped 200g (8oz) frozen scampi, thawed
4. Serve with crusty French bread, or boiled rice.	Serves 4

This text is recognizable as a recipe in form and style. Indeed, the form is partly defined by the style, so that the verbs under *method* are finite (*fry*, *add*) and under *ingredients* non-finite (*chopped*, *drained*). The noun phrases contain determiners under *method* but not under *ingredients*. The *method* column has preposition phrases (*in the butter*) and post-predicate modification (*stir well*, *simmer gently*) while the *ingredients* column has neither preposition phrases nor predicate modifiers. Thus the *methods* column exhibits cohesion, but the *ingredients* column is just a list which does not even exhibit concord (*4 15ml (table) spoon*). The *methods* are the phrase structure rules of combination—one gets as far as *the* in *fry the onion* before going to *ingredients* (or lexicon) to locate the referent. Thus the first two or three words in the left-hand column are read first and then the entire right-hand column is read next before the reader returns to the left-hand column. When this process is accomplished you have passed the understanding test and generated *Scampi Provençale*, a description which is neither English by grammar (a noun + modifier combination) nor by lexical selection.

Recipes are a unique genre whose formal and stylistic properties, which closely parallel a set of instructions for making a sentence, are what makes them recipes. Because a recipe is a written genre, it provides an undisputed illustration of its unique character. The unique character of speech events is harder to demonstrate only because they are spoken rather than written. Speech events are genres whose properties are formally deployed speech acts.

The formal properties of speech events

In his paper on the structure of speech events, Levinson argues that 'activity type' is a better term than 'speech event'. He defines an activity type as 'any culturally recognized activity, whether or not that activity is co-extensive with a period of speech or indeed whether any talk takes place in it at all' (1979: 368). A telephone conversation is an activity co-extensive with a period of speech, whereas a hundred-metre sprint would not be expected to contain talk. In determining the function of any utterance, 'we depend both on the meaning of the words which serve to differentiate the utterances, and on the possible roles which utterances can play within such a game' (367). This suggests that to understand properly the structure of an activity type or speech event is to account for the way the language is deployed in it. On the assumption that all talk belongs to some speech event, this holds out the promise that a developed account of activity type structure can account for language use.

Levinson defines activity types as 'goal defined, socially constituted, bounded, events with constraints on the participants, setting and so on, but above all on the kinds of allowable contributions. Paradigm examples would be teaching, a job interview, a jural interrogation, a football game, a task in a workshop, a dinner party and so on' (368). Utterances have force 'by virtue of the expectations governing the activity' (372). This would account for the different forces of *pass* in the television general-knowledge contest, *Mastermind*, and in a game of bridge, as noted in Chapter 5—and in a game of football (where the understood subject is the addressee).

The style of a speech event

The goal-directed nature of speech events reflects the intentionality of language use. So the goal of a television chat-show interview, for example, might be to get the 'guest' to talk freely and entertainingly in a number of topic areas (career, future plans, etc.) to three kinds of audience (interviewer, studio audience, home audience). This is a simplification, but one that enables us to consider the strategies that might enable this goal to be achieved. Since 'the various levels of organization within an activity cohere and can be seen to derive as rational means from overall ends' (390), it ought to be possible to specify the style by which the overall end(s) of a speech event such as a chat-show interview are achieved, in just the same way as we showed in the much simpler case of a recipe how the style or 'means' were constitutive of the form or structure of the genre.

Working with data drawn from a television chat-show, I am going to show how the language used is constrained by the goals and setting of the activity type and can best be explained (perhaps only be explained) as constitutive of the event. Consider the following interrogative structure used by a chat-show 'host' to Sir Edmund Hillary:

20 I wonder its er you are one of the sort of great adventuring figures of of this century and one wonders er you know where that all starts from and stems from did you have the er any sort of sense of destiny as a as a child

The final interrogative structure contains a repaired false start (*the er any*), a hesitation (*er*), a hedge (*sort of*) and a redundant repetition (*as a as a*), as the schematic representation below shows:

20′

  did you have (the)   any   sense of destiny as a (as a) child

<

             er   sort of

Only the non-parenthetical items in the upper line represent the propositional content of the question put; all the other items seem to work against its content. A similar schematic representation of the other parts of this turn show the same property:

20″

   you are one of the   great adventuring figures of (of) this century

<

          sort of

20‴

   (I wonder) (it's)

               [20″] [and]

        er

20⁗

   one wonders   where that all . . . .

<

       er you know

These schematizations show how overblown statements are moderated by repairs and redundancies (shown in the upper line) and the hedges and hesitations (shown in the lower line). Perhaps this is the language of flattery. Given the inherently threatening nature of an interview which clashes with the goal of promoting free and entertaining talk, the 'guest' has to be put at ease. This is accomplished by overstating their achievements. But these Quality-flouting overstatements have to be mitigated by hedges and other devices, or they run the risk of seeming ironical.

Checking understanding (1)

Schematize the following questions put by the host to Sir Edmund Hillary in the same chat-show, either in the way demonstrated above or in some other effective way of your own. Label each item in your schematized version as hedge, hesitation, etc. You may find features not commented on in the schematization given above.

21 How determined were you er yourself to be the the er first man to to climb Everest

22 Was there er er a physical or specialist advantage that you had er yourself in in enabling you to to to climb Everest I mean were you a better climber than anybody else or were you physically stronger or what

Example (22) also illustrates the way that the inherent threat of questions is mitigated. The interviewee appears to be asked to choose between two answer options, physical advantage or better technique. This question is put twice, with the hedge *I mean* before the second formulation, indicating that the interviewer doubts the clarity of the first formulation. But the second formulation ends with *or what*, i.e. an invitation to give any answer at all. In this way the force of the question is mitigated, since any answer is a good answer. And the implied compliment that the interviewee is both physically stronger and has superior technique can now be modestly denied without providing a dispreferred answer. The way questions were asked in (20) and (21) displayed similar mitigating techniques. In (20) the interviewer speculates on the impossibility of providing an answer to the question (shown by *I wonder, one wonders*) and in (21) the question presupposes that the interviewee was *determined* but leaves him the option of indicating the degree of his determination.

An interviewer must ask questions. Theoretically, questions constitute a threat which are liable to frustrate the goal of the activity. Therefore it is characteristic of this speech event that the interviewer employs a range of techniques to mitigate their force.

Checking understanding (2)

A number of other questions asked by the host in this chat-show are given below. Show how each is designed to mitigate the inherent threat of the speech act:

23 You also of course you you played a er a um a extraordinary episode in your career er if I remember arightly was it you rescued er did you not er er um um a masterpiece an Italian masterpiece

24 Do you agree with that do you

25 But once you saw it and once it was there what you I mean you had to conquer it had you

26 Finally I'd like to ask you its er er a daft question I know but I've always wanted to ask this of somebody who's obviously displayed great courage and you had to have that at least to climb Everest what frightens you

The limited space available does not permit an exhaustive account of the goal-directed style of this activity type. Instead, I am going to cite several single examples of data which show a range of the goal-directed strategies employed by this chat-show host. A is the interviewer, B the interviewee.

Strategy Do not pursue controversial topics or allow a controversial speaker to continue.

27 B: It's impossible for us to stop the change
A: Yes
B: And I deplore this
A: Yes
B: But what can one do about it
A: Yes conversely of course I mean I'd like to ask all three of you this too

Strategy Respond encouragingly by exaggerating interest (28), displaying polite incredulity (29), etc.

28 B: He said there's a psychic wall around there
A: Extraord
B: And I believe him

29 A: I mean what is it that you having had close contact with these people um have gained from THEM from

   B: Knowledge

   A: Knowledge

   B: Self-knowledge

   A: Really

Strategy Defer by elevated description of referents.

30 A: They were an amazing breed

31 A: Well in a moment you can swap mountaineering yarns with my next guest

Strategy Compliment off-record by understatement.

32 A: You say once said of yourself you had a rather nice phrase

Strategy Use concessives to imply that situations described are untypical.

33 A: What made you though when you were a child feel insecure

Checking understanding (3)

Identify some of the goal-directed strategies in the following exchanges:

34 B: I arrived at a very lucky epoch when the BBC was I think in a curious way at the height of its prestige and power

   A: Yes I suppose also of course I mean there were sort of drawbacks to that it was a rather compared to today what's the word um a sombre

   B: Austere

   A: Austere yes austere is is the word

   B: Yes

   A: Would that not be so we're now talking about Lord Reith aren't we and people like that

35 A: But you are seventy now aren't you

   B: Yes I am yes I am

   A: Are you still and in rude health still

Speech acts, speech events, and knowledge of language

This chapter has shown how a speech act has a role to play in a larger speech event and how each particular utterance has distinct, activity type determined properties. The goal-directed use of language in an activity type is therefore a third candidate system which might account for pragmatic usage, alongside the politeness status of language in use discussed in Chapter 7 and relevance in Chapter 8. Language use has a predictable quality which can be accounted for as the stylistic realization of the structure of a speech event.

One issue raised by this account of pragmatic usage is to do with the balance of power between the speech act and the speech event context. Take a sentence like

36 Thank you for not smoking

which we discussed in Chapter 1 in the context of its display as a notice on a secretary's office door. Would this notice have the same illocutionary force if it appeared on the milkman's bill? Since the context does not hold, presumably not. The Gricean account would suggest that a different implicature should be inferred. Hence a different speech act is performed with a different illocutionary force. But at the same time the illocutionary force of (36) transforms the context in some way, so that the secretary's notice and the milk bill are both contexts created to some degree by the same speech act. This returns us to a consideration of the relation of context and language: is the language of the chat-show prescribed by the external context (the context-as-given view) or is the context created by the particular assemblage of linguistic values displayed in the chat-show?

A second issue raised by this account of pragmatic usage has to do with knowledge of language. The phrase 'knowledge of language' has been used in a very particular way by Chomsky in his book of that title (1986). In many places in his work, Chomsky draws a distinction between knowing a language on the one hand and the use of language on the other. In *Knowledge of Language*, he draws a distinction between the external manifestation of language and the internal knowledge underlying our ability to use it. He describes how generative linguistics, of which he was the original pioneer, shifted the focus in language study 'from the study of language regarded as an externalized object to the study of the system of knowledge attained and internally represented in the mind/brain' (1986: 24). In *Knowledge of Language*, the external manifestation of language is termed E-language and the internal representation I-language. Chomsky has some harsh things to say about the value of studying E-language, arguing that what we know about language as revealed in our ability to discriminate the grammars of sentences like

37 They left room empty

and

38 They left the room angry

is the proper study of linguistics, and the way we choose to deploy language pragmatically is not part of that knowledge. There is a general consensus that knowledge of language (the domain of syntactic theorists) and knowledge of the rules of use (the domain of pragmaticists) are two different knowledge domains. Thus the study of the grammar of *what's it for* and the study of the use of *what's it for* in a variety of contexts as an utterance with a variety of possible illocutionary forces are different disciplines. Indeed, the latter, because it is a study of language as action, is not strictly linguistic at all. It is the study of an aspect of a theory of action rather than a theory of language.

Although this distinction is clear, the narrow view of the study of I-language can only be sustained if one regards as primary data sentences like (37) and (38) and the lower-case strings in (20):

20 I WONDER ITS ER you are one of the SORT OF great adventuring figures of OF this century and one wonders ER YOU KNOW where that all starts from and stems from did you have THE ER any SORT OF sense of destiny as a AS A child

Are the upper-case strings whose functions are entirely pragmatic to be regarded as agrammatical and somehow outside our knowledge of language and the domain of syntactic description? And yet we have strong intuitions as to which syntactic constituents the upper-case strings are attached to. Is this not a reflection of our knowledge of language? Of language which could not be I-language without its E-language function? And ought not a properly thought-through representation of our knowledge of language to be able to account for both the upper- and the lower-case data in (20)?

Raising pragmatic awareness

1. Work with a partner. You should each choose a different example from the utterances cited in this chapter and write an entry for it in a dictionary of speech acts. Your entry should discuss its possible role in a speech event. Exchange entries and tell your partner what you think of theirs.

2. This exercise works best in a small group. Choose a word like *intelligent, stupid, generous, mean, young, old*. Think of several synonyms for your chosen word and then imagine these synonyms in the following sentence frames: *she's/he's/they're/you're so/completely/100 per cent....* Discuss the speech events in which each of these utterances would be expectable.

3. This exercise works best in a small group. Imagine an activity type setting such as ordering a meal in a restaurant, talking to a tutor, booking a holiday. Then decide on language forms you would expect to find in this speech event—register, lexis, structure, turn-taking, adjacency pairs, etc. (*Acknowledgement:* the ideas in (2) and (3) are Kelly Glover's.)

Further reading

Levinson (1979).

10

Project work in pragmatics

This chapter contains suggestions for project work with a pragmatic orientation, and discusses the types of project which are viable and the issues involved in successful data collection and transcription.

10.1 *The nature of pragmatic investigation*

Many linguists, although not by any means all pragmaticists, view their subject as a science. They see the purpose of linguistics as bringing order to the untidy set of data that we call language. Even speech act theorists such as Austin, who denied that meaning could be accounted for as an orderly representation of states of affairs in the world, replaced a truth-conditional account of meaning with what we might call an 'intention-conditional' account. So although Austin rejects the account of meaning which treats language as a consequence of states of affairs in the world, he replaces it with an equally exhaustive alternative, speech act theory, which is designed to account for all intentional uses of language and for nothing else.

Recognizing the scientific basis of linguistics has important consequences for the way we investigate language. Rather as one might observe the revolution of visible planets around a star and form the hypothesis that their motion suggested the presence of a further, as yet undiscovered, planet and then set out to test this hypothesis, so in linguistic investigation, too, a favoured method is to test hypotheses. Thus, to take a quite arbitrary example, the other day I overheard someone say to a two-year-old

1   Why don't you use your spoon

whereupon the two-year-old obligingly picked up her spoon and tried to feed herself with it. If two-year-olds can understand indirect speech acts, I reasoned, my fifteen-year-old son shouldn't have any trouble either. And so the next time I saw him eating with his fingers, I said, trying to capture the intonation pattern of the original utterance:

2   Why don't you use your knife and fork

Unfortunately he responded to the propositional content rather than to the illocutionary force of my utterance.

One could easily imagine potentially investigable topics in this area that might well, given a little thought, be turned into testable hypotheses. These potentially investigable topics might include

- family members show that they are displeased with one another by responding to the propositional content rather than the illocutionary force of each other's utterances, typically treating indirect speech acts as though they were direct speech acts;
- some indirect parental requests are complied with by children and some are not, the determining factors perhaps being age of child, gender of child, gender of parent, time of day, subject of request, etc.;
- when two-year-olds do not comply with indirect requests, it is not through choice but rather the result of a lack of pragmatic understanding;
- when parents and children talk to each other, indirect requests are more commonly associated with money talk than with personal hygiene talk.

Each of these topics is potentially investigable. A typical way to proceed would be to try and frame a testable hypothesis. For example, one might hypothesize that two-year-olds responded equally (un)cooperatively to indirect and to direct requests. And then one might set out to test this hypothesis by designing an experiment in which a sample of two-year-olds was selected and stimulated to action by a series of requests, some expressed directly and some expressed indirectly. The data resulting from such an experiment might be best collected on videotape. Once the data had been collected, they could be analysed and a finding would emerge, either that the hypothesis was proved or that it failed for some reason. If it turned out that the sample of two-year-olds complied more readily with direct than with indirect requests, this finding would presumably have implications for the way adults should talk to two-year-olds on occasions when they wanted to get them to do things. And the research might suggest follow-up experiments: for example, it might be useful to try and design an experiment to determine whether two-year-olds failed to respond to indirect requests because they were failing to understand their pragmatics or because they did not like being talked to indirectly.

This kind of research is usually called 'empirical' research because it studies real, observable phenomena, in this case the reactions of two-year-olds to a series of direct and indirect requests. The research method outlined above is typical:

- frame a testable hypothesis (or series of hypotheses) suggested by some observation about the way the world appears to work;
- design an experiment which will enable you to collect data which test this hypothesis;
- collect the data under experimental conditions;
- quantify the data in order to determine whether or not the hypothesis is proved;
- consider the implications of the findings and whether follow-up experiments would be useful.

Very often empirical research of this sort tries to determine whether there is a significant, as opposed to a chance, association between two variables. So that, for example, you might try to establish whether there is a significant association between age and compliance with indirect speech acts.

Earlier I said that recognizing the scientific basis of linguistics has important consequences for the way we investigate language. But this does not mean that all pragmaticists think of the area of linguistics they are interested in as essentially scientific. Nor does it mean that every aspect of pragmatics readily lends itself to empirical methods of investigation. In fact, precisely because pragmatic meaning depends so much on inference, which is not an observable phenomenon, there are lots of ways of investigating language use that are not contrived experiments of the kind suggested for the investigation of two-year-old responses to indirect speech acts. If you were interested in conversation, for example, you would rarely want to design an experiment to collect sets of data that would be easily comparable. In fact, you could argue that we got further in our analysis of the conversation in the travel agent's by trying to understand it in terms of the sequential properties of talk rather than by investigating how frequently the three speakers made use of particular pragmatic strategies. In this case, the data were not collected as part of a controlled experiment at all, but instead challenged us to devise a system of description able to account for an example of real-world language.

Obviously, very different techniques are involved in researching two-year-old talk by means of the kind of hypothesis suggested above and researching the structure of conversation by accounting for it as we did in Chapter 6. The first approach is often called 'quantitative' because it requires a substantial quantity of data whose regularities can be determined, often by detailed statistical means. The second approach is often called 'qualitative' because its results rely more on the insight of the researcher than on objectively measured associations between sets of variables. Pragmatic research makes use of both of these approaches. And when you identify the area you wish to research, it is usually fairly clear which method is likely to give the better result.

10.2 *Collecting data*

You may be collecting your data because you wish to test a hypothesis. In this case your data will usually be elicited, as in the hypothetical two-year-old project discussed above. When this is the case, you will need to design elicitation experiments very carefully to make sure that you are actually measuring what you seek to measure rather than some other phenomenon. This means that all the non-relevant variables need to be eliminated. More often in your own work, you will probably collect your data first and have only a fairly general idea of what you hope they will show before you have collected them.

There are some fairly well-established 'dos' and 'don'ts' when it comes to data collection. One of the most obvious relates to the so-called 'Observer's Paradox', or effect that the observer or collector has on the nature of the data itself: if you tell someone you would like to ask them a number of questions, they will provide you with data that reflect this situation and are very unlikely to represent their natural speech style. So it is important to find a means of collecting data which is not influenced by the collection procedure itself.

Similarly, if you tell your friends to have a natural conversation while you record it on tape, you will get anything but a natural conversation. In fact, in most situations you are unlikely to be able to collect representative data if your informants know that they are being recorded. On the other hand, there is an ethical issue: it is widely agreed that one ought not to make use of revealing data provided by informants without their consent. And indeed, you often need to know things about your informants (such as their ages or nationalities or status in an organization) that may well not be revealed in the data they provide, so you will need to talk to them anyway. Therefore you have to make a decision:

● whether to obtain the prior consent of your informants before you collect data from them;
● whether to ask permission to use the data after they have been collected;
● not to ask permission at all.

The decision you make will typically depend on the circumstances in which the data are collected and the kind of talk that is expected to occur.

Asking permission before collecting data You would obviously need to ask permission before collecting data if you were hoping to record your own job interview, or if you were recording a business meeting or a doctor–patient encounter.

Asking permission once the data has been collected Some years ago a colleague and I conducted a small-scale research project in which we decided that reliable data could only be obtained if permission was not sought until after the data had been obtained, and that the nature of the project and the transaction involved were such as to justify this. Every afternoon for four weeks we recorded every transaction that occurred between 4 and 5 p.m. in the tourist information office in Durham. We were hoping to find out whether native and non-native speakers used the same pragmatic strategies to achieve the same end—that of finding overnight accommodation in the local area. Although the staff of the tourist information office obviously knew they were being recorded, if we had told the tourists as they walked through the door that they were going to be recorded, the data would obviously have been distorted. So the transactions were recorded covertly.

As each informant left the counter, they were approached by a research assistant who explained to them that they had been recorded as part of a research project whose purpose was to study the ways in which people make requests, with the ultimate aim of developing teaching materials that would help non-native-speaker visitors in the future. They were asked whether they would agree to the conversation they had just had being analysed or whether they would prefer it to be erased. As it happened, only two informants asked for their conversations to be erased. Both were non-native speakers who said that if they had known they were being recorded they would have spoken better English. In the case of all the rest who gave their consent, we were then able to ask about their native/non-native-speaker status, their language-learning backgrounds, ages, etc.

Recording without asking permission Many researchers would consider it acceptable to record short anonymous bursts of talk without obtaining the speaker's consent. For example, I might pretend to be an innocent bystander if I happened to be fortunate enough to be passing with my pinhead microphone and concealed tape-recorder and saw a motorist returning to their car just as a traffic warden was attaching a parking ticket. Because this material is in the public domain and might equally be recorded by a passing television crew, and since the identities of the informants will remain unknown, this might be considered the type of situation that it would be ethical to record without the consent of the informants. Unlike the other situations discussed, it is also not clear that data being obtained in this way are going to be used at all—pragmaticists collect masses of data rather as tourists take masses of photographs, but only a small part of all the data we record in this way will ever be transcribed.

There are a number of other points to keep in mind when you collect data. These include:

Whenever possible, do a pilot collection exercise first. This will enable you to see whether the data you are collecting are (a) audible and (b) useful for the purposes you have in mind.

Give some thought to whether you need to use all the data or just some part of them. There are circumstances when excluding any of the data you collect would render them an incomplete record of the speech event recorded. There are other occasions on which some random sample, such as the second ten minutes of a classroom interaction, might be preferred just because it is a random sample, and directly comparable, therefore, with other samples selected according to the same criterion. There are still other occasions when you are looking for particular types of data, such as inserted sequences between a question and the eventual answer, which probably means that you will have to transcribe all the data collected and then select your target data from the whole. If you have thought these issues through before you begin your data collection, you will probably be able to collect your data more economically and are likely to collect only data that are genuinely useful.

Do not be too ambitious: one hour of conversation involving several speakers can take many days to transcribe. So limit the amount of data you set out to collect to what you can practically transcribe and usefully analyse.

If you collect data featuring more than two or three speakers, when you come to transcribe it you are guaranteed to have problems in some places determining who the speaker is. This problem can sometimes be overcome by recording your data on video, but this is usually impractical. Another option is to be present during the speech event and note the opening words of each speaker. To do this, you will need to number the speakers, perhaps according to their locations around a table. But even this method is far from foolproof, as you will quickly discover. There are also practical problems

associated with recording a many-speaker event: inevitably some speakers
will be nearer the microphone than others, so some will be harder to
transcribe. And the transcription will be harder still in the sections where
several speakers talk at the same time, such as at points of agreement or
when schism occurs, i.e. a larger group becomes two smaller groups for a
number of exchanges so that two conversations run concurrently.

Once you have tried to collect your own data, you will become aware of the
need to plan carefully—nothing is more frustrating than to have data which
do not really reveal what you had hoped they would or which are so difficult to hear that you can never get an accurate enough transcription to work
with.

10.3 *Transcription conventions*

When you make a transcription, you will need to make decisions about the
notation conventions you employ and about how to set the transcription out
on the page.

Notation

Conventional transcriptions of conversations use standard orthographic
script rather than phonemic transcription. This is fortunate, since the task of
transcription would be overwhelming otherwise. (Of course, you are always
able to give a phonetic representation of an item in close discussion if you
need to.) Most standard orthographic transcriptions are adapted to show how
items like *and* and *your* are actually spoken, so that you might expect to use
representations like *n* and *yer*. You also need to indicate hesitations like *er*
and *um*, other fillers and uptake signals like *uh*, *uh-uh* and *yeah*, and audible
breathing (*hh*) and indrawn breath (*.hh*). You may decide to indicate any
particularly marked representation of a lexical item. In the travel agent data,
for example, *burit* represents B's characteristic realization of *but it*.

A more difficult issue is whether and how to represent intonation and
pitch. Most transcribers avoid standard punctuation marks altogether
because they can only represent broad interpretations of the functions of
utterances and are in many ways ambiguous. The easiest solution is only to
indicate very marked examples, so that distinctive pitch prominence might
be marked by capitalizing the appropriate segments (e.g. you WHAT) and the
louder of two simultaneous utterances by underlining. There are more elaborate systems for marking intonation contours such as the one worked out by
Crystal and Davy (1969: 24–40), but they are very laborious to employ and
require a degree of skill to interpret too.

More important in many ways than marking intonation is marking features
of conversational sequencing. For example, you will almost always need to
mark pauses in talk. The most widely used convention is parentheses, with
the length of pause indicated in tenths of a second, so that '(2.5)' would
represent a pause of 2.5 seconds. Short pauses can also be marked with

parentheses and points, with '(.)' equal to a one-syllable-length pause, and '(..)' equal to a two-syllable-length pause. Sometimes the micro-pause that we expect at transition relevance places (TRP) does not occur, so that the utterances of the two speakers are 'latched', a phenomenon which is usually indicated by an '=' sign. In our earlier discussion of the travel agent data, I said that A indicated his displeasure by the speed of his response when B asked him which weekend he wanted to travel on. The two utterances are in fact latched, that is, they occur with no discernible pause between them, a phenomenon that we can now indicate:

3   B: (13.0) well there's a shuttle service (0.4) um (.) sixty pounds one way
         (2.5) er (2.3) when do you want to go
     A: I want to go at the weekend
     B: (0.3) what weekend=
     A: =next weekend

Another sequencing phenomenon that needs to be marked is the 'overlap' of two speakers. The start of an overlap is usually marked by a double slash '//' and the end of the overlap by an asterisk '*', which may be indicated in both speakers' utterances. We came across this phenomenon very frequently in the travel agent data:

4   B: we're not British Rail //agents*
     A: //you're* not a//gents I see*
     M: //but I'll*give you a rough idea

This exchange illustrates how using different symbols to mark the start and end of an overlap can make a transcription clearer.

You will also need a convention to indicate that the transcription is uncertain or that there is a contribution which you are unable to transcribe. This may be done with either single or double parentheses. Thus the double parentheses in the assistant's utterance below indicate that her contribution is not transcribed:

5   A: (0.2) and h//and*
     B: //((   ))*
     A: how often do they go

You may also want to indicate an important non-linguistic feature. This may be done with square brackets. So that if one of a group leaves, you might insert '[G leaves the room]' or if there is laughter, '[Laughter]'. It would have been appropriate to have included such a direction in the travel agent transcript at the point where the manager comes up to the counter, viz.

6   B: what happens if he wants the last fl//ight*
     A: //if I*want to come back on
         the//last flight on the Sunday night*
     B: //((   )) they don't put*on an extra plane do they
     M: (1.4) [advances to counter] well theoretically if it's full they're
         supposed to put a back-up plane on

Although these are relatively widely agreed conventions, there is considerable minor variation in the way that different linguists use and adapt them to their own purposes. There is nothing to prevent you using conventions that are especially suited to your own data, as long as you provide a key indicating how the conventions are to be understood. For example, you might decide that it would be appropriate to mark overlap only in the text that was being overlapped by the new speaker, and that indicating the end of overlap was essentially redundant since it would be indicated naturally at the point one speaker gives up the floor. If you used this convention, (5) would be represented as

5′ A: (0.2) and h and
B: //((   ))
A: how often do they go

and (4) as

4′ B: we're not British Rail agents
A: //you're not agents I see
M: //but I'll give you a rough idea

You must decide for yourself whether this more economical system is as clear as the more elaborate system described earlier.

Setting the transcription out on the page

This is a much trickier area than it might appear to be. You only realize the complexities of the problem and the effects of the decisions you make once you have tried a few ways. Five of the central issues are discussed below.

1. Start each new speaker at the left-hand margin. If you have an adequate way of indicating latched utterances and overlaps, in theory a transcription in which all new speakers, even when overlapping the previous speaker, began at the left-hand margin would be transparent. However, as soon as you have more than two speakers, this becomes problematical, as the following example shows:

4″ B: we're not British Rail //agents*
A: //you're* not a//gents I see*
M: //but I'll*give you a rough idea

This is not only difficult to read, but might also give the impression that A and M simultaneously overlap B.

2. Wherever there is a TRP, start the new turn at the left-hand margin. This convention not only solves the problem indicated in (4″), it also shows where TRPs occur. Notice how this means that a speaker who self-selects at a TRP will also start a new line at this point. In the travel agent data, when the customer tries to get the assistant to take the turn and eventually has to continue himself, the data were represented as follows:

7 B: I can tell you what it is to go to Edinburgh
A: yes (1.0) by plane
B: by plane

I chose this method of representing the data when you first came across them in Chapter 6 because they are easy to read in this form when you are unfamiliar with transcription conventions, but a more accurate representation perhaps would have been

7' B: I can tell you what it is to go to Edinburgh
    A: yes
       (1.0)
    A: by plane
    B: by plane

or even

7'' B: I can tell you what it is to go to Edinburgh
    A: yes
       (1.0)
    B:
    A: by plane
    B: by plane

This convention also enables a transcriber to distinguish a TRP from a genuine in-turn pause such as occurs when the manager searches for the right continuation:

8 M: er yeah the flight's a standby guarantee (..) yeah you you turn up and you've got to er (1.0) if they can't get on one flight they'll put you on the next any of the next two

Some transcriptions that start a new line at each TRP also employ a capital letter at the start of each turn.

3. Start the next speaker at the point in the line where the previous speaker terminates. This method has the advantage of capturing the notion that talk continues naturally, but has the disadvantage that it does not enable TRPs to be unambiguously transcribed. Both this and the first method may be suitable for very short examples of data, but are not as satisfactory for longer conversations.

4. Use running lines for each speaker. This method has the advantage that it enables aizuchi (supportive interjections—see page 119) to be marked as they occur without breaking the record of the speaker's talk. It works rather as music for an orchestra would be scored. If we had been using this convention, the final sequences between the manager and the customer in the travel agent's would not have looked as we set it out:

9 A: sixty-eight sixty(0.6) good thank you very much (.) I //thin*
    M: //that's* from
    London sir
    A: that's from London (.) either way I've got to get myself (.)
    M: yeh
    A: to the right//place*
    M: //yes*
    A: yeh I'll think about it
    M: yeh
    A: thanks very much that's very helpful (.) bye-bye

but rather as follows

9' A: sixty-eight sixty (0.6) good thank you very much (.) I thin
    M: that's from

    M: London sir

```
A:                  that's from London (.) either way I've got to get

A:  myself (.)   to the right place yeh I'll think about it
M:          yeh          yes                              yeh

A:  thanks very much that's very helpful (.) bye-bye
```

There are clearly some advantages to this method, which allows aizuchi to be marked in a natural way and captures the notion of continuing talk. It is particularly suited to talk where the contributors offer very unequal contributions, such as an instruction-giving or an explanation sequence in which the instructed party does little more than indicate understanding. However, it is a rather cumbersome method, which becomes very wasteful of space as well as difficult to follow as soon as three or more speakers are involved.

5. Use columns for each speaker. This is an uncommon method of transcription, but can be used quite effectively where the encounter is very unequal. For example, a teacher–pupil exchange which followed a question–answer format might lend itself to this method of representation. One advantage of the method is that utterance types as well as data can be represented in this format. So if we had transcribed the opening of the travel agent encounter in this way, we would be able to parallel the transcription with a typification of the contributions in the same format:

10

A:	B:
can you help me I have to go to Edinburgh (.) somebody told me it was cheaper to go by plane than by train (.) is that right	(1.5) well we're not British Rail agents so I don't know the difference
oh I see	I can tell you what it is to go to Edinburgh
A: request for information	B: refusal of information
A: rejection of refusal	B: offer of part information

Whichever method you choose for transcribing your data and however you adapt it to your own needs, you will discover how time-consuming making a good transcription is. We are unfortunately still some years away from having a computer programme with voice recognition capable of turning multi-speaker natural talk into a transcription, although with a bit of luck this book will still be in print when the software is available and you will be able to throw away most of the section you have just been reading. Meanwhile, you have to make do with existing technology. In this respect, you will find the transcription task much easier if you work with a transcriber rather than a tape-recorder. A transcriber usually comes with a foot control. Each time you use the control to stop the tape, the tape automatically rewinds a few words so that you can hear the problem passage again. This means that you can type the transcription as you control its pace with the foot control and simultaneously check difficult passages.

Another very useful aid is a computer programme which allows you to insert new material or delete misheard original material while at the same time adding or taking away the appropriate number of spaces on linked lines. Imagine, for example, that as I listen to the travel agent data again, I discover that I had misheard A's contribution in

11 B: that's a saver (0.7) burit it's a standby
    A: a st//andby*
    B: //you ha*ve to book it in advance but um (.)

and that I now realize that A actually says not *a standby* but *it's a standby*. If I insert *it's*, B's overlap will no longer be in the right place. Software is available which enables the relative positions of utterances to be maintained when insertions and deletions are made to linked lines. If you can afford this software, it obviously makes the task of revising a transcription much easier.

It should be repeated that making a good transcription is very time-consuming indeed, and that you can only find out by trial and error which kind of notation suits your data best. Expect to listen to your tape many times—you will be surprised to find that even with the clearest tapes there are tiny things that you misheard or had never noticed before. And, just for security, always work with a copy of the original tape.

10.4 *Investigable topics*

It may seem rather odd to come last to discussing possible topics for project work. But now that you have considered the nature of pragmatic investigation and the problems associated with data collection and transcription, you may have a better idea of what topic areas are practical.

This section should not be taken as prescriptive or constraining—indeed, there are many other areas that can be investigated besides the few suggested below, and in many ways other than those outlined above. What follows is a short list of investigable areas, numbered for convenience:

1. Conversational strategies: how does turn-taking work—in general terms and in a particular conversation? According to what principles and by what means does the speaker select the next speaker? Who self-selects at TRPs and with what effects? How does a potential speaker show their intention to be the next speaker? What sort of interventions occur: requests for clarification, confirmations of understanding, aizuchi, repair—both self- and other-initiated and self- and other-completed? What are the mechanics of interruption—is there an interruption trigger? How long does it occur before the actual interruption? Are there interruption markers? What determines whether the existing speaker or the interrupter secures the floor? How does topic shift occur—is it natural or contrived? Is it preceded by a formulation of the gist of what had gone before? Is an agenda adverted to? Is topic a viable unit of analysis? Do discussions of topic have internal structure? How are conversational methods, such as insertion sequences, adjacency pairs and presequences, used? How are contributions cued, and how does any contribution project beyond its moment of utterance?

2. Language forms and their pragmatic effects: the characteristic pragmatic strategies of particular speakers or writers—can rhetorical strategies such as coupling (repeating structures), irony, overstatement, metaphor be analysed in terms of their pragmatic properties and effects?

3. Activity types and the institutional use of language: the structure and pragmatic properties of seminars, interviews, etc. Also talk types: the structure of telephone conversations, ordering sequences in restaurants, contributions to radio phone-ins, etc. To what extent are these speech events goal-oriented and to what extent do they determine their own structures? How are expectations signalled and how are prototypes, or best examples, implied and referred to? How is talk constrained and how do participants indicate constraints on allowable contributions? Determining the functional role assumed by a speaker and assigned to other speakers.

4. Focusing on power and distance, 'relation-indicating devices' (Matsumoto, 1988)—how speakers encode these; how speakers get their own way. Facework—how speakers use politeness strategies to acknowledge the face wants of others.

5. Audience design—how speakers signal that they take their audiences into account. Co-authorship—how conversations and speech encounters are co-authored by participants; signals of agreement and mutual recognition of ends; successful negotiation.

6. The acquisition of pragmatics: what is to be acquired and how it gets acquired—studies of toddlers and infants and their recognition and production of pragmatic effects; the role of pragmatics in enabling first-language acquisition. The acquisition of a second pragmatics—sociopragmatic skills, honorific language, achieving pragmatic effects.

7. Adding to pragmatic description: can you add a term of your own to the growing list of terms such as 'gist', 'formulation', 'cue', which have been borrowed from everyday use and applied to conversational phenomena? Show how your term is motivated and how it accounts for a typical and repeated pragmatic effect.

8. Context: does the external social structure determine the way talk is organized and the type of contributions that occur, or is the context created by the talk itself?

9. Ethnomethodological accounts of language use: showing how language use is expectable, regular, and recognizable by members of a community. Providing an ethnographic account of the way that talk and life are entwined. Showing how membership is indicated in the use of language and has both including and excluding functions.

10. Relevance: just how does relevance theory enable us to characterize particular contributions to talk and account for the way these contributions are understood? The search for another account for the fundamental pragmatic property of communication to set against relevance theory—candidate notions might include 'indexicality', 'implicitness', 'intentionality', or a term of your choosing.

11. The explanatory nature of pragmatics—show how some pragmatic feature such as a maxim hedge or an indirect speech act can account for systematic language behaviour.

12. 'Folk' views of talk—investigating the extent to which people's beliefs about pragmatic uses of language (politeness, interruption, etc.) reflect the phenomena that are actually observed. The degree of match between metapragmatic 'folk' terms and pragmatic metalanguage.

13. When talk goes wrong—what is unexpectable but occurring and what we might hypothesize would never occur. Recognizing the regulative aspects

of talk. Coping with pragmatic misfires. How lasting are the effects of misfires in talk-in-interaction and how are they repaired?

Further reading

For transcription conventions, Atkinson and Heritage (1984: ix–xvii).

Part III

Pragmatic explanation

11

Pragmatic theory and application

'oft of one wide expanse had I been told'
(John Keats, *On first looking into
Chapman's Homer*)

Like this chapter, this book began with a quotation: 'We all know what light is; but it is not easy to tell what it is'. Of course, we now find it quite easy to tell what light is, and no doubt one day we will have an equally developed understanding of language and of the usage principles that we study when we study pragmatics. But our present situation is a bit like Dr Johnson's: we know what pragmatics is, 'but it is not easy to tell what it is'. This is why the first words of mine in this book were 'I am not going to try and define pragmatics in this first chapter'. Nor am I going to try to define pragmatics in this last chapter, although I will try to draw out the significance of the ground covered in the intervening chapters.

In the second sentence of the first chapter I said I would write about some of the aspects of language use that are of particular interest to pragmaticists. The chapter went on to enumerate the pragmatic features of language use (appropriacy, indirectness, indeterminacy, relevance) and language under-standing (inference based on the use of language in context). Each of these observations about language was of special salience at some stage in the chapters that followed. For example, in Chapter 7 we defined politeness in terms of hearer-expected appropriacy; in Chapter 5 we problematized the notion of indirectness (and of directness for that matter), and in our discussion of Relevance Theory in Chapter 8 we noted that an implicated meaning is an inference based on two kinds of premise, explicated meaning and knowledge of context.

In the following sections we will be considering whether the systematic descriptions of pragmatic phenomena suggested in Chapters 2, 3, 4, and 5 have explanatory power, i.e. whether they can account for the systematic nature of observed language use.

The pragmatic domain and pragmatic description

Most pragmatics textbooks follow a different strategy from the one taken in this book, and typically begin with a definition of pragmatics. Levinson, for example, begins by describing the historical origin of the term 'pragmatics'

definitions

before rehearsing a number of candidate definitions (1983: 5–35). These include

- the study of language from a functional perspective;
- the study of the context-dependent nature of language use and language understanding;
- the study of the effects of language use on the grammar of language;
- the study of non-conventional, or, more narrowly perhaps, non-truth-conditional meaning, possibly to be understood as speaker- or utterance-meaning rather than sentence-meaning.

In a similar way, Green begins by defining pragmatics as 'the study of understanding intentional human action' (1989: 3), and Mey as 'the science of language as it is used by real, live people for their own purposes and within their limitations and affordances' (1993: 5).

Although it seems odd to begin a book, as I did, without defining its subject, the fact of the matter is that the wide range of phenomena we have been investigating do not fit neatly under a single definition. What is for sure is that pragmaticists take a special interest in language as it is used, which is why the term 'utterance', a metapragmatic 'folk' term used to describe sentences used in talk, has been a keyword in so many of the chapters.

More difficult even than defining pragmatics is the task of delimiting its domain. Broadly, we have been distinguishing between 'conventional' meaning and pragmatic meaning, taking 'conventional' meaning to be a meaning associated with linguistic expressions whenever they are used and pragmatic meaning to be the meaning that is associated with them in particular contexts. This was shown to be an inadequate distinction in the case of generalized conversational implicatures, however, which occur irrespective of the context and yet cannot be conventional meanings since they are cancellable.

In deciding what to include in this book, I have had to draw fairly arbitrary lines. For example, although we have discussed deixis as a relation between a point of origin and a referent, we have nowhere described the actual process of reference assignment—surely a pragmatic phenomenon. Take a phrase like

1 the children

Hawkins (1978) treats *the* as a quantifier whose entailment invokes a reference to all the members of some speaker–hearer shared set which is pragmatically defined. Thus the addressee knows that semantically I am entailing all the children in some set when I say

2 Do bring the children when you come on Sunday

and that pragmatically the set consists of just the number of children that the speaker knows the addressee to have. So semantically *the* is non-problematical, entailing all the members in the set referred to; but pragmatically the number referred to is liable to vary on different occasions of use, so that when I am talking to Maggie and Andy *the* refers to their two children, and when I am talking to John and Victoria *the* refers to their three children, and if I were rash enough to say

2 Do bring the children when you come on Sunday

to a head teacher, well . . .

Thinking about the semantic and pragmatic meanings of *the* in this way enables us to see that deixis is a special kind of reference that identifies a referent in relation to the point of origin of the utterance, while the reference effected by the use of *the* depends on speaker–hearer shared knowledge about the membership of some set. Yet another kind of reference occurs when we say *Maggie and Andy* or *John and Victoria*, intending to pick out by that description some referent(s) in the world in a way that can only be pragmatic. So whilst the expressions we use to effect reference have stable semantic meanings, the references we effect with them must be pragmatically determined. The distinction between what our words mean and what we mean by our words, as Atkinson, Kilby and Roca so aptly put it (1988: 217), is seen working in the area of reference just as we saw it at work in the case of implicature or speech acts.

The status of pragmatic description

So if we accept (a) that definitions of pragmatics are elusive and (b) that no treatment such as this one even aims to exhaust the pragmatic domain, what have we been doing together? One thing we have been doing in the areas we have identified is to attempt a systematic description. Our description has been systematic to the extent that in each area treated a wide range of data has been brought together and shown to have common properties. A cynic might say that this is all we have been doing, just providing labels for categories of phenomena that seem to share common properties, so that grouping deictic phenomena is the pragmatic equivalent of listing nouns or adjectives. But in fact we have gone some way beyond that: just as a syntactician is interested in criteria for adjectivehood, so we have been trying to determine not just what data is presupposition triggering but, more importantly, what we mean by 'presupposition'—not what appears to be a presupposition, if you like, but what a presupposition appears to be. And no pragmaticist is interested only in the use of language; he or she is interested rather in usage principles, in trying to find a grammar that accounts for the way language is put to use, on the assumption that language would not be as it is if it were not used to communicate with.

When I said earlier that we had distinguished semantic meaning as 'conventional' and pragmatic meaning as 'non-conventional', I was in a sense following an established practice that regards pragmatics as a useful catch-all for supposedly non-conventional data. In his chapter in the *Cambridge Survey* Horn dismisses this 'repository' approach (1988: 114), and in Chapter 6 I argued that pragmatic meaning is entirely conventional when judged by the criteria of expectability, and that it makes little sense to talk of any aspect of language or language use as 'non-conventional'. Indeed, the force of the last three chapters has been precisely that politeness is a self-regulating principle which occurs just to ensure that we talk to others as they would be talked to; that, as Sperber and Wilson argue, 'Every act of ostensive communication communicates the presumption of its own optimal relevance' (1986: 158), so that things are said in the optimal and therefore most conventional possible way in relation to the meaning the speaker seeks to convey; and that speech acts have a conventional role to play in speech events. In a sense, pragmatics has 'come of age' (Horn 1988: 113) when it no longer needs to accept 'non-conventional' status.

There is another way in which pragmatics may be seen to have come of age. In earlier work it was common to argue either that syntax needed to be pragmatically sensitive (a strong argument against an autonomous syntax), in order to account for data such as pre-verbal *please* in indirect speech acts, or at least that an autonomous syntax would have to generate a large number of pragmatically anomalous sentences (e.g. interrogative sentences containing pre-verbal *please* and functioning as direct speech acts) which would then have to be filtered out. In fact a great deal of energy was expended, not only on pragmatic description, but on challenging the autonomous status claimed for syntax by producing endless examples, the most obvious explanation of whose grammatical status was pragmatic. In our discussion of compact structures in Chapter 3 we were able to take a more constructive line as we were in discussing the syntactic status of maxim hedges, arguing essentially that syntactic structures and pragmatic effects are linked, without prejudice to the prior status of one or the other.

In these two ways it seems that pragmatics has shrugged off its inferiority complex, and no longer sees itself as a discipline that has to fight over disputed linguistic territory.

Explanation or description

If we were to achieve, not merely a description of pragmatic phenomena as they occur when language is used, but a proper 'grammar' of pragmatics, we would expect such a usage theory to have explanatory power, to be able to account for the way things are, and indeed have to be. The cynic who believes we have merely been providing labels for categories of pragmatic phenomena obviously does not think that pragmatic theories are explanatory at all. These category terms are the equivalents in the domain of pragmatics of terms in the domain of syntax such as 'noun' or 'adjective', which merely describe categories.   Yet Horn claims for the Quantity maxim, 'make your contribution as informative as is required', that it has 'generality, explanatory power and consequences for simplifying grammatical and lexical description' (1988: 117). And in Chapter 3, we saw how a grammatical position is reserved for maxim hedges, which are themselves derived from the principles of conversational cooperation, and that Quantity-based implicatures account very neatly, as Horn (1972) shows, for the lexical gap indicated in Fig. 11.1.

some	all
sometimes	always
permit	oblige
or	and
none	*nall
never	*nalways
forbid	*nobliged
nor	*nand

Fig. 11.1

It is data such as these which do suggest that pragmatics has explanatory power and, as well as being a description of the way we use language, additionally provides *usage* principles.

There is another sense—in some ways a more telling one—in which pragmatic systems are explanatory. One might reasonably ask why pragmatics should be expected to provide an explanatory account of syntactic phenomena or lexical gaps. A syntactic phenomenon is only required to have explanatory power in the syntactic module, for example. Indeed, where possible we try to account for the properties of each level of language without recourse to information drawn from our knowledge of the systems at another level. In this light, pragmatics certainly has explanatory power in the area of language use, as we have seen. We were able to show in Chapter 3, for example, how Teletext subtitling can be accounted for and predicted on the basis of pragmatic criteria, and we could use pragmatic systems to generate predictable, 'grammatical' subtitles algorithmically from spoken text. In Chapter 5 we saw how Mr Logic systematically responds to propositional content and not to pragmatic meaning, and could use the pragmatic principles identified to generate predictable, 'grammatical' 'Mr Logic' utterances for other contexts. Similarly, the English–Malay, Malay–English code-switching in the following examples taken from letters written by bilinguals is clearly triggered at pragmatic or metapragmatic boundaries (taken from Stapa, 1986: passim; English represented by small capitals, Malay by lower-case):

3 MAYBE you have already known this because MALAYSIA'S NEWS can get there
   I GUESS you are in the middle of winter
   but the north part ESP Kedah AND Perlis are very hot. It is the beginning of the dry season I THINK. OH YEA, BEFORE I FORGOT, N—— I—— sends her regards
   I hope YOU ARE ALWAYS FINE WITH ALL THE WORKLOAD

More simply still, the utterance

4 It's the taste

both states something (although not all that much in this example) and conveys something additional (that the taste is good in the case of instant tea and rotten in the case of school dinners). The fact that there is this implied meaning can then be presented as a problem: how can an utterance convey a meaning that is nowhere explicitly stated (that the taste is good) and that is in many respects more important than the meaning that is stated? It seems to me that Grice's theory of conversational implicature does explain this. Much the same could be said of speech act theory, which explains why a phenomenon like pre-verbal *please* is grammatical in some instances.

In Chapter 3 we considered the arguments for treating pragmatics as an epiphenomenon. These were rejected on the grounds that the pragmatic features of the utterances which the Teletext subtitles did not represent required a syntactic characterization too, although their motivation could only be pragmatic. Thus it is not credible to consider syntax an autonomous system that, by a fortunate accident, is open to pragmatic or semantic interpretation.

This approach runs counter to the view of Chomsky:

> We must distinguish between the literal meaning of the linguistic expression produced by S and what S meant by producing this expression ... The first notion is the one to be explained in a theory of language. The second has nothing particular to do with language; I can just as well ask, in the same sense of 'meaning', what S meant by slamming the door. (1976: 76)

This view is supported by the pragmaticist, Morgan:

> It has become fairly obvious in the past few years that a good part of comprehension must be ascribed not to the rules of language that assign meanings to sentences as a function of the meanings of the parts, but to our ability to somehow infer what the speaker's intentions were in saying what he has said, with the literal meaning it has. But this ability is not, in general, a strictly linguistic ability—in fact, I think it is often not a linguistic ability at all, but the application to linguistic problems of very general common-sense strategies for inferring intentions behind all kinds of acts. (1978: 264)

Morgan continues:

> Conversational pragmatics of the sort Grice discusses is not really conversational at bottom, but the application of general principles of interpreting acts, applied to the sub-case of communicative acts, and more particularly, verbal communicative acts. (1978: 265)

Elsewhere Chomsky does concede that there is a pragmatic competence, which he defines as 'knowledge of the conditions and manner of appropriate use' (1980: 224). But he strictly separates this knowledge of the rules for use from knowledge of language itself. Perhaps the Teletext data could be argued to show knowledge of the rules for use only: but you are left to decide whether the lexical gap data examined first in Chapter 3 and again in this chapter show that knowledge of language itself includes knowledge in the pragmatic domain, and whether it is really true that knowing 'what S meant by producing the expression' *some* (i.e. knowing that the speaker meant 'not-all') 'has nothing particular to do with language'. And rather strikingly, Relevance Theory, by claiming that 'not-all' is an explicature of *some* (in order to free the category of implicature exclusively as a term of description for context-dependent inferences), treats it as a meaning resulting from an inference, part of knowing 'what S meant by producing an expression' and yet at the same time as truth-conditional.

'I see no great harm in this book'

As was said before, this is the last expository chapter in this book. So I should take this opportunity to thank you for reading this far. (Does this count as thanking, or do you want me to say:) Thank you!

When this book was first conceived, as is the custom, the publisher asked me to provide a proposal indicating the structure of the book, and how it would sit among existing books in the same field. And again, as is the custom, the publisher then sent the proposal to three outside anonymous readers for their comments. The least enthusiastic of the three concluded his (or was it her) report with the following sentence:

5   I see no great harm in this book and it could even be quite fun

You must now decide whether your judgements coincide with those implied in this sentence.

Why, one wonders, do we feel such a need to be implicit?

Checking understanding: solutions and suggested answers

1 Using and understanding language

(1)
A1: A calculates that B will take *Mr Major* to refer to the Prime Minister although the true referent is a horse.
B1: *Oh* implies that B has only just heard some surprising news—this makes the utterance more polite than it would have been without *oh*.
A2: Although B has nowhere indicated that he takes *Mr Major* to refer to the Prime Minister, A assumes it and uses *No the horse not the Prime Minister* to contradict something that B had never stated.
B2: B implies that the Prime Minister is a *grey* character.

(2)
Ich bin ein Berliner
Ich is deictic because the person it refers to can only be determined by identifying the speaker on this occasion.
President Kennedy implies that he will stand by (West) Berlin when the city is threatened by the Wall, and perhaps that he empathizes with the people of the city. He implies that anything that happens to them, happens to him too. President Kennedy reassures the Berliners.
One would have come to different conclusions if the speaker and/or the location had been different. Since we know that President Kennedy is not literally a Berliner, we know that he is conveying an indirect meaning and must therefore look for the likeliest or most relevant inference.

2 Deixis: the relation of language to its point of origin

(1)
Gestural
Which finger did he bite?/This little finger on the right
Are you ready? Wait for it! Wait for it! NOW
It's behind (indicating just where for somebody who can't find the item referred to)
Symbolic
I bet you weren't expecting this example

I know more about pragmatics now than I did before
I always hide behind a tree (behind in relation to the seeker)
Non-deictic
And then this strange guy walks in and vomits
Now that wasn't very nice
So I hid my money behind the bookcase (the back of the bookcase does not require any context to be fully determined)

(2)
1. How about
We're not all daft you know
Our understanding of history will always stand us in good stead

2. How about
Look at him over there—I bet he drinks Carling Black Label
He was born in 1564, he wrote 37 plays, he died in 1616 and I'm sure I don't need to tell you who he was. (This sentence isn't anaphoric or deictic—is it?)

In any case, the distinction between deixis and anaphora is not all that secure. An anaphoric reference picks out a referent identifiable in a discourse of which the speaker and addressee are both, in a sense, co-authors. In the notorious case of *Let him have it Chris*, *him* and *it*, if *it* is taken to refer to the gun used to shoot the policeman, do look deictic in the sense that one could only identify the referents if one knew the context.

3. If Salman Rushdie is using *we* and *us* exclusively, he means that only he should be tolerant. But if he is using the pronouns inclusively, he means that those who have declared the *fatwa* should also show tolerance. The exclusive reading is apologetic and the inclusive reading is more accusatory. If the use is non-deictic, then he is treading a middle course between apology and accusation—but it's difficult to see why he should have used *we* and *us* at all if he intended this meaning. It clearly is not easy to determine the intended reference here.

(3)
1. At first sight it appears that *go* is used for movement away from the speaker and *come* for movement towards the speaker. But this example shows that when the addressee is at the location to which the speaker is travelling, the addressee rather than the speaker becomes the deictic centre. Thus movement towards the addressee triggers the use of *come*.

2. *Somewhere* is clearly not deictic because there is no context to consult in order to determine the place referred to. Is the *else* of *somewhere else*, which indicates that no speaker-determined place is being picked out, sufficient for us to say that the expression is deictic?

3. I am indebted to Zhang Qian of South-East University, Nanjing, for posing this neat problem, and to Kelly Glover for helping me to tidy up the explanation. It seems to me that

12   To the left of Mark

is deictic because it will always be interpreted as to the left from the speaker's (or addressee's) perspective (= Sue).

13   On the left of Mark

could be deictic (left from speaker's or addressee's perspective) (= Sue) or non-deictic (left from Mark's perspective) (= Dave).

14 On Mark's left

is typically regarded as non-deictic, i.e. identifying the referent does not depend on knowing the point of origin of the utterance.

If you agree with this verdict, you need to think about why it should be the case. One solution could be to do with English being a Head + Adjunct order language, i.e. we expect the head word (e.g. the preposition in a preposition phrase) to come first. *On the left* is the head in *on the left of Mark* so the order is expectable. But in *on Mark's left*, the head word *left* comes second. When this word order occurs in a predominantly Head + Adjunct language, the whole phrase will tend to be viewed as a single compound word, a head in its own right, as it were, so that *Mark's left* becomes a new non-deictic term to describe what is on the left in relation to Mark irrespective of the speaker's perspective.

(4)

1. I suggest

21'   Now what have you found to say of our past
21''   What have you now found to say of our past (but barely grammatical in this position)
21'''   What have you found now to say of our past
21''''   What have you found to say of our past now

In fact, Hardy actually wrote **21''**.

2. **21'** could be non-deictic, **21''** and **21'''** are deictic and perhaps symbolic, and **21''''** is gestural (certainly it has a prosodic gesture).

3. It seems that the use of *now* is progressively more gestural when it occurs towards the right-hand end of the sentence. Since we place elements we want to focus at the right-hand end of sentences, this is not surprising.

4. There isn't any definitive answer to this question so far as I'm aware. What interests me is that, to the extent that either of these expressions is deictic, *now* seems more deictic than *then*. If you could show that one use is preferred in one place and one in another, would you want to draw any conclusions about the locals?

(5)

2. Heritage writes: 'Consider our example, "That's a nice one", being said by a visitor to a host while both are looking at a photograph album . . . It is obvious that "nice" could mean a number of things in such a context. The visitor could be admiring the composition of the shot, or suggesting that the photograph was a good likeness of the host, or indeed that the host looked particularly well in the photograph . . . . Quite a differently organized search [for an appropriate meaning] will be initiated if the utterance is directed by a girl to her boyfriend in front of a jeweller's window. Once again, the referent may be identified by the girl's pointing to a particular ring, but the ring's property of niceness must be looked for in quite a different way. And different properties again will be looked for in a greengrocer's lettuce described as "nice".' (1984: 143)

3 Implicit meaning

(1)

3   If I knew that everyone believed in God, I should have said so, so *Some people believe in God* implies that not everyone does.

4   If I knew that Damon Hill had won the World Championship, I should have said so, so *Damon Hill did well in his first season in Formula 1* implies that he did not win the Championship.

5   If I had more than £100 in the bank, I should have said so, so *I've got £100 in the bank* implies not more.

6   If I knew that Linford Christie could run 100 m in less than 9.9 seconds, I should have said so, so *Linford Christie can run 100 m in 9.9 seconds* implies not less.

(2)

Quantity—a helper will pass just one light-bulb rather than two to their colleague on the stepladder;

Quality—a helper will supply a light-bulb of the appropriate quality (i.e. new rather than burnt out) and kind (e.g. bayonet-type or screw-type, as required);

Relation—a helper will supply assistance that is relevant to the stage in the operation (e.g. will secure the stepladder when their colleague is climbing it rather than before or after);

Manner—a helper will make the nature of their assistance clear (e.g. will make it evident that they are really securing the stepladder rather than being ambiguous or dilatory about it).

(3)

16 is ironical and therefore flouts Quality. The hearer acquainted with Joyce's book knows that what is stated cannot be the intended meaning, since it is blatantly false, and therefore comes to the conclusion that another meaning is intended—in this case the opposite of the one stated.

17 By providing a response which is not an answer to the question asked, my daughter intends to direct me away from an unwelcome line of questioning. It is an attempt to flout relevance. Many pragmaticists doubt whether any utterance can ever be irrelevant, as an addressee will always attempt to work out how even an apparently irrelevant utterance, such as this one, is related to what has gone before. Perhaps we should say of Eleanor's contribution to **17** that the relevance is given but not obvious.

18 flouts the maxim of Manner since *current* is ambiguous. *Ahead* is given a particularly literal sense by the television advertisement which shows human-like pylons striding 'ahead' across open country. There are therefore more perspicuous ways of indicating the forward-looking nature of the company than the one chosen. Advertisements and jokes are often 'understanding tests' (Sacks 1974: 346) of this sort.

19, 20 and **21** are flouts on Manner like **18**. In **19** *we have the lead* is ambiguous, with one sense contradicting what is entailed by *cordless*; in **20** the second multiplication sign is used in a less than maximally perspicuous way to represent the lexical item *by* in the phrase *by far*; in **21** the spelling of *fourmost* suggests the number *four* and reminds us that a Land Rover is a four-wheel-drive vehicle.

22 Quantity—tautology.

23–26 Quality—metaphor, overstatement, understatement, rhetorical question.

It's the taste flouts Quantity (insufficient information) and Manner (obscure), and therefore triggers an inference process in which the addressee looks for the likeliest meaning that is relevant in the context that obtains—that the taste is 'good' in the case of something being advertised on television and 'bad' in the case of a school dinner.

(4)

No answers are offered for (1).

2. Here are some tentative suggestions—do they coincide with your ideas?
Well—hedges Quantity;
if you asked me for a straight answer, then I shall say that...in terms of the averages of departments...you would...find that...there...wasn't very much in it one way or the other—the proposition;
as far as we can see—hedges Quality;
looking at it by and large—?hedges Quality, ?intensifies Quantity;
taking one time with another—?intensifies Quantity, ??has truth value;
then—intensifies Relation;
in the final analysis—intensifies Manner;
it is...true to say that—intensifies Quality;
...probably... hedges Quality;
at the end of the day—intensifies Relation;
in general terms—?hedges Quality, ?hedges Manner;
...probably... hedges Quality;
not to put too fine a point on it—?intensifies Relation, ?intensifies Manner;
...probably... hedges Quality;
as far as one can see—hedges Quality;
at this stage—hedges Quantity.

(5)

Examples **5** and **39** are straightforward:

5 Entailment—not less; implicature—not more
39 Entailment—not more; implicature—not less

Do you agree with my judgements on **40** and **41**:

40 Entailment—not less; implicature—not more (in fact she has six because on Fridays she has Tatiana's as well as her own/*in fact she has four because on Fridays Tatiana has hers for her);

41 Entailment—not more; implicature—not less (in fact she eats four because on Fridays Tatiana eats her fish for her/*in fact she eats six because on Fridays she eats Tatiana's as well as her own).

Whatever your opinions, do you agree that my suggested answers are based on the notion that *have* cannot entail less than what you assert you have, and *eat* cannot entail more than you say you eat?

(6)

1. Because **58** appears at the beginning of the academic year and because of the pictorial representation, we infer that W.H. Smith sell everything necessary for study except uniforms. **58′** implies that the videos sold at W.H. Smith are so moving that you will need a handkerchief; and because the advertisement appears just before Christmas, it might also be inferred that if you buy someone a weepie video from W.H. Smith as a present, you will have to go somewhere else to buy them handkerchiefs too. These examples show the non-conventional nature of implicature because the reasoning processes that enabled us to calculate the implicature in **58** will not work algorithmically for **58′**: i.e. you would be wrong to infer that **58′** implies that W.H. Smith sell everything necessary for Christmas except hankies.

2. The implicature is non-conventional in the sense that it varies with the context. If the car was Sue's, B's utterance would imply that she was with Bill, and if it belonged to a friend of Bill's who Sue did not get on with, B's utterance might be taken to imply that Sue was not with Bill.

(7)

Examples **60–62** flout the maxim of Manner and example **63** flouts the maxims of Quality and Manner. In **60**, *clapped out* is a calculated ambiguity implying that John Major's career could be finished. **61** is a deliberately obscure way of drawing attention to the misspelling *neccessary* by highlighting the homophone in *seeing double/double 'c'*. The speaker might be taken to imply that the optician does not inspire confidence. In **62**, the speaker implied that the manufacturer of the fireworks was less than successful by suggesting the brand-name was inappropriate. The speaker is obscure in the sense that he treats the brand-name as a description. In **63** the graffiti suggest that the car is dirty by implying that it is not white. This is an obscure way of recommending that the car should be washed.

(8)

The utterance is complicated by irony; but ignoring that aspect of it, in the case of **64** two conditions need to obtain for the sentence to be true: (a) single men with good fortunes need to be in want of wives and (b) everyone has to be of this opinion. In the case of **64′**, only the first condition needs to be satisfied for the sentence to be true. Thus *it's true that* in **64′** does not add truth value to the utterance, but instead intensifies the Quality maxim.

(9)

The assignment of contrastive or any other non-natural stress typically results in an implicature because the unmarked, most perspicuous realization of the proposition does not occur. **65** implies that other washing-powders may remove dirt but will leave your washing smelling unpleasant. You might like to think of other examples of non-natural stress assignment and consider their effect. This understanding of **65** reminds us that **65′**, which seems to mean only what it says, could in theory have a non-conventional meaning too. Thus we have to infer that it does mean only what it says.

(10)

When he gets to *in*, and although the utterance is not complete, the speaker realizes that what he intends to say will imply that David Smeaton, a BBC reporter, is a prisoner in the gaol on Dartmoor. He therefore uses *rather more precisely* to intensify Quality and to intensify Manner, so that the listeners are assured of the appropriacy of *on*.

(11)
At the most literal level of meaning *I see* means *I am looking and therefore I see*. We often think of *I see* as having the secondary meaning *I understand*. In either case it counts as a pseudo-turn in the interaction which, by not advancing the conversation further through flouting the maxim of Quantity, implies that the speaker is dissatisfied with what has been said and that the other speaker should provide a more satisfactory contribution. Because this use of *I see* always works in this way, it has become conventionalized, and no longer requires an inferencing procedure for the implicature to be recovered.

(12)
68 To those who understand cricket, *England are following on* entails England having scored 200 runs fewer than their opponents and therefore implies that England did not do well in their first innings. The question, then, is whether A's overstatement *that's impossible* is a response to the entailment or the implicature of the preceding utterance. If a response to the entailment, it contradicts B; if a response to the implicature, B is not contradicted (and therefore not insulted). Which do you think A's *that's impossible* responds to?

69 *Even* conventionally implicates that the proposition to which it is attached, in **69** *the Labour Party front bench*, is at one end of a scale. Knowing who the speaker is enables us to work out which end of the scale the Labour Party front bench is at, and further to infer the conversational implicature that the Labour Party front bench is nothing to write home about.

As in **69**, *even* in **70** gives rise to the conventional implicature that the action of bringing a wife into Horley Town Hall is at one end of a scale. Thus *I have not even brought my wife into Horley Town Hall* conversationally implicates that Horley Town Hall is not much to write home about. **70** shows that such implicatures are psychologically real, as the speaker goes on to confirm it by saying *that's what I think of Horley Town Hall*.

71 The book title *My Family and Other Animals* gives rise to the conversational implicature that the author's family are animals (as opposed to humans) and therefore less than human. This suggests that *other* is used to mean different examples (an entailment) of the same type (a conventional implicature) as in *I have another (= an other) one, other girls like herself,* and *the other woman*. So this example is like **69** and **70**, where the conversational implicature is triggered by a conventional implicature.

72 conversationally implicates what **73** entails, that it is the handwriting of others rather than that of the speaker which is never criticized. **73** gives rise to the implicature that the speaker's handwriting is nothing to be proud of, presumably triggered by the greater Quantity of information being conveyed as an entailment than would usually be expected. These examples also show that language is inescapably implicit, since **73** is an attempt to make explicit the implicature in **72**, but in the process it gives rise to a further implicature which is not present in **72**.

(13)

A: Mr Major's at Wincanton today
Implicature: Mr Major = the Prime Minister; Wincanton = the racecourse.
Calculation: these are the most relevant ways to understand the references.

B: Oh is he. I didn't know that
Implicature: *he* refers to Mr Major, the Prime Minister; *oh is he* is an expression of surprise, and not a question.
Calculation: *Mr Major* is the closest/only eligible antecedent and *he* tends to confirm a human referent; there is a conventional implicature associated with *oh* which implies that what has just occurred or been discovered was unexpected and very recent—this suggests that an expression of surprise is a likelier meaning than a challenge expressed through a question.

A: No, the horse, not the Prime Minister
Implicature: B was wrong to take *Mr Major* to refer to the Prime Minister.
Calculation: *The horse* and *Mr Major* are co-referential and this, taken with a mutual understanding of how B had calculated the previous implicature, enable the inference to be drawn that A is indicating that B was wrong to take *Mr Major* to refer to the Prime Minister

B: Oh the grey
Implicature: This counts as disparaging the Prime Minister by suggesting he is grey.
Calculation: B states that the horse is grey. This is not an expected contribution and is therefore likely to mean something else. Mr Major (the PM) is also often referred to as *grey*. Thus although B seems to be saying that Mr Major the horse is grey, he is implying a disparaging view of Mr Major the Prime Minister.

(14)
The subtitler typically (although not invariably) excludes items which do not add truth value to the utterance, such as NOW in 1 and BUT in 3. Maxim hedges like SORT OF THING in 6 and intensifiers like JUST in 11 and 12 are excluded. Another principle is to delete lexical items whose entailments can be recovered as implicatures: good examples are the deletion of BOTH in 2, ALSO in 4, IN BETWEEN in 7, and FOR ME in 30. This also applies to the conventional implicature OH in 19, which must be recovered as a conversational implicature in context. Notice that the auxiliary assertion WHICH WAS LOVELY in 21, which is not vital to the main assertion, is also excluded. The principles guiding deletion of spoken language can be determined by comparing 1, where *didn't you* survives, with 14, where COULDN'T YOU does not. Neither contributes propositional content but, unlike 14, 1 is a genuine question in which *didn't you* is necessary to show the speaker's intention.

These data may suggest that speakers have the option of allowing an implicature to arise or conveying what would have been the implicated meaning explicitly. Earlier (**72** and **73**) we saw that this is not always the case. In these data, the 'explicit' version, *her son and her daughter by her first marriage had BOTH left home*, allows the speaker the option of stressing BOTH, which would then act as a trigger to the addressee, advising them of an implicated meaning to be recovered. One can even think of examples where stress is hardly required, such as 'Tim and Julia went to the cinema together', where *together* seems to trigger the implicature that this is significant in some way beyond the stated meaning. As we saw with **72** and **73**, this analysis suggests that implicitness is a natural and unavoidable property of language. So if I decide to try and make explicit what is an implicature in 'Tim and Julia went to the cinema' (implicature: together) by uttering 'Tim and Julia went to the cinema together', another implicature arises.

(15)
The following are only suggested possible answers, since the implicatures will vary with the context

1 Explicature: I assert that the team referred to won the (football) match; Implicature: variable, but might include, *they did well* or *they did badly*.

2 Explicature: It is the taste that I am speaking of; Implicature: variable but might include, *the taste is good* or *the taste is bad*.

9 Explicature: I assert that smoking damages the health of people such as yourself; Implicature: variable, but might include *Why do you smoke* or *You should stop smoking*.

13 Explicature: I assert that time flies = passes quickly; Implicature, variable, but might include, *Act now* or *Did the event we were talking about take place so long ago*.

63 Explicature: I assert that the object indicated is also available in white; Implicature: variable, but on a white car, *This car needs cleaning*.

(16)
The joke turns on the fact that the implicature of *a husband* in the father's original utterance is a man who is not yet a husband, as opposed to a man who is already a husband. This is clearly the most relevant way to understand *a husband* in this utterance, so that in this case the implicature has nothing to do with Quantity-based scalar implicature. The fact that the addressee must first recover the implicature that arises from the father's use of *a husband* and then from the speaker's shows that it is particular to its context. Horn (1988: 132) cites *I slept in a car* as implicating that the car was not mine, since if it had been I should have said so by saying *I slept in the car* or *I slept in my car* (Quantity) and *I broke a finger yesterday* as implicating that it was mine (the most Relevant understanding). Similarly, *Brian went to a funeral* implicates that it was not his own (the most Relevant understanding). (Notice that we could also treat *a husband* as underdetermined and the appropriate understanding as an explicature.)

(17)
1. In **82** the deictic centre is projected forwards: thus (/wəz/) is the expected realization, since it refers to a past in relation to a forward-projected centre. Because it is more natural to shift the centre than to want to talk about plans that are no longer current, the marked (/wɒz/) is reserved for the latter, i.e. **83**.

2. The unmarked realization of <some> is usually associated with the more expectable non-specific reference and the marked realization with the less expectable specific reference, as **84** and **85** show. In **86** the speaker has a

choice between <some> and <any>. Since <any> does not presuppose the existence of the phrase it determines, it is always non-specific. There is therefore no need for non-specific <some>, so specific <some> appropriates the unmarked realization.

These are important examples, because they show that the phonological form is not in a fixed relationship to meaning.

(18)

1. **88** Implicature: good because loud.

88′ Implicature: both good and loud.

88″ Implicature: various, could include *despite being loud, and loud as a bonus, and loud as was required.*

2. **89** My favourite breakfast is *bacon* and *fried bread* (a logical conjunction)
*What is my favourite breakfast bacon and . . . ;
*Bacon which is my favourite breakfast t and fried bread ('t' = trace of moved item).

90 *You have seen tennis played at Wimbledon* and *I have seen football played in Newcastle* (a logical conjunction).

*What have you seen played at Wimbledon t and I have seen football. . . . ;
*Football which you have seen tennis played at Wimbledon and I have seen played t in Newcastle.

3. **91** and **92** are more difficult to decide about than **89** and **90**. Do you agree with my judgements as set out below?

91 Logical conjunction: *I went to the store* and ( ) *bought some whisky.*
Non-logical conjunction: I *went to the store* and *bought some whisky*

Where did I go t and buy some whisky/What did I go to the store and buy t/The whisky which I went to the store and bought t.

92 Logical conjunction: *I forgot my book* and ( ) *couldn't do my homework.*
Non-logical conjunction: I *forgot my book* and *couldn't do my homework*

?What did I forget t and couldn't do my homework/*What did I forget my book and couldn't do t/*My homework, which I forgot my book and couldn't do t.

Implicatures: **91** the whisky was bought in the store; **92** I couldn't do my homework because I forgot my book.

(19)

all the (.) we—he decides to be more implicit and leave the hearer to recover the implicature that *we* is used exclusively to refer to the speaker and his fellow students.

only one person—he decides to be more explicit in choosing *only*, perhaps because he does not trust the addressee to understand that not enough people presented their work unless he adds *only*.

in the end—he decides to be explicit; again, we could speculate as to what this extra degree of explicitness tells us about how the speaker rates his experience. It seems to give rise to the implicature that the activity being described had little face validity for the students.

I think that was something that will help me—was something that makes explicit what would otherwise be implicit, but it is so easily recoverable an explicature that you wonder why the speaker feels it necessary to be so very explicit.

when I compare my (.) the things I had written down with hers (.) what the girl said—the speaker is very exact here and draws a distinction between the written form of his work and the spoken form in which he perceived hers. His repair *my → the things I had written down* is quite natural. But then why does he make himself so explicit with *hers*?

It is salutary to realize that we evaluate people and their relationships to us and others to some extent on the basis of the degree to which their talk is implicit.

4 Presupposition

(1)
2 The speaker has paid for something and tendered more than the sum required; the addressee is going to give change amounting to more than twenty pence; the addressee will be sympathetic to a request to give the change in particular denominations and has a variety of coins available.

3 Some people will want to smoke; the person who wrote the notice does not want these people to smoke; these people will be sympathetic to a request not to smoke.

(2)
1. **8** My son exists/existed (definite description); the speaker had a husband before (*second* is iterative).

9 My varlet exists (definite description); the speaker was unarmed before (*again* is iterative); the speaker had armed (*un-* presupposes an action had been completed which is now to be reversed).

10 The three referred to had met before (*again* is iterative) and will meet again (question introduced by *when*).

11 Someone keeps the gate (question introduced by *who*); *the gate* exists (definite description).

12 Someone is there (question introduced by *who*).

13 The king exists (definite description); the king escaped our hands (embedded question introduced by *how*).

14 The food of love exists (definite description); the musicians were playing before (*play on* is a continuing state description, and closely related to iteratives).

2. **15** Entailment(s): Sue has used the telephone to convey a message;
Conventional presupposition(s): Sue exists; her telephone calls exist; she had made telephone calls before;
Pragmatic presupposition(s): These might include the notion that there is some point in saying this, that the addressee will understand it and be interested in it, etc.;

Implicature(s): These might include the implicature that her telephone calls do her no credit, or that making a call was predictable.

(3)
16 and **18** also presuppose that the doctor exists (definite description) and that I visited the doctor, **17** also presupposes that my son exists (definite description) and that my son became a faster runner than me. These examples show that temporal clauses too give rise to presuppositions.

(4)
Former Prime Ministers exist/existed (*the*).
There has been at least one successor to the Prime Minister referred to (*former*).
The former Prime Minister was barely tolerated by the Queen (*who* + non-restrictive relative).
The Queen exists/existed (*the*).
The former Prime Minister stopped taking notes (*regrets*).
The former Prime Minister once took notes (*stopped*).
The former Prime Minister allowed exports to Iraq (*when* + temporal clause).
Iraq exists (definite description).
One of the former Prime Ministers was a difficult person to accept (*tolerated*).
('The former PM was (not) tolerated by the Queen' has the same presupposition.)

(5)
These are my suggested examples—are yours as good, or better?

Temporal: I chickened out before I got married;
Factive: The Prince never ignores the fact that his plants like being talked to;
Definite descriptions: The straightforward pragmatics book can never be written;
Change-of-state: The second time I began to learn Russian I found it even harder.

(6)
These are my suggested examples—are yours as good, or better?

7' I wonder what you are thinking, or even if you are thinking (suspension)

12' Whenever I see the curtains move in my bedroom, I shout 'Who's there?', and in a way I half hope that one day there will be someone there (?suspension/?cancellation)

16' I began jogging after a visit to the doctor, although to be honest I'd jogged a bit before then (cancellation)

20' Her successor managed to win the election that followed—not that it was a problem given the opposition (cancellation)

27' It was the Scots who invented whisky—in as far as anyone can be said to have invented it (suspension)

28' If you had sent me a Christmas card last year, I would have sent you one this year. As you got one from me this year, you must have sent me one last year (cancellation)

(7)
The potential presuppositions pre-empted metalinguistically are
7' you are thinking about something
12' there is someone there
16' I had not jogged before my visit to the doctor
20' winning the election was difficult (metalinguistic negation)
27' someone invented whisky
28' you sent me a Christmas card last year

5 Speech acts: language as action

(1)
3–5 You will have listed lots of situations and speech acts. One of my favourites is the contrast between the use of *sorry* to invite the speaker to repeat their utterance and the use of *I'm sorry* with an accompanying scowl to dare the speaker to do this. Here the same proposition seems to be used for two entirely opposite purposes.

(2)
Examples of explicitly performative utterances that are often cited include
I second the motion
I name this ship QE2
I promise you won't regret it
I bet you five pounds you can't eat a kilo of chocolate
I refuse to accept your explanation
I apologize

(3)
The counter clerk takes *do you sell postage stamps* as an indirect speech act requesting a stamp or stamps. In fact Mr Logic asks whether one of the felicity conditions on buying stamps obtains, from which she infers that he wishes to buy some. Whilst she responds to the illocutionary force of his utterance, his 'logic' consists in treating it only as a locutionary act. The absurdity of this strategy is confirmed by the question mark that appears over her head when he does this a second time. Mr Logic could hardly have calculated the perlocutionary effect of treating the address term *smart arse* as a mistaken attempt to use his name.

(4)
1. *Could we have some more coffee* is a conventionally indirect way of requesting. Notice that there is a scale of politeness which includes *might* (most formal), *may*, *could*, and *can* (least formal). This kind of politeness encodes greater distance between speaker and hearer as you move up the scale. She obviously felt that he was not quite formal enough with the waitress, as indicated by *you should say may we*. When challenged, she tries to justify her objection to *could* by appealing to its literal meaning. This is really more or less beside the point, since he uses the literal meaning to refer to a felicity condition on having more coffee. Moreover, her preferred

replacement, *may*, merely makes reference to another felicity condition, whether it is permissible to have more coffee. She is quite right to protest that he didn't mean it literally, but then if he had used *may* to begin with, who is to say that she would not have protested that 'it could mean' *have you got permission*? In fact they are just having a quarrel, which followed from her not liking the way he was encoding his attitude to the waitress.

Later she made a lot of fuss and said she could not eat toast, and so asked for some bread. But when it came, she did not like the look of that either and ended up eating toast. This enabled him to get his own back with the observation: *you had a piece of toast in the end*, clearly an indirect way of scoring a point.

2. You are supposed to say *no* with fall–rise intonation, which counts as inviting the assistant to tell you. But it was late, I was tired and thinking of sorting the children out when I got home, and why should I have heard of their miserable oil anyway, and so I rather rudely said *no* with falling intonation, to which the assistant replied *I see I can't interest you*. This interesting example shows how the same lexical item can have quite opposite illocutionary forces and perlocutionary effects depending on the intonation pattern assigned to it. A week or two later I stopped again at the same garage. There was a different assistant this time, but she tried just the same utterance on me. I didn't feel keen to go through the charade of fall–rise *no*, nor did I want to repeat the rudeness of falling *no*, so I decided to try *yes* instead. It had just the same perlocutionary effect as falling *no*. Why didn't I think of it the first time!

3. Not only are the formulas interesting here (e.g. my first utterance counts as an indirect instruction to stop smoking) but the sequential properties of the three interactions are very similar: I begin with information about the smoking status of the location, which is inevitably responded to with a checking question. Either these two turns are sufficient to bring the smoking to an end or, more usually, I have to make some broader comment about smoking in the area, which is sufficient to ensure compliance with the illocutionary purpose of my first utterance. These data show how a series of speech acts in a predictable sequential structure constitute a recognizable speech event.

(5)
1. What about: *Let me tell you that naturally I hate music* or *May I tell you that naturally I hate music*. Both function as assertions.

2. What about: *this comes as a surprise—you never studied pragmatics before*. This functions as a question. It is easy to find examples with *this comes as a surprise* + imperative (e.g. this comes as surprise—tell me again), but I can't think of any examples where *this* and the proposition contained in the imperative utterance are co-referential—can you? If I could, I'm sure the utterance would function as a question.

(6)
These are my suggested answers. Are yours comparable?

37 This is a Building Society

Implicature: we do not lend money for buying cars;
Speech act: refusal to meet a request.

38 Not at all

Implicature: this contradiction is supportive;
Speech act: invitation to describe symptoms.

39 I don't know what to say

Implicature: there are no words sufficient to convey my feelings;
Speech act: expression of sympathy or condolence.

6 Talk

(1)
Some suggestions follow. You will probably have found other, equally good,
examples of your own.

1. B: (1.5) well we're not British Rail agents so I don't know the differ-
    ence (1.4–5)

So projects the imminent end by indicating the beginning of the final, conse-
quential part of the sentence.

2. B: Ron with the shuttle saver (1.25)

The term of address selects the speaker.

3. A: (0.2) and h// and*
    B: //((   ))*
    A: how often do they go (1.38–40)

A has to compete for the turn.

4. M: (0.8) yeh (1.26)

M delays confirming that he has been included in the conversation. By virtue
of being an incomplete proposition, the previous turn (*Ron with the shuttle
saver*) had asked him to confirm the openness of the channel of communication before B resumed her turn. Perhaps he resents B's strategy. Or
perhaps he is too important to answer B immediately.

5. B: we're not British Rail //agents*
    A: //you're* not agents I see (1.96–7)

A does not want B to complete a turn which contains a proposition that A
has earlier categorized as an unacceptable contribution.

(2)
1. First-pair part of an adjacency pair:
A: are you guaranteed a seat (1.22)

2. Use of address term:
B: Ron what happens if he wants the last flight (1.75)

3. One-word or short *wh*-phrase clarification request:
B: what weekend (1.14)

4. Clarification request involving repetition:
B: that's a saver (0.7) burit it's a standby
A: a standby (1.19–20)

5. Tag used as an exit technique:

B: and coming back they er (3.4) er (0.4) you're coming back Sunday aren't you (1.63–4)

6. Place where there is a natural next-turn taker:

B: what happens if he wants the last fl//ight*

A: //if I*want to come back on the//last flight on the Sunday night*

B: //((   )) they don't put* on an extra plane do they

→M: (1.4) well theoretically if it's full they're supposed to put a back-up plane on (1.79–85)

(3)

1. Long single-unit turn:

A: ah ha (.) so it's forty either way and it starts at seven-forty on Saturday from London and nine-forty from Edinburgh on Sunday (.) until what time on Sunday night (1.67–9)

The absence of a verb in the *until* 'clause' indicates that this is a single unit.

2. Short single-unit turn:

A: oh I see (1.6)

3. Long turn resulting from lack of next speaker self-selection:

A: Nineteen-forty (.) now what happens if you turn up for the nineteen-forty flight and they get you on any of the next two does that mean Monday (1.5) or do they guarantee to do something about it on Sunday night (1.71–4)

4. There are many pauses, especially while B looks up the information which she needs to complete her turn. Although there are no lapses because this is an event with a clearly defined purpose rather than incipient talk, there are a number of what might be termed potential lapses, where the initiative rests with A but he seems undecided as to how to proceed. For example,

M: in theory (2.1) whether or not it works in practice I don't know

A: (3.0) now if I buy a ticket from you then it costs I I pay you a hundred pounds //(.) n* (1.87–90)

(4)

Three-part turn:

B: (13.0) well there's a shuttle service (0.4) um (.) sixty pounds one way (2.5) er (2.3) when do you want to go (1.11–12)

well is oriented to the preceding turn and *when do you want to go* to the succeeding turn.

7 Politeness phenomena and the politeness status of language in use

(1)

Some of the striking politeness features of these texts include:

Text A

1 The redundant *I know* is a way of expressing empathy; *but it was very helpful to me* gives a reason for imposing; *I appreciate* is an overt expression of gratitude and *what you did*, because it is verbal rather than a nominal such

as *your action/your help*, is strongly on record; *I feel indebted to you* makes a small act of assistance look more than it is. Going on record as incurring a debt is very rarely meant sincerely in a non-debt culture like Britain. Why does the writer say *for agreeing to register* rather than *for registering*—does this imply that I had any real choice in the matter? (I did not feel good when I got this letter. I thought it was over the top.)

Text B

This letter makes use of the powerful *we*. The level of formality also distances the writer from the reader, so that she uses *we acknowledge receipt of* rather than *thank you for* and *regarding the above* instead of *your flights*. Imagine I get home from work and my wife tells me the washing machine isn't working (i.e. implies I should do something about it) and I reply *we were extremely concerned to learn of the problems you encountered, but trust you will appreciate that we are unable to comment before an investigation has been made*. Well, you would not be reading this now because I'd have been permanently hospitalized long ago. This sentence is a good illustration of the distancing effects of politeness. We talk to our friends in plain language (*as soon as we find out what happened*) and to those we know less well in a more formal register (*as soon as we are in possession of the facts*). The use of *would* in the conditional sentence (which is prohibited in pedagogic grammars for learners of English as a second language) expresses a remote possibility and therefore tries to be as non-coercive as possible. Apology is two-sided, in the sense that it not only costs the apologizer something to apologize, especially when it is *most sincere*, but it obliges the recipient to accept it. This imposition is moderated by referring to it as a *kind* act. (When I got this letter, I did not expect to get much out of the promised follow-up letter because too much distance was already being placed between the airline and myself. But I did enjoy the letter because it contained a most unfortunate typing error: the typist hit the key to the left of the one aimed at in the last letter of *grateful*.)

Text C

The employer is the powerful *we* whose actions are mostly expressed verbally rather than nominally (*we place*, *we provide*, *would appreciate*, but *a value*), thus stressing that the employer is the agent of action; the employee is a powerless *temporary worker* whose actions are expressed entirely nominally (*workers*, *opinions*, *comments*). It is unclear what the employer's underlying motives are in asking the employee to complete the survey form that came with this letter, although a reason is given and stressed with the use of *therefore*; *would appreciate* invites or coerces the employee to earn the employer's gratitude. (My wife did not fill the questionnaire in.)

Text D

Although purporting to address residents in an impersonal way by suggesting a general rule (a politeness strategy), the illocutionary targets are casual non-residents who are being told indirectly that drinks are not served after 10.30. This is done rather crudely: the verbal *drink* often has the connotation of drinking to excess. *Must* expresses an on-record imposition of obligation without any redress. (If I had been a resident, I might have been quite pleased to see that riff-raff were to be chucked out at 10.30. There is a certain directness about this notice, which does not treat addressees and illocutionary targets as quite as important as they might like—the inclusion of some formula like *respectfully reminded* might make them feel better.)

Text E
This postcard, which we get all too frequently where we live, brings you very bad news (no water for several hours) but is set out to look more like an invitation to a Buckingham Palace garden party. There is an attempt to minimize the inconvenience with the warning that one possible course of action would be *inadvisable*; *dangerous* might be a more accurate term. Both of the last two sentences are impersonal. (Most people find this an acceptable way of conveying unpalatable news.)

(2)
1. **11** treats you as an equal by claiming kinship (*mate*). The elliptical structure *Got* (rather than *have you got*) implies closeness.

12 begins with an apology (*I'm sorry*), admits the inconvenience caused (*bother*), and is pessimistic about whether the request will be met (*you haven't by any chance . . . have you*).

The speaker of **11** encodes much less distance between themselves and the addressee than the speaker of **12** does. I might make the assumption that the speaker of **11** was 'working-class' and the speaker of **12** 'middle-class', since it is in the interests of those who suppose themselves to be 'under' to claim equality and those who suppose themselves to be 'over' to try to maintain distance between themselves and others. This is why the kind of politeness middle-class parents teach their children is like that of **12** rather than that of **11**, hoping by that means to give their children a head-start in life.

2. **13** is a direct order, made all the stronger by the use of *up*, which has the effect of making the verb *eat* perfective, i.e. altering its meaning to 'eat till you have finished'.

14 is an indirect way of telling me to eat.

In **13** I show how much more powerful I am than my addressee, and in **14** the speaker shows how much less powerful she is than me.

3. I don't know what you said. I might say something like

15 Would it be all right if I left Honey with you on Wednesday morning— I'd like to go shopping by myself for a change

16 I don't know how to put this. I don't suppose you could do me an immense favour, but we've been invited to stay with the Trolls on Saturday night and you know how they hate babies. I don't suppose there's any chance that we could possibly leave Howler with you is there. I can let you have everything you'll need

What is being requested in **15** is much less of an imposition than what is being requested in **16**.

Taken together, these three pairs of utterances show that the distance between speakers, the extent to which their power-statuses are equal or unequal, and the degree to which one speaker imposes on the other all affect the way we talk to each other.

(3)
You will have been able to assign some of the comments made in Checking

Understanding (1) to positive and negative strategies. Here are some more suggestions:

Text A

Positive politeness: *I know it must have made a very difficult day even more fraught* (writer can see the world from addressee's perspective); *it was very helpful to me* (gives a reason for imposing).

Negative politeness: *I appreciate what you did and I feel indebted to you* (goes on record as incurring a debt).

Text B

Positive politeness: *We were extremely concerned to learn of the problems you encountered* (expression of sympathy); *you will appreciate that we are unable to comment* (asserts a common perspective).

Negative politeness: *receipt* (without the definite article) (an impersonalizing strategy); *we would be grateful if you would...* (does not presume addressee's compliance); *kindly accept our most sincere apologies for the inconvenience caused* (apology).

Text C

Positive politeness: *we place a high value on our temporary workers' opinions* (expression of approval); *we . . . would appreciate your comments* (shows interest in addressee); *therefore* (gives a reason for imposing).

Text D

Negative politeness: *Residents wishing to drink...* (imposition stated as a general rule).

Text E

Negative politeness: INTERRUPTION OF WATER SUPPLY (the problem stated nominally without any apparent agent); *it would be inadvisable* and *it is essential* (the writer impersonalizes).

(4)

Here are two suggestions:

1. If a non-resident casual drinker were to ask if Text D was aimed at them, this could always be denied.

2. In Text E, *it would be inadvisable* is an understatement. So if an addressee were to ask whether it was dangerous or even not permitted to draw hot water, the writer could always assert that they had merely said that it would be inadvisable.

8 Relevance theory and degrees of understanding

(1)

These are my suggestions—yours may be different but equally plausible. If B had inferred the intended explicature of *at the weekend*, she would have understood the time A was referring to. Being unaware of the context in which B was working, A did not have the contextual resources (?or cognitive abilities) to understand B's non-deictic use of *weekend*. Because of the different contexts in which each is operating, the most accessible interpretation of *weekend* for A is the least accessible for B, and vice versa.

(2)
A two-stage process is required to understand this part of the joke. Firstly the meaning of *there* in *I nearly got stuck there* must be explicated as *in that style of speaking*. This enables us to recover the implicature that camp style comes too naturally to the teller for his comfort.

(3)
Implicated premise: there were two (elderly) people in his grandfather's bedroom; Implicated conclusion: his grandfather was having a good time.

(4)
1. That *she's doing very well* can only be seen to be ironic when what follows the pause is understood—therefore the first-pass reading has to be rejected and an extra processing burden is placed on the audience.

2. The non-standard use of English is regarded as humorous by the regular native-speaker audience, but the non-native-speaker experimental audience first have to identify it as non-standard (no mean feat); even if they do this satisfactorily, they lack the native-speaker context in which it is comic because incongruous.

3. So *you'll be forgiving* has to be understood as treating *forgive* as dynamic rather than stative; for speakers of languages where there is no co-occurrence constraint such as the *be + *ing*/stative verb constraint in English, it is by no means intuitive that *forgive* is a stative verb.

4. The audience needs to conclude that the speaker must have meant 'bad English' rather than *bad language*, 'grammar' rather than *grandmaster*, and 'brushing up' rather than *touching up*. And the process of replacing the spoken items with native-speaker-like ones requires *bad language* to be processed as an idiom and the 'right sense' of *touching up* to be identified.

5. As well as the innuendo associated with the 'wrong sense' of *touching up*, there is also the association with painting, so that *my grandmaster needs touching up* maintains a consistent, if unlikely, inappropriate meaning.

The processing effort required to recover all these meanings is very considerable. Did you recover all of them when you attempted the activity?

(5)
1. Explicature and implicature: An audience must explicate *to put your suit on with a shovel*. My experimental audience had assumed that the speaker had a shovel with him at the time he put his suit on, rather than the more grotesque notion that his suit had been shovelled on in stages like snow. Without the right explicature, the implicature that he looked very untidy indeed cannot be inferred.

2. Hearer resources: Unless an audience already knows that Patrick Moore is renowned for his untidy appearance, it is very difficult to explicate *to put your suit on with a shovel* in the required way, or to understand that *admiring a photo of Patrick Moore* is ironical.

3. Recovering meanings: Given sufficiently long to consider all the ways in which *to put your suit on with a shovel* might be explicated, a hearer would presumably recover the exotic explicature intended here. But without

knowledge about Patrick Moore and given the unexpectable nature of the explicated utterance, there is not sufficient opportunity to process it.

4. Accessibility: No relevant explicature can be recovered when the effort of trying to recover a relevant meaning outweighs the benefit of recovering it.

5. Garden-path utterances: *Admiring a photo of Patrick Moore* is an understanding test to the extent that not all audiences would be expected to treat it as ironical and infer that Patrick Moore's appearance evokes a comic rather than an admiring response. Indeed, a hearer would need to know about Patrick Moore's appearance to infer what they already knew, that he is of untidy appearance.

9 Speech events

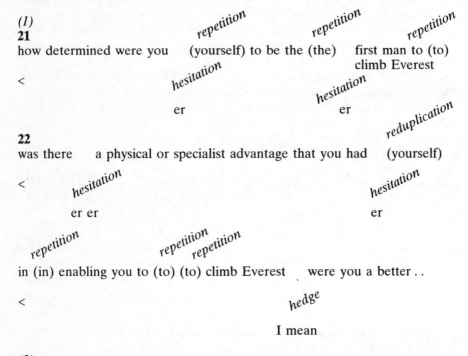

(1)
21
how determined were you   (yourself) to be the (the)   first man to (to) climb Everest

er   er

22
was there   a physical or specialist advantage that you had   (yourself)

er er   er

in (in) enabling you to (to) (to) climb Everest   were you a better . .

I mean

(2)
23 *if I remember arightly was it*—the parenthetical question is used as a request for reassurance that the right question is being asked; *did you not*—this provides the interviewee with a let-out and indicates that the questioner thinks he already knows the answer to the question he is asking, thus flouting the Quality maxim.

24 the reduplication suggests that the question is tentative.

25 *what* suggests a question is coming, although it is immediately followed by the repair *you I mean you had to*; the tag *had you* turns a statement into a question, so that a suggested answer is already provided for the interviewee.

26 *what frightens you* is a question that threatens the positive face of the addressee. So the fact that a face-threatening question is coming is signalled a long way ahead, and the threat is minimized by the interviewer typing his question as *daft*.

(3)
Some suggestions are given below which you can add to yours or compare yours with (A = interviewer, B = interviewee):

34
B: *very lucky epoch*—elevated description; *I think*—hedge; *in a curious way*—hedge;
A: *yes*—agreement marker preceding heavily hedged disagreement; *I suppose*—hedge; *also*—hedge; *of course*—hedge; *I mean*—hedge; *sort of*—hedge; *compared to today*—sets critical comment in limiting context; *what's the word*—allows interviewee to choose word; *um*—hesitation;
A: *would that not be so*—seeking agreement, with pessimistic *would* and *not*; *aren't we*—appeal for confirmation.

35
A: *but*—conventionally implicates a contrast, conversationally implicates that the contrasted element is of minor significance; *now*—by stating explicitly what could be implied conversationally, the interviewer implies that the interviewee is very active for his age; *aren't you*—tag inviting agreement;
B: *yes I am yes I am*—the reduplication with which the interviewee confirms his age indicates that he does not feel threatened by the awkwardness of the topic;
A: *are you still*—the conventional implicature associated with *still*, that being healthy is surprising at this age, invites a negative answer to the question *are you still in (good) health*; hence the interviewer repairs and substitutes a declarative with an elevated description (*rude health*) for the intended interrogative.

References

Alexander, J.C., Giesen, B., Munch, R. and Smelser, N. (eds) (1987). *The macro–micro link*. Berkeley: University of California Press.
Atkinson, J.M., and Heritage, J. C. (eds) (1984). *Structures of social action*. Cambridge: Cambridge University Press.
Atkinson, M., Kilby, D.A. and Roca, I. (1988). *Foundations of General Linguistics*, 2nd edn. London: Allen and Unwin.
Atlas J., and Levinson, S.C. (1981). '*It*-clefts, informativeness, and logical form', in Cole (1981: 1–61).
Austin, J.L. (1962). *How to do things with words*. Oxford: Clarendon Press.
—— (1970). *Philosophical papers*. Oxford: Oxford University Press.
—— (1971). 'Performative-constative', in Searle (1971: 13–22).
Bauman, R., and Sherzer, J. (eds) (1974). *Explorations in the ethnography of speaking*. Cambridge: Cambridge University Press.
Bever, T.G., Katz, J. and Langendoen, D.T. (eds) (1976). *An integrated theory of linguistic ability*. New York: Crowell.
Blakemore, D. (1992). *Understanding utterances*. Oxford: Blackwell.
Brown, P. and Levinson, S.C. (1978). 'Universals in language usage: politeness phenomena', in Goody (1978: 56–311); reprinted with new introduction and revised bibliography as
—— (1987). *Politeness: some universals in language usage*. Cambridge: Cambridge University Press.
Burton-Roberts, N. (1989). *The limits to debate*. Cambridge: Cambridge University Press.
Carston, R. (1988). 'Implicature, explicature, and truth-theoretic semantics', in Kempson (1988: 155–81); reprinted in Davis (1991: 33–51).
Chomsky, N. (1976). *Reflections on language*. Glasgow: Fontana.
—— (1980). *Rules and representations*. Oxford: Blackwell.
—— (1986). *Knowledge of language: its nature, origin, and use*. New York: Praeger.
Cole, P. (ed.) (1978). *Syntax and semantics 9: Pragmatics*. New York: Academic Press.
—— (ed.) (1981). *Radical pragmatics*. New York: Academic Press.
—— and Morgan, J.L. (eds) (1975). *Syntax and semantics 3: Speech acts*. New York: Academic Press.
Comrie, B. (1976). 'Linguistic politeness axes: speaker–addressee, speaker–reference, speaker–bystander', *Pragmatics Microfiche* 1/7.

Crystal, D., and Davy, D. (1969). *Investigating English style*. London: Longman.

Davis, S. (ed.) (1991). *Pragmatics: a reader*. Oxford: Oxford University Press.

Duranti, A., and Goodwin, C. (1992). *Rethinking context*. Cambridge: Cambridge University Press.

Gazdar, G. (1979). *Pragmatics: implicature, presupposition, and logical form*. New York: Academic Press.

Glover, K.D. (1995). 'A prototype view of context and linguistic behaviour', *Journal of Pragmatics* 19.2.

Goody, E.N. (ed.) (1978). *Questions and politeness*. Cambridge: Cambridge University Press.

Green, G.M. (1989). *Pragmatics and natural language understanding*. Hillsdale, NJ: Laurence Erlbaum Associates.

Grice, H.P. (1967a). William James lectures: 'Logic and conversation', in Cole and Morgan (1975: 41–58) and Davis (1991: 305–15).

—— (1967b). William James lectures: 'Further notes on logic and conversation', in Cole (1978: 113–28).

—— (1968). 'Utterer's meaning, sentence-meaning, and word-meaning', *Foundations of Language* 4: 1–18; reprinted in Searle (1971: 54–70) and Davis (1991: 65–76).

Grundy, P. (1989 and 1991). 'Obviously, natural language, maxim hedges, x-bar syntax—OK?', *Linguistica Silesiana* 10 and 12.

—— (1992). 'Relevant to whom: the role of pragmatics in defining linguistic communities', in F.J.H. Dols (ed.), *Pragmatic grammar components*. Tilburg: Tilburg University Press.

—— (1994). 'Context–learner context', in P. Franklin and H. Purschel (eds), *Intercultural communication in institutional settings*. Frankfurt: Peter Lang.

Gu, Y. (1990). 'Politeness phenomena in modern Chinese'. *Journal of Pragmatics* 14/2: 237–57.

Hall, E. (1976). *Beyond culture*. Garden City, NY: Anchor Press.

Hanks, W.F. (1992). 'The indexical ground of deictic reference', in Duranti and Goodwin (1992: 43–76).

Harman, G.H. (ed.) (1974). *On Noam Chomsky: critical essays*. New York: Anchor Books.

Harnish, R.M. (1976). 'Logical form and implicature', in Bever *et al.* (1976: 464–79) and Davis (1991: 316–64).

Hawkins, J.A. (1978). *Definiteness and indefiniteness: a study in reference and grammaticality prediction*. London: Croom Helm.

Heritage, J. (1984). *Garfinkel and ethnomethodology*. Cambridge: Polity Press.

Hofstede, G.H. (1980). *Culture's consequences*. Beverly Hills: Sage.

Holmes, J. (1986). 'Compliments and compliment responses in New Zealand English', *Anthropological Linguistics* 28: 485–508.

Hopper, P.J. and Traugott, E.C. (1993). *Grammaticalization*. Cambridge: Cambridge University Press.

Horn, L. (1972). *On the semantic properties of the logical operators in English*. Mimeo: Indiana University Linguistics Club.

—— (1984). 'Toward a new taxonomy for pragmatic inference: Q-based and R-based implicature', in Schiffrin (1984: 11–42).

—— (1985). 'Metalinguistic negation and pragmatic ambiguity', *Language* 61/1.

—— (1988). 'Pragmatic theory', in the *Cambridge Survey*, Vol. 1: 113–45. Cambridge: Cambridge University Press.

—— (1989). *A natural history of negation*. Chicago: University of Chicago Press.

Kaplan, D. (1978). 'On the logic of demonstratives', *Journal of Philosophical Logic* 8: 81–98; reprinted in Davis (1991: 137–45).

Karttunen, L. and Peters, S. (1979). 'Conventional implicature', in Oh and Dinneen (1979: 1–56).

Kasper, G. (1990). 'Linguistic politeness: current research issues', *Journal of Pragmatics* 14/2: 193–218.

Kelly, O.J.G. (1984). 'Language and culture: an ethnomethodological approach to Sara-Kaba society'. Unpub. MA dissertation, University of Durham.

Kempson, R.M. (ed.) (1988). *Mental representations: the interface between language and reality*. Cambridge: Cambridge University Press.

Kiparsky, P., and Kiparsky, C. (1971). 'Fact', in Steinberg and Jakobovits (1971: 345–69).

Lakoff, G. (1971). 'Presupposition and relative well-formedness', in Steinberg and Jakobovits (1971).

Lakoff, R. (1972). 'Language in context', *Language* 48: 907–27.

—— (1973). 'The logic of politeness: or minding your P's and Q's', *Papers from the ninth regional meeting of the CL*. Chicago: CLS.

Leech, G.N. (1983). *Principles of Pragmatics*. Harlow: Longman.

Levinson, S.C. (1979). 'Activity types', *Linguistics* 17: 365–99.

—— (1983). *Pragmatics*. Cambridge: Cambridge University Press.

Loveday, L. (1984). 'Pitch prominence and sexual role: an exploratory investigation into the pitch correlates of English and Japanese politeness formulae'. *Language and Speech* 24: 71–89.

Matsumoto, Y. (1988). 'Reexamination of the universality of face: politeness phenomena in Japanese', *Journal of Pragmatics* 12: 403–26.

—— (1989). 'Politeness and conversational universals—observations from Japanese', *Multilingua* 8: 207–22.

McCawley, J.D. (1981). *Everything that linguists have always wanted to know about logic*. Oxford: Blackwell.

Mey, J.L. (1993). *Pragmatics: an introduction*. Oxford: Blackwell.

Morgan, J.L. (1978). 'Two types of convention in indirect speech acts', in Cole (1978: 261–80) and Davis (1991: 242–53).

Nwoye, O.G. (1992). 'Linguistic politeness and sociocultural variation of the notion of face', *Journal of Pragmatics* 16: 309–28.

Oh, C.-K. and Dinneen, D.A. (eds) (1979). *Syntax and semantics* 11: *Presupposition*. New York: Academic Press.

Ross, J.R. (1967). 'Constraints on variables in syntax', in Harman (1974: 165–200).

—— (1975). 'Where to do things with words', in Cole and Morgan (1975: 233–56).

Russell, B. (1905). 'On denoting', *Mind* 14: 479–93.

Sacks, H. (1974). 'An analysis of the course of a joke's telling in conversation', in Bauman and Sherzer (1974: 337–53).

——, Schegloff, E.A. and Jefferson, G. (1974). 'A simplest systematics for the organization of turn-taking in conversation', *Language* 50/4: 696–735; reprinted in Schenkein (1978: 7–55), with changes.

Sadock, J.M. (1974). *Toward a linguistic theory of speech acts*. New York: Academic Press.

Schegloff, E.A. (1987). 'Between micro and macro: context and other connections', in Alexander *et al.* (1987: 207–34).

—— (1992). 'In another context', in Duranti and Goodwin (1992: 191–228).

—— and Sacks, H. (1973). 'Opening up closings', *Semiotica* 7/4: 289–327.

Schenkein, J. (ed.) (1978). *Studies in the organization of conversational interaction*. New York: Academic Press.

Schiffrin, D. (ed.) (1984). *Meaning, form, and use in context: linguistic applications*. Washington, DC: Georgetown University Press.

Schmerling, S.F. (1972). 'Apparent counterexamples to the coordinate structure constraint', *Studies in the Linguistic Sciences* 2/1.

—— (1975). 'Asymmetric conjunction and rules of conversation', in Cole and Morgan (1975: 211–32).

Searle, J.R. (1965). 'What is a speech act?', in M. Black (ed.), *Philosophy in America* (1965); London: Unwin, Hyman (1965: 221–39) and Davis (1991: 254–64).
—— (1969). *Speech acts*. Cambridge: Cambridge University Press.
—— (ed.) (1971). *Philosophy of language*. Oxford: Oxford University Press.
—— (1975). 'Indirect speech acts', in Cole and Morgan (1975: 59–82).
—— (1979). *Expression and meaning*. Cambridge: Cambridge University Press.
Sperber, D. and Wilson, D. (1986). *Relevance: communication and cognition*. Oxford: Blackwell.
Stalnaker, R.C. (1987). *Inquiry*. Cambridge, Mass.: MIT Press.
Stapa, S.H. (1986). 'Code switching among Malay–English bilinguals'. Unpub. MA dissertation, University of Durham.
Steinberg, D. and Jakobovits, L. (1971). *Semantics*. Cambridge: Cambridge University Press.
Strawson, P.F. (1952). *Introduction to logical theory*. London: Methuen.
Tarski, A. (1944). 'The semantic conception of truth', *Philosophy and Phenomenological Research* 4: 341–75; reprinted in Tarski, *Logic, semantics and metamathematics*. London: Oxford University Press, 1956.
Zimmerman, D.H. and Boden, D. (eds) (1991). *Talk and social structure: studies in ethnomethodology and conversation analysis*. Cambridge: Polity Press.

Glossary

activity type (or speech event) a goal-directed, culturally recognizable routine (Levinson, 1979).

adjacency pair a fundamental unit of talk consisting of a sequence of two paired units produced by different speakers so that the first triggers an appropriate second. Examples include greeting + greeting, invitation + acceptance/refusal (Schegloff and Sacks, 1973).

anaphora a reference to a previous item, or 'antecedent', in a discourse.

communication the act of conveying a meaning from one party to another.

context any relevant element of the social structure. Context may impinge on or be created by the use of language.

contextual resource the term Sperber and Wilson (1986) use to describe the knowledge schema(ta) required by a hearer in order to understand an utterance.

conventional meaning a meaning associated with a particular morpheme, lexical item, or structure. Most conventional meanings contribute to the truth-conditions of the sentence of which they are a part, although there are conventional meanings without truth value. For example, *well* has the conventional meaning that what follows is a dispreferred contribution (i.e. not quite what the hearer was hoping for): this meaning, although conventionally associated with *well*, has no truth value.

conversation a series of utterances exchanged between two or more speakers, typically of comparable status, which follow a regular pattern of turn-taking.

cooperative principle the central presumption underlying Grice's theory of conversational implicature (1967a and b) which enjoins speakers to make relevant, expectable contributions.

defeasibility the term used to describe the cancellability status of a meaning. Some meanings are defeasible (e.g. that I have only one child in *I have a child*), others are not defeasible (e.g. that I have at least one child in *I have a child*).

deixis the property of a restricted set of demonstratives such that their reference is determined in relation to the point of origin of the utterance in which they occur. Examples include *I, here*, and *now*.

E-language, I-language a distinction drawn by Chomsky (1986) between language which is externalized (E) and internalized knowledge of language (I).

entailment a meaning that is always associated with an expression so that on every occasion when the expression occurs the meaning occurs. For example, I can never say that one football team 'beat' another without entailing that the first team scored at least one goal more than the second.

explicature   a term used by Sperber and Wilson (1986) to describe the logical form of a sentence whose indeterminacies have been resolved, typically by a process of inference.

face   a person's sense of self-esteem (positive face) and desire to determine their own course of action (negative face) postulated by Brown and Levinson (1978) as the psychological feature addressed by politeness. Hence **face-wants** (= need to have face respected), **face-threat** (= threat to self-esteem or to freedom of action), **facework** (= language addressed to the face-wants of others). B&L suggest that face is a universal feature of personality which politeness addresses, but some commentators think this view of face too Western-oriented.

factivity   the property of a set of predicates in whose domain subject or complement clauses are presupposed (Kiparsky and Kiparsky, 1971).

felicity condition   a condition which must be in place for a speech act to be performed appropriately (Austin, 1962).

form   linguistic structure (as opposed to function). Thus a sentence is a form, while an utterance is a sentence put to use, i.e. given a function.

grammaticalization   the process by which an item comes to have a systematic relation to other items.

honorific   language forms used to encode the high social status of the addressee.

implicature   an inferred meaning (Grice, 1967a); an inferred meaning with a different logical (i.e. non-truth-preserving) form from that of the original utterance (Sperber and Wilson, 1986). In Grice's theory, the inference process by which a hearer derives a conversational implicature is calculable, and the implicature is defeasible and non-detachable (if the context holds, any item with the same meaning will have the same implicature); according to Grice, implicatures may be 'generalized' (inferred irrespective of context—i.e. *some* will always implicate *not all*) or 'particularized' (particular to the context of the utterance in which they arise).

indexicality   the encoding of points of reference, or 'indices', that occurs in the use of language.

indirect speech act   a functional use of language effected by the use of a form other than the one prototypically associated with the function concerned. For example, *would you mind opening the window* is a request expressed in an interrogative form.

inference   a conclusion derived from premises. A deductive inference is necessarily valid, i.e. will always yield the same conclusion; an inductive inference is probabilistic, i.e. it may not yield the same conclusion when additional premises are adduced. Pragmatic inferences are usually presumed to be inductive, although Sperber and Wilson argue that in Relevance Theory implicatures are deductive inferences. A hearer will frequently be led to infer a meaning as the result of a 'trigger', a feature of the utterance that leads the hearer to suspect that the literal meaning is not the (only) meaning that the speaker seeks to convey.

intentionality   According to some accounts, pragmatics is the study of the way in which intentionality is reflected in language use. Speech acts very obviously reflect intentionality.

literal meaning   There is a generally (but not universally) held belief that words and sentences have an invariant literal meaning and that all non-conventional, non-literal meanings are inferences.

logical form   the representation of a sentence in a form that may be adjudged true or false.

maxim   the term Grice (1967a) uses for the four sub-principles of his cooperative principle. The four maxims enjoin the speaker to strive to provide well-founded, appropriately informative, relevant contributions to conversation in a perspicuous manner.

maxim hedge   a metalingual gloss on the extent to which the speaker is abiding by one of the conversational maxims. Examples include *I mean* and *by the way*.

meaning   the sense that is conveyed in a communicative act. Conventional linguistic meaning is usually thought of truth-theoretically, i.e. if you know whether a sentence is a true or false description, you know what it means. Grice distinguishes conventional meaning and non-conventional or inferred meaning (meaning$_{nn}$).

negation   maps one value (false) onto another by means of a negative particle; the negative particle is also used metalinguistically as a way of objecting to some aspect of an utterance on any grounds except its conventional, semantic meaning.

performative   the use of language to accomplish action.

politeness   the relationship between how something is said and the addressee's judgement as to how it should be said. In Brown and Levinson's model (1978), politeness is seen as redressive, and computed as a function of speaker–hearer power–distance differential and degree of imposition.

pragmatics   the study of language used in communication and the associated usage principles.

presupposition   a meaning taken as given which does not therefore need to be asserted; variously defined as 'semantic presupposition' (non-defeasible, contributes to the truth-conditional meaning of the sentence), 'conventional implicature' (non-defeasible, non-truth-conditional), and 'pragmatic presupposition' (cancellable where inconsistent with speaker/hearer knowledge about the world).

presupposition projection   the ability of complex sentences to inherit the presuppositions of the component sentences embedded within them.

proposition   a linguistic representation of a state of affairs with a truth value.

reference   Most descriptions refer to different referents (persons, objects, notions) on each occasion when they are used. The function of picking out an object in the world is called referring.

relevance   According to Sperber and Wilson (1986), every utterance is relevant merely by virtue of being uttered. If we know how it is relevant, we know what the speaker means.

repair   a term used in conversation analysis to describe the correction or adjustment by speaker or hearer of some part of what is said.

sentence   the formal output of a grammar in which constituent items are combined in a limited set of rule-determined configurations.

sequence   a term used to describe the grammar of conversation as a variety of sequentially ordered turn-types.

speech act   the performative, or action-accomplishing, aspect of language use, and particularly the (illocutionary) force associated with an utterance.

speech event   see 'activity type'.

talk/talk-in-interaction   a term used to describe conversation, which draws attention to the underlying principle of turn-taking.

turn   the principal unit of description in conversational structure.

usage   the principles which underlie allowable 'use'.

utterance   a sentence used by a speaker for some purpose. Thus *I'm Peter* is both a sentence (it has a determinate grammar) and an utterance (I use it to introduce myself).

Index